Exploring Oracle Internals
Tips and Tricks for the Oracle DBA

Ben Prusinski

RAMPANT TECHPRESS

Dedication

Writing a book requires thousands of hours to develop quality material. It truly is a labor of love. Equally important is the selfless help provided by kind individuals to lend their valuable insight into editorial reviews and technical guidance for the author while writing the book. As such, I am extremely indebted and thankful to many folks who have been wonderful and generous to help me during the writing of this book. I hereby dedicate my book to the following individuals:

My parents and family, everyone at Rampant Tech Press, fellow Oracle ACEs and all of my professional colleagues over the years who have guided and mentored me to become a solid Oracle database professional. I also wish to extend my thanks to Don Burleson who provided me with many hours of assistance in terms of editorial and technical expertise to write this book. I also wish to thank my friends who were patient and understanding of my commitments to writing and spending weekends on the book rather than surfing at the beach or attending weekend parties.

- Ben Prusinski

Exploring Oracle Internals
Tips and Tricks for the Oracle DBA

By Ben Prusinski

Copyright © 2010 by Rampant TechPress. All rights reserved.
Printed in the United States of America.
Published in Kittrell, North Carolina, USA.

Oracle In-Focus Series: Book 35

Series Editor: Donald K. Burleson

Production Manager: Robin Rademacher

Production Editor: Valerre Aquitaine

Cover Design: Janet Burleson

Printing History: May 2011 for First Edition

Oracle, Oracle7, Oracle8, Oracle8i, Oracle9i, Oracle10g and Oracle 11g are trademarks of Oracle Corporation.

ISBN 10: 0-9823061-2-1
ISBN 13: 978-0-9823061-2-3
Library of Congress Control Number: 2009934294

Table of Contents

Using the Online Code Depot.. 1
Conventions Used in this Book... 2
Acknowledgements 3

Chapter 1: Introduction to Oracle 11g Database Internals 4

Chapter 1: Introduction... 4
    Chapter 2: Oracle 11g Memory.. 4
    Chapter 3: Locks with Oracle 11g... 5
    Chapter 4: Latches and Oracle 11g.. 5
    Chapter 5: Hidden and Undocumented Oracle 11g Parameters 5
    Chapter 6: Exploring V$ and the Oracle 11g Data Dictionary....... 5
    Chapter 7: X$ Tables for Oracle 11g.. 6
    Appendices 6
  New Features Overview for Oracle 11g Release................................. 6
    New Feature: Invisible Index 6
  Partitioning New Features.. 11
    System Partitioning.. 11
    Interval Partitioning 13
    Virtual Column Based Partitioning.. 14
    Reference Partitioning 18
  New Feature: Active Data Guard 20
  New Feature: ADR Monitoring Tools 20
  Automatic Memory Management 29
  Oracle 11g Internals Summary 30
  The Oracle 11g Kernel Architecture 30
    Undocumented Tools.. 32
    Poorly Documented Tools.. 32
  Summary 32

Chapter 2: Oracle 11g Database Internals: Memory 34

  Oracle 11g Memory.. 34
  Oracle 11g Database Architecture 34
  Inside the Oracle 11g System Global Area (SGA) 40
    Automatic Memory Management (AMM)..................................... 43
    Oracle 11g Advisors for SGA and PGA Memory........................... 44

Shared Pool..*47*

Streams Pool...*54*

Large Pool..*55*

Java Pool..*56*

Other Components Within the Oracle 11g SGA...........................*57*

Inside the Oracle 11g Program Global Area (PGA)............58

Semaphores and Oracle 11g...*61*

Mutexes and Oracle 11g..*61*

Wait Events and Mutexes for Oracle 11g.................................*63*

How Mutexes in Oracle 11g Differ from Operating System Mutexes64

Windows Memory and Threads and Oracle 11g.....................65

UNIX and Linux Shared Memory and Oracle 11g................67

Stack Traces for Oracle 11g Shared Memory..............................*71*

Understanding the Oracle 11g Memory Call Stack......................*72*

Summary 75

Chapter 3: Oracle Internals: Locks and Oracle 11g.........76

Introduction..76

What Are Locks?..76

Database Isolation Levels and Serialization for Transactions......*78*

Types of Locks within Oracle 11g......................................81

DML Locks..*81*

Lock Management and Escalation 91

Lock Management for Oracle RAC Environments......................*92*

Locking Mechanism for Oracle 11g RAC.................................*92*

Enhancements to Lock Management with Oracle 11g............98

Serializing Locks with Oracle 11g..*98*

Locking Tables Explicitly..*98*

Useful Tips and Tricks for Locking Problems....................100

Oracle 11g Database Waits: Insufficient ITL Slots...................*101*

Avoiding Deadlock Conditions..*103*

Lock Contention Issues and Solutions...............................104

Summary 105

Chapter 4: Oracle Internals: Latches.............................106

What are Latches?..106

How Do Latches Work with Oracle 11g?................................*107*

Types of Latches within Oracle 11g 109
Exploring Latches with Dynamic Performance Views 113
How Latches Differ From Locks 119
Tips for Latch Contention Issues with Oracle 11g 121
Tuning Latch Contention Issues for LRU Chain Latches *126*
Additional Tips for Tuning Oracle 11g Latches *127*
Summary 128

Chapter 5: Hidden Parameters in Oracle 11g 129

Purpose of Hidden Parameters for Oracle 11g 129
How to Locate Hidden Parameters for Oracle 11g *129*
Explanation of Key Hidden Parameters for Oracle 11g 142
New Features for 11g and Hidden Parameters *142*
Summary 144

Chapter 6: Exploring New *v$* Tables in Oracle 11g 146

New Features for the *v$* Tables and Oracle 11g Data Dictionary 146
Purpose of v$ Views for Oracle 11g *146*
Categories for Oracle 11g Database Administration with v$ Views *147*
General Oracle 11g Database Administration 148
Performance Tuning Oracle 11g *151*
Comprehensive Listing of Oracle 11g Dynamic v$ Performance Views 153
Investigating Oracle 11g Internals with V$ Views 163
Scripts and Tips for v$ and Data Dictionary - Oracle 11g 164
Summary 165

Chapter 7: Inside the x$ Tables of Oracle 11g 167

Classification of x$ Tables 167
Exploring Oracle 11g Database Internals with x$ Tables *170*
Oracle 11g New Features – Useful x$ Tables *178*
Using the X$ Tables for Oracle 11g Analysis 180
Scripts using X$ Tables with Oracle 11g *180*
Summary 199
Book Conclusion 200

Appendix A: Internal Tools for Oracle 11g 201

DBX 201
Using DBX for Debugging Oracle 201

Using DBX for Tracing Oracle 11g Memory Process:.....................................*202*
Truss 203

Appendix B: Oracle 11g Trace Events..**205**

Oracle 11g Database Trace Level Events 205

Appendix C: ORA-0600 Troubleshooting.....................................**231**
Appendix D: References..**232**

Chapter 1: Introduction 232
Chapter 2: Oracle 11g Memory 233
Chapter 3: Database Locks...234
Chapter 4: Database Latches..234
Chapter 5: Hidden Oracle 11g Parameters 235
Chapter 6: V$ Views..235
Chapter 7: X$ Tables for 11g..235
Appendix A: Oracle 11g Database Internal Toolkit 235
Appendix B: Oracle 11g Trace Events 236
Appendix C: ORA-0600 236
Appendix E: Strace 237
Appendix F: Using GDB for Oracle 11g.......................................237
Appendix G: Orakill for Windows and Oracle 11g 237

Appendix E: Using Strace **238**

Strace for Oracle 11g and Linux...238
Command Options for Strace with Linux for Oracle 11g...............................*238*

Appendix F: Using GDB with Oracle 11g **243**

Introduction to GDB with Oracle 11g...243
Oracle 11g Trace Stack with GDB..*245*

Appendix G: Orakill for Windows **248**

Orakill for Windows..248

Index..**251**
About the Author **255**

Using the Online Code Depot

Purchase of this book provides complete access to the online code depot that contains sample code scripts. Any code depot scripts in this book are located at the following URL in zip format and ready to load and use:

rampant.cc/insider_secrets.htm

If technical assistance is needed with downloading or accessing the scripts, please contact Rampant TechPress at rtp@rampant.cc.

Conventions Used in this Book

It is critical for any technical publication to follow rigorous standards and employ consistent punctuation conventions to make the text easy to read. However, this is not an easy task. Within database terminology, there are many types of notation that can confuse a reader. For example, some Oracle utilities such as STATSPACK and TKPROF are always spelled in CAPITAL letters, while Oracle parameters and procedures have varying naming conventions in the database documentation. It is also important to remember that many database commands are case sensitive, and are always left in their original executable form, and never altered with italics or capitalization. Hence, all Rampant TechPress books follow these conventions:

Parameters – Database parameters will be *lowercase italics*. The exception is parameter arguments that are commonly capitalized (KEEP pool, TKPROF), which will be ALL CAPS.

Variables – Procedural language (e.g. PL/SQL) program variables and arguments will also remain in *lowercase italics* (i.e. *dbms_job*).

Tables & dictionary objects – Data dictionary objects are referenced in lowercase italics (*dba_indexes*, *v$sql*), ncluding *v$* and *x$* views (*x$kcbcbh*, *v$parameter*) and dictionary views (*dba_tables*, *user_indexes*).

SQL – All SQL is formatted for easy use in the code depot and displayed in lowercase. Main SQL terms (select, from, where, group by, order by, having) will appear on a separate line.

Programs & Products – All products and programs that are known to the author are capitalized according to the vendor specifications (CentOS, VMware, Oracle, etc). All names known by Rampant TechPress to be trademark names appear in this text as initial caps. References to UNIX are always made in uppercase.

Acknowledgements

This type of highly technical reference book requires the dedicated efforts of many people. Even though we are the authors, our work ends when we deliver the content. After each chapter is delivered, several Oracle DBAs carefully review and correct the technical content. After the technical review, experienced copy editors polish the grammar and syntax.

The finished work is then reviewed as page proofs and turned over to the production manager, who arranges the creation of the online code depot and manages the cover art, printing distribution, and warehousing.

In short, the authors play a small role in the development of this book, and I need to thank and acknowledge everyone who helped bring this book to fruition:

Robin Rademacher for production management including the coordination of the cover art, page proofing, printing, and distribution.

Valerre Q Aquitaine for help in the production of the page proofs.

Janet Burleson for exceptional cover design and graphics.

John Lavender for assistance with the web site and for creating the code depot and the online shopping cart for this book.

With my sincerest thanks,

Ben Prusinski

Introduction to Oracle 11g Database Internals

Introduction

Welcome to Oracle 11g Insider Tips and Tricks! The journey to the world of inside tips and tricks for Oracle 11g will be quite an adventure. Oracle 11g Release 1 came out in July 2008 for public general release on Linux and Windows platforms.

The focus of this book will be on how to understand Oracle 11g database internals. As part of the survey for Oracle 11g database internals, how to best leverage and make use of the many hidden utilities, tools and features with Oracle 11g that previously either have scant documentation or have been exclusively in the realm of Oracle internal support engineers will be examined. As part of the investigation into Oracle 11g, some of the new features will be explained as they pertain to the discussion of Oracle 11g database internals and undocumented features when relevant. In this chapter, new features for Oracle 11g will be surveyed with an introduction to Oracle 11g database internals. First to be illustrated are what each chapter will include.

Chapter 2: Oracle 11g Memory

This chapter will cover in great detail the new memory model introduced in the Oracle 11g release in terms of how the SGA (System Global Area) and PGA (Program Global Area) allocate memory as well as new techniques for best understanding complex topics with memory management for Oracle 11g environments. The differences between operating system platforms in terms of how UNIX versus Windows allocates and manages memory for Oracle with tips on best tuning Oracle 11g for these platforms will be investigated.

Chapter 3: Locks with Oracle 11g

Locking is one of the frequently misunderstood core concepts of the Oracle database engine. In the locking chapter, a detailed treatment of Oracle 11g locks and how to best avoid performance issues with locking so that applications can run fully optimized with Oracle 11g databases will be covered.

Chapter 4: Latches and Oracle 11g

Latches are a distant cousin to locks within the Oracle 11g database engine. This chapter visits the methods in which latch behavior affects Oracle database operations and performance.

Chapter 5: Hidden and Undocumented Oracle 11g Parameters

In the Oracle database, the majority of tricks and tips that perform the black magic for the Oracle expert are hidden in the realm of undocumented database parameters. Chapter 5 journeys to this arena to show how these unknown features can best assist the Oracle professional with troubleshooting and tuning the Oracle 11g environment.

Chapter 6: Exploring *v$* and the Oracle 11g Data Dictionary

Hundreds of gems exist with the Oracle 11g and previous releases for the Oracle database master. These are the *v$* dynamic performance views such as *v$session* which can be used to tune, monitor and troubleshoot Oracle 11g database internals. A comprehensive look will be provided on how these can be used by the Oracle professional to solve complex problems.

Chapter 7: *x$* Tables for Oracle 11g

The dynamic performance *v$* tables are built upon the hidden *x$* tables which form the core of the Oracle database dictionary. Chapter 7 will explore useful *x$* tables to master Oracle 11g internals.

Appendices

Many tools and tips will be included for system utilities, trace events and methods to resolve Oracle core dump internal errors.

New Features Overview for Oracle 11g Release

With the Oracle 11g database new release, many new features have been added since Oracle 10g. In summary, among these new features include the following:

- New index type with invisible indexes
- New partitioning features
- Oracle 11g Active Data Guard
- Monitoring features with the ADR utility
- New features for backup and recovery with RMAN
- Automatic Storage Management (ASM) new features
- Data warehousing new features
- Automatic Memory Management
- Security new features
- Database replay and Rapid Application Testing new features

New Feature: Invisible Index

Oracle 11g introduces a new index type called the invisible index. The invisible index provides added functionality in that it can be used for testing performance scenarios and affects how the Oracle Cost Based

Optimizer (CBO) behaves. For example, when the invisible index is used, the CBO ignores the index as if the index did not exist. If the Oracle 11g initialization parameter *optimizer_use_invisible_indexes* is set to TRUE, then the CBO will see the index. By default, the parameter is set to FALSE so that the CBO ignores the invisible index when using execution plans. The syntax to create a new invisible index with Oracle 11g is similar to other *create index* statements as shown in this example:

```
SQL> CREATE INDEX emp_inv_idx ON scott.emp(ename)
  2    TABLESPACE USERS
  3    INVISIBLE;

Index created.

SQL> show parameter optimizer_use_invisible

NAME                                  TYPE          VALUE
------------------------------------- ------------- --------------------
optimizer_use_invisible_indexes       boolean       FALSE
SQL>
```

Now check to find the index has been created and is an invisible index with the following query.

```
SQL> SELECT INDEX_NAME, INDEX_TYPE, VISIBILITY
  2    FROM ALL_INDEXES
  3    WHERE INDEX_NAME LIKE 'EMP%';

INDEX_NAME                      INDEX_TYPE                   VISIBILIT
------------------------------- ---------------------------- ---------
EMP_LOWER_IDX                   FUNCTION-BASED NORMAL        VISIBLE
EMP_INV_IDX                     NORMAL                       INVISIBLE
EMP_DEPARTMENT_IX               NORMAL                       VISIBLE
EMP_EMAIL_UK                    NORMAL                       VISIBLE
EMP_EMP_ID_PK                   NORMAL                       VISIBLE
EMP_JOB_IX                      NORMAL                       VISIBLE
EMP_MANAGER_IX                  NORMAL                       VISIBLE
EMP_NAME_IX                     NORMAL                       VISIBLE

8 rows selected.
```

The key difference is use of the *invisible* statement in the syntax to create the invisible index. To see the affect of the invisible index on the optimizer behavior, use autotrace to show the execution plan.

Notice in the following example that the query performs a full table scan against the scott.emp table since the index is invisible.

```
SQL> select empno, ename, sal
2  from scott.emp
3  order by ename;

    EMPNO ENAME           SAL
---------- ---------- ----------
      7876 ADAMS          1100
      7499 ALLEN          1600
      7698 BLAKE          2850
      7782 CLARK          2450
      7902 FORD           3000
      7900 JAMES           950
      7566 JONES          2975
      7839 KING           5000
      7654 MARTIN         1250
      7934 MILLER         1300
      7788 SCOTT          3000
      7369 SMITH           800
      7844 TURNER         1500
      7521 WARD           1250

14 rows selected.

Elapsed: 00:00:00.03

Execution Plan
----------------------------------------------------------
Plan hash value: 150391907
----------------------------------------------------------
| Id  | Operation          | Name | Rows  | Bytes | Cost (%CPU)| Time     |
----------------------------------------------------------
|   0 | SELECT STATEMENT   |      |    14 |   196 |     4  (25)| 00:00:01 |
|   1 |  SORT ORDER BY     |      |    14 |   196 |     4  (25)| 00:00:01 |
|   2 |   TABLE ACCESS FULL| EMP  |    14 |   196 |     3   (0)| 00:00:01 |
----------------------------------------------------------
Statistics
----------------------------------------------------------
          0  recursive calls
          0  db block gets
          7  consistent gets
          0  physical reads
          0  redo size
        803  bytes sent via SQL*Net to client
        420  bytes received via SQL*Net from client
          2  SQL*Net roundtrips to/from client
          1  sorts (memory)
          0  sorts (disk)
         14  rows processed
```

Now one can test the impact on the cost-based optimizer if the invisible index is made into a normal and visible index with the *alter index...visible* command as shown in the query:

```
SQL> ALTER INDEX EMP_INV_IDX VISIBLE;

Index altered.
```

When the query is rerun against the scott.emp table, the results should access the new index as shown in the following example query:

```
SQL> set timing on
SQL> set autotrace on
SQL> select ename, empno, sal
  2  from
  3  scott.emp
  4  order by empno;

ENAME           EMPNO        SAL
---------- ---------- ----------
SMITH            7369        800
ALLEN            7499       1600
WARD             7521       1250
JONES            7566       2975
MARTIN           7654       1250
BLAKE            7698       2850
CLARK            7782       2450
SCOTT            7788       3000
KING             7839       5000
TURNER           7844       1500
ADAMS            7876       1100
JAMES            7900        950
FORD             7902       3000
MILLER           7934       1300

14 rows selected.

Elapsed: 00:00:00.05

Execution Plan
----------------------------------------------------------
Plan hash value: 4170700152
----------------------------------------------------------
| Id | Operation                   | Name  | Rows | Bytes | Cost (%CPU)| Time     |
------------------------------------------------------------------------------------
|  0 | SELECT STATEMENT            |       |   14 |   196 |    2   (0)| 00:00:01 |
|  1 |  TABLE ACCESS BY INDEX ROWID| EMP   |   14 |   196 |    2   (0)| 00:00:01 |
|  2 |   INDEX FULL SCAN           | PK_EMP|   14 |       |    1   (0)| 00:00:01 |
------------------------------------------------------------------------------------

Statistics
----------------------------------------------------------
        406  recursive calls
          0  db block gets
         81  consistent gets
          7  physical reads
          0  redo size
        803  bytes sent via SQL*Net to client
        420  bytes received via SQL*Net from client
          2  SQL*Net roundtrips to/from client
         11  sorts (memory)
          0  sorts (disk)
         14  rows processed
```

Toggle the index type back to invisible using the *alter index...invisible* command on the index as well.

```
SQL> ALTER INDEX emp_inv_idx INVISIBLE;

Index altered.
```

One can also test by making the primary key index for *pk_emp invisible*:

```
SQL> alter index scott.pk_emp invisible;

Index altered.

SQL> set autotrace on
SQL> select ename, empno, sal
  2  from scott.emp
  3  order by empno;

ENAME           EMPNO        SAL
---------- ---------- ----------
SMITH            7369        800
ALLEN            7499       1600
WARD             7521       1250
JONES            7566       2975
MARTIN           7654       1250
BLAKE            7698       2850
CLARK            7782       2450
ENAME           EMPNO        SAL
---------- ---------- ----------
SCOTT            7788       3000
KING             7839       5000
TURNER           7844       1500
ADAMS            7876       1100
JAMES            7900        950
FORD             7902       3000
MILLER           7934       1300

14 rows selected.

Elapsed: 00:00:00.01

Execution Plan
----------------------------------------------------------
Plan hash value: 150391907
----------------------------------------------------------
```

Id	Operation	Name	Rows	Bytes	Cost (%CPU)	Time
0	SELECT STATEMENT		14	196	4 (25)	00:00:01
1	SORT ORDER BY		14	196	4 (25)	00:00:01
2	TABLE ACCESS FULL	EMP	14	196	3 (0)	00:00:01

```
Statistics
----------------------------------------------------------
        240  recursive calls
          0  db block gets
         55  consistent gets
```

```
    5  physical reads
    0  redo size
  803  bytes sent via SQL*Net to client
  420  bytes received via SQL*Net from client
    2  SQL*Net roundtrips to/from client
    7  sorts (memory)
    0  sorts (disk)
   14  rows processed

SQL>
```

The beauty of using the invisible index feature for Oracle 11g is that it allows the developer and DBA staff to test performance for the index without the risk of dropping an index which can be time consuming and a potential risk to the production environment.

Partitioning New Features

Oracle 11g introduces many new features and enhancements for database partitioning. Among the new types and methods for data partitioning include the following:

- System Partitioning
- Interval Partitioning
- Virtual Column Partitioning
- Reference Partitioning

System Partitioning

The new system partitioning feature in Oracle 11g provides the developer or DBA with the ability to implement and manage new partitions without a specific partition key. Instead, each partition is mapped to a tablespace using the extended partitioning syntax for system partitions. Due to lack of partition keys with system partitioning, the usual performance benefits available for partitioned tables do not exist with system partitions.

Another drawback to system partitions is that they cannot be used for partition-wise joins or traditional partition pruning operations. As such,

---

the main benefit of using the new system partitioning is for manageability purposes. An example of the system partition feature is shown in the following example.

First, create a test table for usage with system partitioning:

```
SQL> CREATE TABLE system_part_table (a1 integer, a2 integer)
  2   PARTITION BY SYSTEM
  3   (
  4   PARTITION p1 TABLESPACE USERS,
  5   PARTITION p2 TABLESPACE EXAMPLE
  6   );

Table created.
```

The previous new table was created with two system partitions assigned to USERS and EXAMPLE tablespaces. Of special note is that the syntactical element SYSTEM is used to indicate a system based partitioned table. Now insert some test data into the new system partitions.

```
SQL> INSERT INTO system_part_table PARTITION (p1) VALUES (1,2);

1 row created.

SQL> INSERT INTO system_part_table PARTITION (p2) VALUES (3,4);

1 row created.
```

The status for the new system partitions can be verified with the following query against the *user_tab_partitions* view:

```
SQL> select table_name, partition_name, tablespace_name
  2   from user_tab_partitions;
```

TABLE_NAME	PARTITION_NAME	TABLESPACE_NAME
SYSTEM_PART_TABLE	P1	USERS
SYSTEM_PART_TABLE	P2	EXAMPLE

While system partitioning is useful in cases when other partitioning strategies are not possible, there are limitations to its usage.

User ID = book, password = reader

For example, the following operations are not supported for system partitioning:

- create table as select
- insert into <table_name> as <sub query>
- split partition operations
- Unique Local Indexes are not supported as these require a partition key.

As a workaround to these limitations, one should first create the table with the system partitions and then insert rows for each partition.

Interval Partitioning

Interval partitions build upon the foundation introduced with range partitioning for Oracle 11g. Before Oracle 11g, database administrators had to set explicit ranges of data to use for partition keys. Interval partitioning resolves the limitations built into range partitioning when a specific range is unknown by the developer or DBA creating the partitions for the table. It tells Oracle to automatically set up new partitions for a particular interval when data inserted into tables is greater than the range partitions.

As such, the requirement of interval partitioning dictates that at least one range partition is specified. Once the range partitioning key is given for the high value of the range partitions, this transition point is used as the baseline to create interval partitions beyond this point. The nice thing about the new interval partitioning feature for Oracle 11g is that it eases the management of new partitions for the busy Oracle DBA or development staff. The following exercise will demonstrate how interval partitioning works with Oracle 11g.

First create a new table to use for interval partitioning:

```
SQL> CREATE TABLE sales_interval
  2  (product_id              NUMBER(6),
  3   customer_id             NUMBER,
  4   time_id                 DATE,
```

```
 5  channel_info          CHAR(1),
 6  promo_id              NUMBER(6),
 7  qty_sold              NUMBER(3),
 8  amt_sold              NUMBER(10,2)
 9  )
10  PARTITION BY RANGE (time_id)
11  INTERVAL(NUMTOYMINTERVAL(1, 'MONTH'))
12  (PARTITION t0 VALUES LESS THAN (TO_DATE('1-1-2005','DD-MM-YYYY')),
13  PARTITION t1 VALUES LESS THAN (TO_DATE('1-1-2006','DD-MM-YYYY')),
14  PARTITION t2 VALUES LESS THAN (TO_DATE('1-7-2006','DD-MM-YYYY')),
15  PARTITION t3 VALUES LESS THAN (TO_DATE('1-1-2007','DD-MM-YYYY')) );
```

```
Table created.
```

The above statement creates a table with four new interval-based partitions using a one-month period for the width of the interval with January 1, 2007. The transition point is with t3 partition as the high bound and the other partitions (t0-t2) as the range section with all partitions above it occurring in the interval range. However, like other forms of partitioning, there are some limitations as follows.

Interval partitioning restrictions include:

- Index Organized Tables (IOTs) are not supported by interval partitioning

- Domain index cannot be created on interval partitioned tables

- Only one partitioning key column can be set for the interval partition and it must be either a DATE or NUMBER data type

Virtual Column Based Partitioning

Oracle 11g has another new type of partitioning called Virtual Column Based partitioning. Virtual column based partitioning allows data partitioning to be based on virtual columns as the partitioning key. Virtual columns are a new feature in 11g that allow derivation from a function or expression evaluation results. As such, values for virtual columns are not stored within the table, but rather the values for the virtual columns are evaluated on demand when calculated. Indexes and tables can be partitioned as such on new virtual columns.

For instance, to add a new virtual column to an existing table, SCOTT.EMP, one would execute the following statement.

```
SQL> ALTER TABLE EMP ADD (yearly_sal as (sal*comm));

Table altered.

SQL> desc emp
```

Name	Null?	Type
EMPNO	NOT NULL	NUMBER(4)
ENAME		VARCHAR2(10)
JOB		VARCHAR2(9)
MGR		NUMBER(4)
HIREDATE		DATE
SAL		NUMBER(7,2)
COMM		NUMBER(7,2)
DEPTNO		NUMBER(2)
YEARLY_SAL		NUMBER

```
SQL> select ename, sal, comm, yearly_sal
  2  from emp;
```

ENAME	SAL	COMM	YEARLY_SAL
SMITH	800		
ALLEN	1600	300	480000
WARD	1250	500	625000
JONES	2975		
MARTIN	1250	1400	1750000

Now when the above query is issued against the SCOTT.EMP table, there will be the new virtual column, *yearly_sal*, that can be used in calculations.

If a new table needs to be created that uses virtual columns, issue a CREATE TABLE like that found in the following example.

```
SQL> CREATE TABLE virtual_emp (
  2  empno      NUMBER  PRIMARY KEY,
  3  ename      VARCHAR2(20) NOT NULL,
  4  social_id  NUMBER(9),
  5  sal        NUMBER(7,2),
  6  hrly_pay   NUMBER(7,2) GENERATED ALWAYS AS (sal/2000));

Table created.
```

Note that the key syntax to use when creating tables that make use of virtual columns is the *generated always* phrase. An optional syntax parameter, *virtual*, can be used in addition when creating virtual columns, as shown in the example below.

```
SQL> CREATE TABLE v_emp
  2  (name   VARCHAR2(20),
  3   hr_rate NUMBER(7,2),
  4  income   NUMBER(7,2) generated always as (hr_rate*2080)
  5  virtual
  6  );

Table created.
```

Virtual columns have the following limitations:

- They cannot be created on user defined types LOB or RAW

- Delete or insert operations cannot be performed on virtual columns. If one attempts to do so, Oracle will generate an ORA-54013 error.

- They cannot be created on index-organized tables (IOT), external table, temporary tables, objects, or clusters

- All of the virtual columns used in expressions must belong to the same table

- They cannot be updated by the *set* clause in an UPDATE statement

Next to be given is an example of how to create a virtual column based partition table in the following exercise. First, create a new table called workers.

```
SQL> create table workers
  2  (
  3  emp_id     number  not null,
  4  job_no     number,
  5  fname      varchar2(20),
  6  mname      varchar2(20),
  7  lname      varchar2(20),
  8  salary     number,
  9  bonus      number,
 10  position   varchar2(50),
 11  tcomp      as (salary+bonus) virtual
 12  )
 13  partition by range(tcomp)
 14  (partition p_10g values less than (20000),
 15  partition p_20g values less than (30000),
 16  partition p_50g values less than (60000),
 17  partition p_100g values less than (200000),
 18  partition p_500g values less than (600000),
 19  partition p_more values less than (maxvalue));
```

```
Table created.
```

Now that the new virtual column based partition table has been created, insert some sample test data to see how row placement in the partitions is evaluated.

```
SQL> insert into workers
  2  (emp_id,job_no,fname,mname,lname,salary,bonus,position)
  3  values
  4  (1,1,'Scott','Smith','Henry',30000,1200,'DBA');

1 row created.

SQL> insert into workers
  2  (emp_id,job_no,fname,mname,lname,salary,bonus,position)
  3  values
  4  (2,2,'Howard','M','Ostro',250000,25000,'Director');

1 row created.

SQL> commit;

Commit complete.
```

Virtual column based partitions have the same functionality as that in range or list based partitions. Now take a peek at how the optimizer views virtual based partitions and row position.

```
SQL> select fname, lname, salary, bonus, tcomp
  2  from workers partition (p_50g);

FNAME                LNAME                  SALARY      BONUS      TCOMP
-------------------- ---------------------- ---------- ---------- ----------
Scott                Henry                   30000       1200       31200

SQL> select fname, lname, salary, bonus, tcomp
  2  from workers partition (p_500g);

Howard               Ostro                  250000      25000      275000
```

Here it can be seen that the partitions' return values based on the virtual column based partitions. By viewing the execution plan from *dbms_xplan*, one can view the use of the virtual column based partitions as shown below.

```
SQL> explain plan for
  2  select fname, lname, salary, bonus, tcomp
  3  from workers partition (p_500g);

Explained.
```

```
SQL> select * from table(dbms_xplan.display);

PLAN_TABLE_OUTPUT
--------------------------------------------------------------------Plan    hash    value:
475732617

----------------------------------------------------------------------------
| Id | Operation            | Name    | Rows  | Bytes | Cost (%CPU)| Time
   | Pstart| Pstop |
----------------------------------------------------------------------------

PLAN_TABLE_OUTPUT
-----------------------------------------------------------------|     0   |  SELECT
STATEMENT       |          |   1 |   63 |    3   (0)| 00:00:01 |          |      |

|   1 |   PARTITION RANGE SINGLE|         |   1 |   63 |    3   (0)| 00:00:01 |    5 |    5 |

|   2 |      TABLE ACCESS FULL  | WORKERS |   1 |   63 |    3   (0)| 00:00:01 |    5 |    5 |

----------------------------------------------------------------------------

PLAN_TABLE_OUTPUT
-----------------------------------------------------------------------
9 rows selected.
```

The nice thing about virtual column based partitions is that they allow the development staff to create partitions based on business requirements when other types of partitioning are limited in terms of flexibility and when business rules call for partitioning based on specific needs for the application.

Reference Partitioning

Oracle 11g provides an additional new type of partitioning called reference partitioning which allows for partitioning by using the parent table referenced by a foreign key constraint. It allows for use of existing parent-child relationship-based partitioning enforced by active primary key and foreign key constraints. The partition *by reference* clause is used to create reference partitions as shown in the following example.

First, create a table that is partitioned to the server as the parent table. This table will be referenced by the second table which is to be reference partitioned.

```
SQL> create table parent_emp(
  2  empno        number  primary key,
  3  job          varchar2(20),
  4  sal          number(7,2),
  5  deptno       number(2)
  6  )
  7  partition by list(job)
  8  ( partition p_job_dba values ('DBA'),
```

```
 9    partition p_job_mgr values ('MGR'),
10    partition p_job_vp  values ('VP')
11  );

Table created.

SQL> create table reference_emp
  2  (
  3  ename      varchar2(10),
  4  emp_id     number  primary key,
  5  empno      not null,
  6  constraint fk_empno foreign key(empno)
  7     references parent_emp(empno)
  8  )
  9  partition by reference (fk_empno)
 10  /

Table created.
```

The reference partition is now created on the child table and both tables can be queried to determine the partition information from the *user_part_tables* view.

```
SQL> select table_name, partitioning_type, ref_ptn_constraint_name
  2  from user_part_tables
  3  where table_name='PARENT_EMP'
  4  or
  5  table_name='REFERENCE_EMP';


TABLE_NAME                      PARTITION REF_PTN_CONSTRAINT_NAME
------------------------------- --------- ---------------------------
PARENT_EMP                      LIST
REFERENCE_EMP                   REFERENCE FK_EMPNO
```

The *reference_emp* child table has been reference partitioned using the foreign key constraint *fk_empno*. Next to be viewed are the high values for the partitions in both tables with the following query:

```
SQL> select table_name, partition_name, high_value
  2  from user_tab_partitions
  3  where table_name='PARENT_EMP'
  4  or
  5  table_name='REFERENCE_EMP'
  6  /

TABLE_NAME                      PARTITION_NAME        HIGH_VALUE
------------------------------- --------------------- --------------------------------
PARENT_EMP                      P_JOB_DBA             'DBA'
PARENT_EMP                      P_JOB_MGR             'MGR'
PARENT_EMP                      P_JOB_VP              'VP'
REFERENCE_EMP                   P_JOB_DBA
REFERENCE_EMP                   P_JOB_MGR
```

```
REFERENCE_EMP                    P_JOB_VP

6 rows selected.
```

Reference partitioning is useful in that partition operations against the parent table are duplicated to the child table, thus reducing errors when manually performing maintenance against both tables. Before Oracle 11g, the developer would have to manually allocate storage for the partition key on both the parent and child table. Now with Oracle 11g, less storage is required and easier maintenance is provided.

New Feature: Active Data Guard

Oracle 11g introduces several new enhancements to improve the operation and maintenance of complex Data Guard standby environments for improved high availability. The many new features with Oracle 11g for Data Guard include the following:

- Real time query standby database

- Redo log compression

- Logical standby enhancements

- Data Guard Broker enhancements

- Fast start failover improvements

- Integration for RMAN with Data Guard

- Snapshot standby database

Further details on the steps for how to configure and setup a physical standby and logical standby database using the new features for Oracle 11g with Data Guard are available in the Oracle 11g Data Guard Concepts and Administration reference guide. This guide is available from the Oracle OTN site located online at http://otn.oracle.com.

New Feature: ADR Monitoring Tools

Oracle 11g has introduced a new monitoring tool called the Automatic Diagnostic Repository (ADR). This new tool, which is available via both

---

command line and from within Enterprise Manager/Grid Control, provides comprehensive reporting and monitoring functions for Oracle trace files, alert log reporting and other features for monitoring the Oracle 11g database environment. Prior to Oracle 11g, trace files were stored by default under the *user_dump_dest* directory.

Before Oracle 11g, the *alert.log* text based file which contains details on the status of the Oracle database was stored by default under the background dump destination directory and now is referenced by a single initialization parameter called *diagnostic_dest*. The previous release parameters for *background_dump_dest, core_dump_dest*, and *user_dump_dest* have been deprecated and replaced by the single parameter *diagnostic_dest* in 11g.

Now these files are managed under the ADR directory structure and can be viewed by the ADR tool. The base monitoring file is stored in XML format in a file called *log.xml*. By default, the diagnostic directory structure is tied to the *oracle_home*, *oracle_base* and *oracle_sid* environment variables.

```
SQL> show parameter diagnostic_dest

NAME                                 TYPE        VALUE
------------------------------------ ----------- -------------------
diagnostic_dest                      string      /u01/app/oracle
```

The Oracle 11g ADR uses a home directory to centralize log file maintenance operations. By default, the ADR home directory is located under the directory structure:

```
<ADR_BASE>/diag/rdbms/<db_name>/<instance_id>.
```

To show the home directory details for ADR, log on to the command line tool *adrci* as follows.

```
[oracle@raclinux1 ~]$ adrci

ADRCI: Release 11.1.0.6.0 - Beta on Tue Jul 29 00:07:57 2008

Copyright (c) 1982, 2007, Oracle.  All rights reserved.

ADR base = "/u01/app/oracle"
```

```
adrci> show home
ADR Homes:
diag/rdbms/ora11g/ora11g
diag/rdbms/ora11g/ORA11G
diag/rdbms/default/ORA11G
diag/rdbms/unknown/ORA11G
diag/rdbms/stdby1/stdby1
diag/clients/user_oracle/host_3681296775_11
diag/clients/user_unknown/host_411310321_11
diag/tnslsnr/raclinux1/listener
diag/tnslsnr/raclinux1/listener1
diag/tnslsnr/raclinux1/listener_stdby1
```

In addition to using the *adrci> show home* command, the location for the ADR configuration can be displayed using the *v$diag_info* view as shown in the next example.

```
Oracle Database 11g Enterprise Edition Release 11.1.0.6.0 - Production
With the Partitioning, OLAP, Data Mining and Real Application Testing
options

SQL> col name format a20
SQL> col value format a50 word_wrapped
SQL> select name, value
  2  from
  3  v$diag_info;

NAME                 VALUE
-------------------- --------------------------------------------------
Diag Enabled         TRUE
ADR Base             /u01/app/oracle
ADR Home             /u01/app/oracle/diag/rdbms/ora11g/ORA11G
Diag Trace           /u01/app/oracle/diag/rdbms/ora11g/ORA11G/trace
Diag Alert           /u01/app/oracle/diag/rdbms/ora11g/ORA11G/alert
Diag Incident        /u01/app/oracle/diag/rdbms/ora11g/ORA11G/incident
Diag Cdump           /u01/app/oracle/diag/rdbms/ora11g/ORA11G/cdump
Health Monitor       /u01/app/oracle/diag/rdbms/ora11g/ORA11G/hm
Default Trace File   /u01/app/oracle/diag/rdbms/ora11g/ORA11G/trace/ORA
                     11G_ora_28603.trc
```

The above query against the *v$diag_info* view provides the DBA or developer with the default locations for the diagnostic trace, alert, incident, core dump, ADR home, ADR base, and health monitor files for Oracle 11g.

If the *log.xml* file is examined, it should be noticed that the default xml alert log file contains all of the entries that are also contained in the text based *alert.log* file. This file is available for backward compatibility with previous releases.

```
SQL> !ls /u01/app/oracle/diag/rdbms/ora11g/ORA11G/alert
log.xml

SQL> !view /u01/app/oracle/diag/rdbms/ora11g/ORA11G/alert/log.xml

<msg time='2008-06-09T18:34:25.057-04:00' org_id='oracle' comp_id='rdbms'
 msg_id='opistr_real:871:3971575317' type='NOTIFICATION' group='startup'
 level='16' pid='7457' version='1'>
 <txt>Starting ORACLE instance (normal)
 </txt>
</msg>
<msg time='2008-06-09T18:34:25.840-04:00' org_id='oracle' comp_id='rdbms'
 msg_id='ksunfy:13399:2937430291' type='NOTIFICATION' group='startup'
 level='16' pid='7457'>
 <txt>LICENSE_MAX_SESSION = 0
 </txt>
</msg>
<msg time='2008-06-09T18:34:25.840-04:00' org_id='oracle' comp_id='rdbms'
 msg_id='ksunfy:13400:4207019197' type='NOTIFICATION' group='startup'
 level='16' pid='7457'>
 <txt>LICENSE_SESSIONS_WARNING = 0
 </txt>
</msg>
<msg time='2008-06-09T18:34:25.918-04:00' org_id='oracle' comp_id='rdbms'
 msg_id='kcsnfy:323:968333812' type='NOTIFICATION' group='startup'
 level='16' pid='7457'>
 <txt>Picked latch-free SCN scheme 2
 </txt>
</msg>
<msg time='2008-06-09T18:34:26.494-04:00' org_id='oracle' comp_id='rdbms'
 msg_id='kcrrdini:15230:1211400554' type='NOTIFICATION' group='startup'
 level='16' pid='7457'>
```

Since the format of the *log.xml* file is not intended for viewing in xml format, it is advised to use the *adrci* interface to view log files. When returning to the ADR interface via the *adrci* command tool, one can dump the help contents to be provided with a list of commands available with ADR, as shown in the code listing below. One can also use the *help extended* command to display more details.

```
[oracle@raclinux1 ~]$ adrci

ADRCI: Release 11.1.0.6.0 - Beta on Tue Jul 29 00:29:52 2008

Copyright (c) 1982, 2007, Oracle.  All rights reserved.

ADR base = "/u01/app/oracle"
adrci> help extended

 HELP [topic]
   Available Topics:
        BEGIN BACKUP
        CD
        DDE
```

```
        DEFINE
        DESCRIBE
        END BACKUP
        LIST DEFINE
        MERGE ALERT
        MERGE FILE
        QUERY
        SET COLUMN
        SHOW CATALOG
        SHOW DUMP
        SHOW SECTION
        SHOW TRACE
        SHOW TRACEMAP
        SWEEP
        UNDEFINE
        VIEW

adrci> help

 HELP [topic]
    Available Topics:
        CREATE REPORT
        ECHO
        EXIT
        HELP
        HOST
        IPS
        PURGE
        RUN
        SET BASE
        SET BROWSER
        SET CONTROL
        SET ECHO
        SET EDITOR
        SET HOMES | HOME | HOMEPATH
        SET TERMOUT
        SHOW ALERT
        SHOW BASE
        SHOW CONTROL
        SHOW HM_RUN
        SHOW HOMES | HOME | HOMEPATH
        SHOW INCDIR
        SHOW INCIDENT
        SHOW PROBLEM
        SHOW REPORT
        SHOW TRACEFILE
        SPOOL

 There are other commands intended to be used directly by Oracle, type
 "HELP EXTENDED" to see the list

adrci>
```

If one wishes to find specific help on a particular topic with ADR, issue the command *help* followed by the topic as shown in the following example.

```
adrci> help dde create incident

  Usage:  DDE CREATE INCIDENT TYPE <type>

  Purpose: Create an incident of specified type.
           If the incident type is associated with an action, the action
will be automatically recommended for the new incident.

  Arguments:
    <type>:  Incident type

  Notes:
    The relation DDE_USER_INCIDENT_TYPE shows available incident types.

  Example:
    dde create incident type wrong_results
```

ADR is basically the alert monitoring on steroids. It further allows for the packaging of incidents and reports to be sent to Oracle customer support for analysis and problem resolution. To view the alert log reports in ADR, issue the *show alert* command:

```
adrci> show alert

Choose the alert log from the following homes to view:

1: diag/rdbms/ora11g/ora11g
2: diag/rdbms/ora11g/ORA11G
3: diag/rdbms/default/ORA11G
4: diag/rdbms/unknown/ORA11G
5: diag/rdbms/stdby1/stdby1
6: diag/clients/user_oracle/host_3681296775_11
7: diag/clients/user_unknown/host_411310321_11
8: diag/tnslsnr/raclinux1/listener
9: diag/tnslsnr/raclinux1/listener1
10: diag/tnslsnr/raclinux1/listener_stdby1
Q: to quit

Please select option: 1
Output the results to file: /tmp/alert_30297_3086_ora11g_1.ado

2008-05-18 18:54:11.768000 -04:00
Starting ORACLE instance (normal)
2008-05-18 18:54:12.946000 -04:00
LICENSE_MAX_SESSION = 0
LICENSE_SESSIONS_WARNING = 0
Shared memory segment for instance monitoring created
Picked latch-free SCN scheme 2
2008-05-18 18:54:14.823000 -04:00
Using LOG_ARCHIVE_DEST_1 parameter default value as
"/tmp/alert_30297_3086_ora11g_1.ado" 1274L, 53223C
```

The ADR monitoring system can also be understood in terms of examination of the following *v$* views:

- *v$hm_check*

- *v$hm_check_param*

- *v$hm_finding*

- *v$hm_info*

- *v$hm_recommendation*

- *v$hm_run*

Now that the basic monitoring functions available with the ADR tools for Oracle 11g have been examined, review how ADR manages incidents with Oracle 11g. Incidents refer to critical database errors that usually generate core dump files. In particular, ADR will automatically generate an incident report for most internal error conditions such as those for ORA-00600, ORA-00700, and ORA-07445. When such internal errors occur, an incident package can be assembled with ADR to send to Oracle internal support for analysis and resolution. The ability to create and package incidents is a robust feature provided by ADR that quickly assists the busy DBA to send diagnostic files to Oracle support during crisis situations.

The following example illustrates how to use the incident feature with ADR for sending critical diagnostic information to Oracle Support.

The first step is to set the ADR home directory since the *ips create package* command supports only a single ADR home at one time.

```
adrci> set homepath diag/rdbms/ora11g/ora11g
adrci> show homes
ADR Homes:
diag/rdbms/ora11g/ora11g


adrci> show incident

ADR Home = /u01/app/oracle/diag/rdbms/ora11g/ora11g:
******************************************************************
0 rows fetched
```

```
adrci> ips create package

Created package 1 without any contents, correlation level typical
```

Once the new incident package is created, as in the previous example, it is now time to add outstanding incidents to the package.

The following ADR commands are used to add the incident and create the necessary zip files to send to Oracle support for analysis.

```
ips add incident <incident_id> package <package_id>

ips generate package <package_id> in <directory>
```

The ADR configuration settings for the incident package creation can be viewed with the *ips show* command:

```
adrci> ips show configuration

************************************************************
IPS CONFIGURATION PARAMETER
************************************************************


-----------------------------------------------------------
PARAMETER INFORMATION:
   PARAMETER_ID                1
   NAME                        CUTOFF_TIME
   DESCRIPTION                 Maximum age for an incident to be
considered for inclusion
   UNIT                        Days
   VALUE                       90
   DEFAULT_VALUE               90


-----------------------------------------------------------
************************************************************
IPS CONFIGURATION PARAMETER
************************************************************


-----------------------------------------------------------
PARAMETER INFORMATION:
   PARAMETER_ID                2
   NAME                        NUM_EARLY_INCIDENTS
   DESCRIPTION                 How many incidents to get in the early
part of the range
   UNIT                        Number
   VALUE                       3
   DEFAULT_VALUE               3


-----------------------------------------------------------
************************************************************
IPS CONFIGURATION PARAMETER
```

```
************************************************************

------------------------------------------------------------
PARAMETER INFORMATION:
    PARAMETER_ID            3
    NAME                    NUM_LATE_INCIDENTS
    DESCRIPTION             How many incidents to get in the late part
of the range
    UNIT                    Number
    VALUE                   3
    DEFAULT_VALUE           3

------------------------------------------------------------
************************************************************
IPS CONFIGURATION PARAMETER
************************************************************

------------------------------------------------------------
PARAMETER INFORMATION:
    PARAMETER_ID            4
    NAME                    INCIDENT_TIME_WINDOW
    DESCRIPTION             Incidents this close to each other are
considered correlated
    UNIT                    Minutes
    VALUE                   5
    DEFAULT_VALUE           5

------------------------------------------------------------
************************************************************
IPS CONFIGURATION PARAMETER
************************************************************

------------------------------------------------------------
PARAMETER INFORMATION:
    PARAMETER_ID            5
    NAME                    PACKAGE_TIME_WINDOW
    DESCRIPTION             Time window for content inclusion is from
x hours before first included incident to x hours after last incident
    UNIT                    Hours
    VALUE                   24
    DEFAULT_VALUE           24

------------------------------------------------------------
************************************************************
IPS CONFIGURATION PARAMETER
************************************************************

------------------------------------------------------------
PARAMETER INFORMATION:
    PARAMETER_ID            6
    NAME                    DEFAULT_CORRELATION_LEVEL
    DESCRIPTION             Default correlation level for packages
    UNIT                    Number
    VALUE                   2
    DEFAULT_VALUE           2

------------------------------------------------------------
************************************************************
IPS CONFIGURATION PARAMETER
```

```
*************************************************************
-------------------------------------------------------------
PARAMETER INFORMATION:
   PARAMETER_ID              7
   NAME                      PURGE_ENABLED
   DESCRIPTION               If automatic purging is allowed for the
IPS schema
   UNIT                      Number
   VALUE                     1
   DEFAULT_VALUE             1

-------------------------------------------------------------
adrci>
```

The zipped files can then be uploaded to Metalink for coordination with Oracle customer support.

In addition to the ADR command line, Enterprise Manager provides a facility called the EM Support Workbench that can be used for managing incidents and reports to send to Oracle internal customer support.

Due to the vast array of commands and functions available with the powerful new ADR monitoring tools for Oracle 11g, it is recommended that one consults the Oracle 11g documentation for the comprehensive syntax and list of functions available for more details on this robust new tool for Oracle 11g monitoring.

Automatic Memory Management

Prior to Oracle 11g, memory configuration was a complex task that required hours of tuning to perfect the optimal solution for database performance. In the past, Oracle DBA staff would need to tune settings for many initialization parameters with regards to the shared pool and many other settings for the SGA and PGA memory areas within the Oracle database. Release 10g improved matters quite a bit with the new *sga_max*, *sga_target*, and *pga_target* initialization parameters. Now with 11g, there is a single new parameter called memory management.

Now that a solid introduction to some of the latest and greatest new features for Oracle 11g have been provided, it is time to begin the voyage to database internals for Oracle 11g.

Oracle 11g Internals Summary

Oracle 11g internals coverage will include a review and explanation on the inner workings of Oracle 11g database memory as well as treatment of how locks, wait events, and latches operate within the context of Oracle 11g database environments. Oracle 11g provides the database practitioner with a suite of performance views in the form of $v\$$ and $x\$$ views that can be used to monitor and assess Oracle 11g database internal details. In addition, operating system tools such as truss, ps, top, and vmstat can provide details on performance and system level details on UNIX platforms, for example.

The Oracle 11g Kernel Architecture

The Oracle 11g database kernel is composed of multiple layers as shown in Figure 1.1. Each of the layers is dependent on services for each layer in the Oracle kernel and communicates with processes across the kernel stack. The first two layers of the Oracle 11g kernel architecture consist of the Oracle Call Interface (OCI) and Oracle 11g User Program Interface (UPI) layers. Beneath the Oracle 11g User Program Interface Layer lies the Oracle 11g Network Services, which was named Net8 in previous releases of Oracle.

Oracle 11g Call Interface	OCI
Oracle 11g User Program Interface	UPI

Oracle 11g
Network Services

Oracle Program Interface	OPI
Oracle 11g Compilation Layer	KK
Oracle 11g Execution Layer	KX
Oracle 11g Distributed Execution Layer	K2
Oracle 11g Network Program Interface	NPI
Oracle 11g Security Layer	KZ
Oracle 11g Query Layer	KQ
Oracle 11g Recursive Program Interface	RPI
Oracle 11g Access Layer	KA
Oracle 11g Data Layer	KD
Oracle 11g Transaction Layer	KT
Oracle 11g Cache Layer	KC
Oracle 11g Services Layer	KS
Oracle 11g Lock Management	KJ
Oracle 11g Generic Kernel Layer	KG
Oracle 11g Layer for Operating System Dependent Services	S

Figure 1.1: *The Oracle 11g Kernel Architecture*

Undocumented Tools

Among the many undocumented tools within the Oracle 11g release, this book will use examples from oradebug and other tools to understand memory management, locking and latching concepts. One note of caution: when using these undocumented tools for Oracle, it is critical that extreme care be exercised or database corruption and/or data loss can result. The prudent usage of these utilities should be taken in a non-production environment for testing as well as use with guidance from Oracle Customer Support.

Poorly Documented Tools

Oracle provides many excellent tools for analysis, monitoring and performance tuning. However, many of these utilities are poorly documented or unknown by most Oracle DBAs. Internal database issues and problems such as the infamous ORA-0600 errors can be investigated and diagnosed with tools such as oradebug.

Among these poorly documented tools that will be covered: oradebug, tkprof, autotrace, and the *sql_tune* packages for Oracle 11g. In addition, one will be shown how to utilize the *dbms_stats* package within the context of Oracle 11g to best tune the database environments.

Summary

In this chapter, the following topics about the new features and tips for Oracle 11g have been introduced:

- Essential new features for Oracle 11g

- Oracle 11g kernel architecture

- Overview of undocumented and hidden features for Oracle 11g

The following chapters will dig deeper into Oracle 11g database internals so that the reader can understand how to diagnose, tune, and resolve complex Oracle database problems using these undocumented and hidden Oracle 11g features.

Oracle 11g Database Internals: Memory

Oracle 11g Memory

This chapter will provide a comprehensive primer for the Oracle professional on the memory structures and architecture for Oracle 11g database environments. As such, previous releases of Oracle will not be covered except to mention critical differences when each topic is introduced. For example, new features for managing and tuning the Oracle 11g System Global Area (SGA) and Oracle 11g Program Global Area (PGA) memory structures as well as how they interact with operating system memory structures for Linux, UNIX, and Windows memory management models will be examined.

The first step is to understand the concepts and features for the Oracle 11g architecture and processes. The key to understanding Oracle 11g memory structures is to first examine how shared memory is allocated and managed by the Oracle database engine. After the concepts behind Oracle 11g memory architecture are shown, some useful tools and tips on how to monitor and manage Oracle 11g memory will be covered. Introducing the logical and physical structures that constitute an Oracle 11g environment is a good place to begin.

Oracle 11g Database Architecture

Oracle 11g provides a robust model for memory management in terms of its interactions between the operating system and database engine. The core concepts of the Oracle database architecture consist of Oracle background processes, the Oracle instance, Oracle specific files, and the Oracle database itself. As shown in the following figure, the architecture of Oracle 11g is extremely robust and complex.

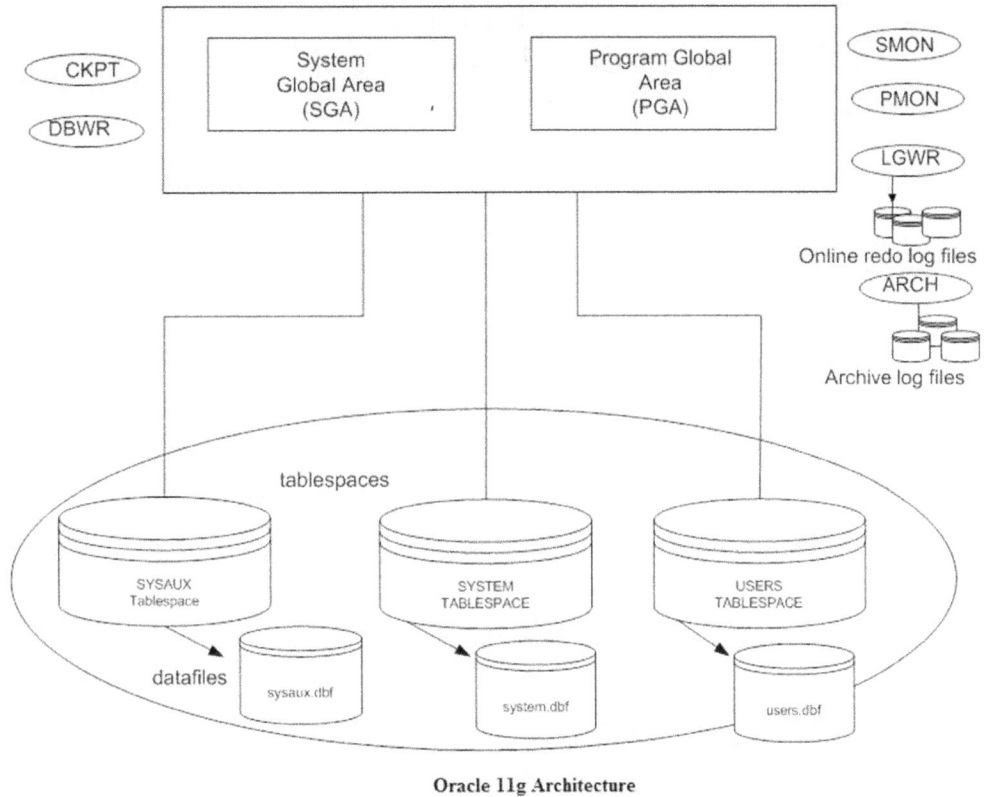

Oracle 11g Architecture

Figure 2.1: *Oracle 11g Architecture*

The fundamental unit of how Oracle 11g stores data is the data block. Multiple data blocks consist of extents and multiple extents form a segment such as an index segment, table segment or rollback/undo segment as shown in the following diagram. Each data block in Oracle is based and stored in the underlying operating system such as Windows or Red Hat Linux in data blocks on that operating system. Oracle stores these data blocks in shared memory within an Oracle instance within the Oracle SGA.

Within an Oracle 11g database environment, there are logical and physical structures. Logical structures consist of tablespaces and segments, whereas physical structures include the shared memory buffers from the Oracle 11g SGA and PGA as well as datafiles and Oracle blocks. The diagram in Figure 2.2 highlights these structures.

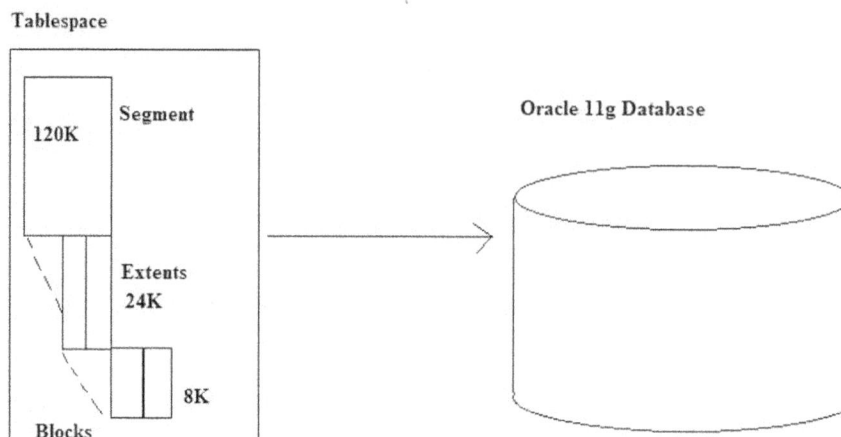

Figure 2.2: *Oracle 11g Logical to Physical Structure*

The basic architecture for logical and physical data structures within an Oracle 11g database environment can be examined by a brief example. The example will illustrate how to view the breakdown by querying the *dba_segments*, *dba_extents*, and *dba_blocks* views.

First, drill down from the tablespace and segment logical view to look at segments and extents.

```
SQL> select header_file, header_block, max_size
  2  from dba_segments
  3  where owner='SCOTT'
  4  and
  5  relative_fno=1;

HEADER_FILE HEADER_BLOCK   MAX_SIZE
----------- ------------ ----------
          1        89049 2147483645
```

By using the SQL*Plus describe on the *dba_segments* view, many characteristics of segments within Oracle 11g can be determined.

```
SQL> desc dba_segments

Name                                        Null?    Type
----------------------------------------    --------  ----------------
OWNER                                                 VARCHAR2(30)
SEGMENT_NAME                                          VARCHAR2(81)
PARTITION_NAME                                        VARCHAR2(30)
SEGMENT_TYPE                                          VARCHAR2(18)
SEGMENT_SUBTYPE                                       VARCHAR2(10)
TABLESPACE_NAME                                       VARCHAR2(30)
HEADER_FILE                                           NUMBER
HEADER_BLOCK                                          NUMBER
BYTES                                                 NUMBER
BLOCKS                                                NUMBER
EXTENTS                                               NUMBER
INITIAL_EXTENT                                        NUMBER
NEXT_EXTENT                                           NUMBER
MIN_EXTENTS                                           NUMBER
MAX_EXTENTS                                           NUMBER
MAX_SIZE                                              NUMBER
RETENTION                                             VARCHAR2(7)
MINRETENTION                                          NUMBER
PCT_INCREASE                                          NUMBER
FREELISTS                                             NUMBER
FREELIST_GROUPS                                       NUMBER
RELATIVE_FNO                                          NUMBER
BUFFER_POOL                                           VARCHAR2(7)
```

Next, examine the contents of the data blocks from the *dba_extents* view.

```
SQL> select extent_id, block_id, segment_type, relative_fno
  2  from dba_extents
  3  where owner='SCOTT'
  4  and
  5  relative_fno=1;

EXTENT_ID   BLOCK_ID SEGMENT_TYPE       RELATIVE_FNO
---------- ---------- ------------------ ------------
        0      89049 TABLE                         1
```

The options available for viewing extents and blocks in Oracle 11g can be revealed with a SQL*Plus describe on the *dba_extents* view as shown below.

```
SQL> desc dba_extents

Name                                        Null?    Type
----------------------------------------    --------  ----------------
OWNER                                                 VARCHAR2(30)
SEGMENT_NAME                                          VARCHAR2(81)
PARTITION_NAME                                        VARCHAR2(30)
SEGMENT_TYPE                                          VARCHAR2(18)
TABLESPACE_NAME                                       VARCHAR2(30)
```

```
EXTENT_ID                              NUMBER
FILE_ID                                NUMBER
BLOCK_ID                               NUMBER
BYTES                                  NUMBER
BLOCKS                                 NUMBER
RELATIVE_FNO                           NUMBER
```

In database releases prior to Oracle 9i, management of database blocks and segments occupied a great deal of a database administrator's time due to the fact that fragmentation issues would occur in the form of either data row migration or row chaining. Manual segment space management was the only method available to administer database segments and blocks and issues, whereas tuning the values for *pct_free* and *pct_used* would complicate the life of many Oracle database professionals.

Fortunately later releases, starting with Oracle 9i, introduced locally managed tablespaces as well as automatic segment space management (ASSM) which reduced the complex nature of tuning these values for database segments and blocks. In a nutshell, these features provided automated methods to tune and manage segments and data blocks without the need for the Oracle DBA to provide specific values for *pct_free* and *pct_used* at the segment and database block level. Instead, the locally managed tablespace model and automatic segment space management (ASSM) provides bitmaps to manage these settings without the need for DBA intervention. As a result, fragmentation and row chaining issues are mainly a thing of the past provided that the Oracle database administrator uses locally managed tablespaces and ASSM with Oracle 9i and later releases of Oracle.

By understanding the nature of how Oracle uses data blocks, one can prevent and manage such problems as block corruption by using the *dbverify* tool. For example, to detect a block corruption problem, run the utility mentioned above against the example tablespace for Oracle 11g on Linux platform as shown here:

```
[oracle@raclinux1 backupset]$ dbv

DBVERIFY: Release 11.1.0.6.0 - Production on Mon Oct 27 00:30:07 2008
```

```
Keyword      Description                      (Default)
-------------------------------------------------------
FILE         File to Verify                   (NONE)
START        Start Block                      (First Block of File)
END          End Block                        (Last Block of File)
BLOCKSIZE    Logical Block Size               (8192)
LOGFILE      Output Log                       (NONE)
FEEDBACK     Display Progress                 (0)
PARFILE      Parameter File                   (NONE)
USERID       Username/Password                (NONE)
SEGMENT_ID   Segment ID (tsn.relfile.block)   (NONE)
HIGH_SCN     Highest Block SCN To Verify      (NONE)
             (scn_wrap.scn_base OR scn)
```

The syntax to use *dbverify* with check for block corruption is shown
below:

```
dbv file=example01.dbf blocksize=8192
```

Make sure that the OS user account has read and write permissions or
an error will occur with Oracle 11g Release 1 due to a bug with *dbverify*.

In addition, Oracle provides block corruption detection and repair with
the Oracle 11g Recovery Manager (RMAN) utility during backup and
recovery processing. To check for block corruption with Oracle 11g
RMAN, you can use the *backup check logical validate database* command to
search for logical block corruption or the *backup check logical database*
command with RMAN to search for both physical and logical database
corruption with Oracle 11g. Note: the RMAN command does not
actually perform a database backup. The following example performs the
check.

```
$ rman target /

Recovery Manager: Release 11.1.0.7.0 - Production on Sun Oct 25 20:17:42
2009

Copyright (c) 1982, 2007, Oracle.  All rights reserved.

connected to target database: TEST (DBID=3791167554)

RMAN> backup check logical database;

Starting backup at 25-OCT-09
using target database control file instead of recovery catalog
```

```
allocated channel: ORA_DISK_1
channel ORA_DISK_1: SID=250 device type=DISK
channel ORA_DISK_1: starting piece 1 at 25-OCT-09
input datafile file number=00048

File Status Marked Corrupt Empty Blocks Blocks Examined High SCN
---- ------ ------------- ------------ --------------- 
59   OK     0             131071       131072           0
  File Name: /test/db/data/system12.dbf
  Block Type Blocks Failing Blocks Processed
  ---------- -------------- ----------------
  Data       0              0
  Index      0              0
  Other      0              1

validate found one or more corrupt blocks
See trace file /u01/oracle/11.1.0/admin/diag/rdbms/test/trace/test_ora_2498616.trc for details
channel ORA_DISK_1: starting full datafile backup set
channel ORA_DISK_1: specifying datafile(s) in backup set
including current control file in backup set
channel ORA_DISK_1: backup set complete, elapsed time: 00:00:03
List of Control File and SPFILE
================================
File Type    Status Blocks Failing Blocks Examined
-----------  ------ -------------- ---------------
Control File OK     0              1760
Finished backup at 25-OCT-09

RMAN>
```

Block corruption can also be detected by querying the
v$database_block_corruption dynamic performance view. To repair block
corruption, the *dbms_repair* package can be used with Oracle 11g.

Now that the essentials of logical and physical structures for Oracle 11g
have been discovered, memory structures will be shown next. Every
Oracle 11g database instance consists of the Shared Global Area (SGA)
and Program Global Area (PGA) memory regions. These memory areas
will be reviewed and explained in the following section.

Inside the Oracle 11g System Global Area (SGA)

Oracle 11g has introduced more automation based on the new
Automatic Memory Management (AMM) methodology introduced with
the Oracle 10g database release to ease tuning and configuration for
SGA memory buffers. Figure 2.3 illustrates with an architecture diagram
of the SGA memory structures how Oracle 11g SGA memory operates.

Oracle 11g System Global Area (SGA)

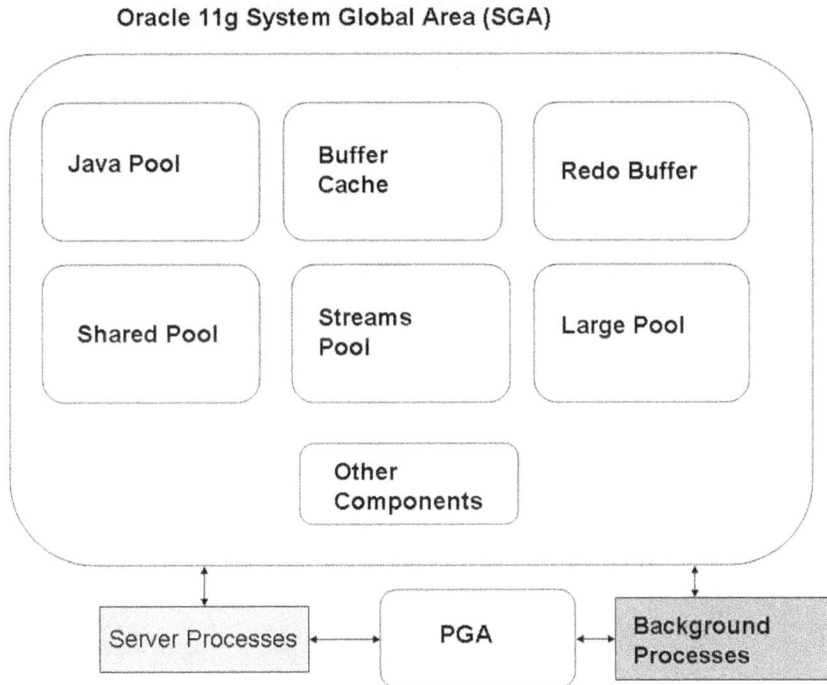

Figure 2.3: *Oracle 11g SGA Memory Structures*

In the past, database administrators would have to tune all of the manual configuration parameters for the Oracle SGA buffers such as the *db_cache_size* and *log_buffer* regions of the SGA. As one can imagine, this cost the busy Oracle DBA a great deal of time and frustration using mostly trial and error results to correctly size the SGA buffers for the Oracle environment.

With the arrival of the Oracle 10g database release, a great deal of tuning and sizing the Oracle SGA has now become a lot easier due to automated settings that are provided with AMM. For example, with Oracle 10g, the Oracle DBA only really needs to set a few parameters such as *sga_target* and *sga_max_size* for the Oracle database and instance and Oracle will take care of the correct sizing for the SGA buffers. Further tuning recommendations can be gathered from either query of the *v$sga_target_advice* dynamic performance view or from one of the new Oracle 11g database advisors which how to use will be revealed shortly. In addition to fewer settings for SGA memory buffers, the Oracle 11g database provides an entire set of advisors to provide recommendations for sizing all of the memory buffers within the Oracle 11g System Global Area.

To view the contents and information on the Oracle 11g SGA buffers, query the *v$sga*, *v$sgainfo*, and *v$sgastat* dynamic performance views as shown in the following queries:

```
SQL> select * from v$sgainfo;

NAME                              BYTES RES
-------------------------------- ---------- ---
Fixed SGA Size                    1300184 No
Redo Buffers                      6184960 No
Buffer Cache Size               100663296 Yes
Shared Pool Size                113246208 Yes
Large Pool Size                   4194304 Yes
Java Pool Size                   12582912 Yes
Streams Pool Size                       0 Yes
Shared IO Pool Size                     0 Yes
Granule Size                      4194304 No
Maximum SGA Size                397557760 No
Startup overhead in Shared Pool  41943040 No
Free SGA Memory Available       159383552
```

The *v$sgainfo* dynamic performance view displays the total Fixed SGA size as well as currently available free SGA memory in bytes along with the size of the main SGA buffers such as the buffer cache and Java pool. In addition, it provides the DBA with the current size of each granule which is the basic building block of memory for the SGA with Oracle 11g. A more in-depth view of the SGA buffers is provided by the *v$sgastat* output:

```
SQL> select * from v$sgastat;

POOL        NAME                                 BYTES
----------- ------------------------------- ----------
            fixed_sga                          1300184
            buffer_cache                      96468992
POOL        NAME                                 BYTES
----------- ------------------------------- ----------
            log_buffer                         6184960
shared pool dpslut_kfdsg                           256
shared pool hot latch diagnostics                   80
shared pool ENQUEUE STATS                          9920
```

```
shared pool   sskgplib                        1048
shared pool   transaction                   386804
shared pool   Wait History Array                 4
shared pool   KCB buffer wait statistic       3352
shared pool   invalid low rba queue            320
shared pool   KCB tablespace encryption        672
shared pool   KQF optimizer stats table       3092
shared pool   bt_qentry                      14304
shared pool   CCursor                      3597672
shared pool   ksunfy: system-global sta       4024
```

Automatic Memory Management (AMM)

With the previous release for Oracle 10g, a new memory sizing and tuning method was introduced called Automatic Memory Management (AMM). This new paradigm for memory sizing and tuning of the Oracle 11g SGA and PGA replaced the many different memory initialization parameters with a few parameters (*sga_max_size*, *sga_target*, *pga_aggregate_target*, *pga_aggregate_target*) to simplify memory management for the hard working DBA.

The Automatic Memory Management (AMM) allows changes to be made for SGA memory management by setting the *sga_max_size* parameter for RAM memory requirements for an Oracle database instance. The benefit further extends in that these database instance parameters are dynamic, meaning that they can be changed by using *alter system* commands without the need for an instance shutdown and restart, thus avoiding downtime to modify memory configuration for Oracle.

Now with the Oracle 11g release, Oracle has further reduced the complexity of memory sizing and configuration with just two parameters: *memory_target* and *memory_max_target*.

According to the Oracle 11g documentation, the *memory_target* database initialization parameter is specific to the entire system wide instance available memory for Oracle 11g. By changing the *memory_target* parameter, the DBA allows Oracle to auto-tune the size of the SGA and PGA as required. However, if one does not configure the *memory_max_target* parameter and only set the value for the *memory_target*

---

parameter, then Oracle will automatically set the value for the *memory_max_target* parameter to the same value as that for *memory_target*.

In addition, if no value is given for the *memory_target* parameter, Oracle 11g will set the default value for *memory_target* to zero. The *memory_target* parameter can be set dynamically without the need for an instance restart with Oracle 11g provided that it does not exceed the value given to *memory_max_target*.

Oracle 11g Advisors for SGA and PGA Memory

Oracle 11g provides advisors which were introduced in the previous 10g release for sizing memory regions within the SGA and PGA. These advisors are excellent tools that provide a baseline estimate for an initial database installation for sizing memory requirements with Oracle 11g.

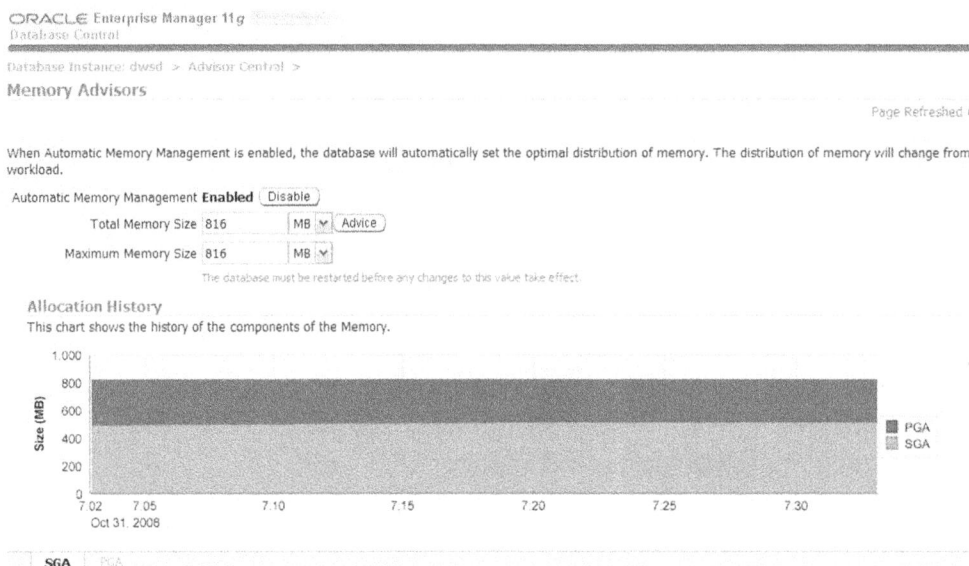

Figure 2.4: *Oracle 11g Memory Advisors*

In the Memory Advisors page from within Oracle 11g Enterprise Manager, current SGA parameters can be examined as shown in Figure 2.5.

Allocation History

This chart shows the history of the components of the SGA.

Current Allocation

Automatic Shared Memory Management **Enabled**

Total SGA Size (MB) **512**

SGA Component Current Allocation (MB)	
Shared Pool	160
Buffer Cache	336
Large Pool	4
Java Pool	4
Other	8

Shared Pool (31.2%)
Buffer Cache (65.6%)
Large Pool (0.8%)
Java Pool (0.8%)
Other (1.6%)

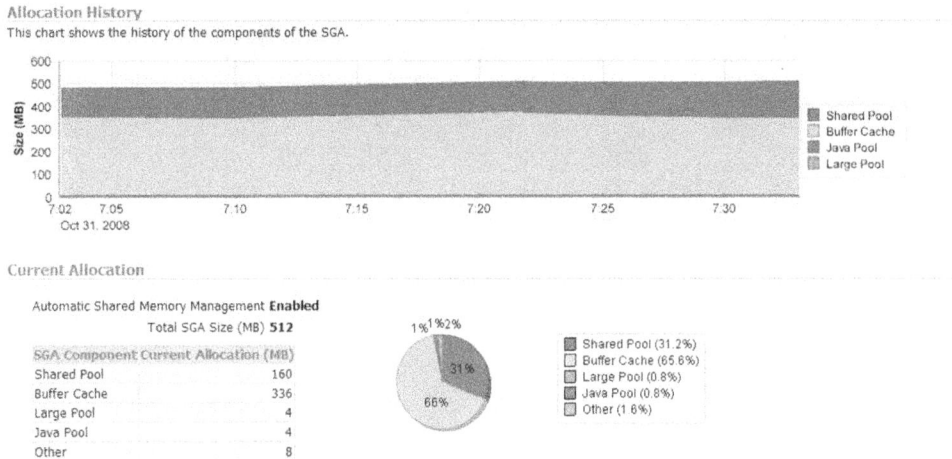

Figure 2.5: *SGA Settings in Oracle 11g Enterprise Manager*

Of note here is that the graphical display presents a comprehensive bird's eye picture of memory settings and configurations for review and analysis.

From the main advisor's menu within Oracle 11g Enterprise Manager, review memory configuration settings for the SGA and PGA as well as obtain recommendations for tuning and optimization for these memory buffers. In the following figure, the current settings are displayed for the PGA memory.

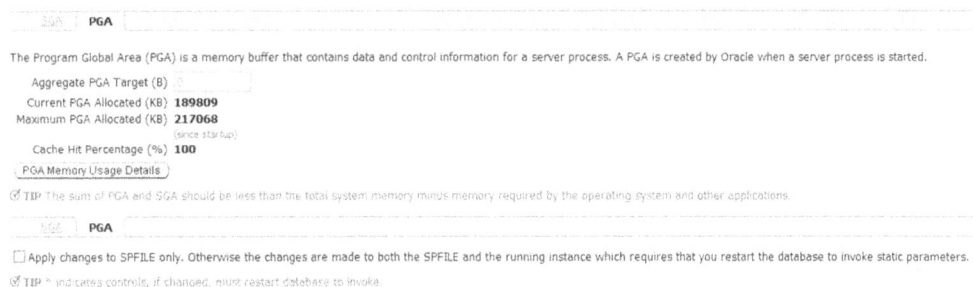

The Program Global Area (PGA) is a memory buffer that contains data and control information for a server process. A PGA is created by Oracle when a server process is started.

Aggregate PGA Target (B)
Current PGA Allocated (KB) **189809**
Maximum PGA Allocated (KB) **217068**
(since startup)
Cache Hit Percentage (%) **100**

PGA Memory Usage Details

☑ TIP The sum of PGA and SGA should be less than the total system memory minus memory required by the operating system and other applications.

☐ Apply changes to SPFILE only. Otherwise the changes are made to both the SPFILE and the running instance which requires that you restart the database to invoke static parameters.

☑ TIP * indicates controls, if changed, must restart database to invoke.

Figure 2.6: *PGA Settings in Oracle 11g Enterprise Manager*

For memory sizing recommendations, click the Advice button in the Memory Advisor main screen and the following graph will be displayed to show recommended settings and expected performance results.

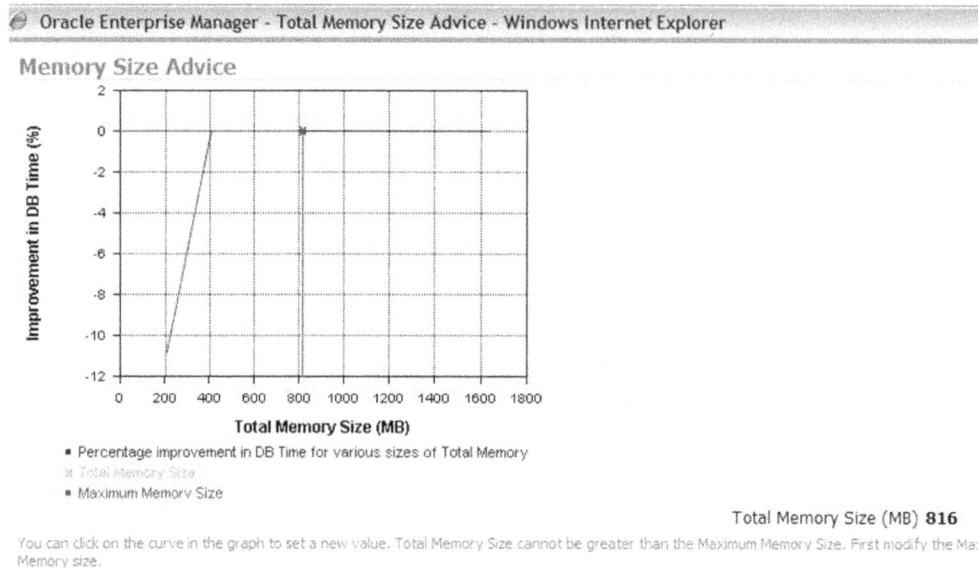

Figure 2.7: *Memory Size Advice in Oracle 11g Enterprise Manager*

Another added benefit of using the Oracle 11g Memory Advisors is the ability to monitor and tune the Oracle 11g PGA memory as shown in the following figure.

PGA Memory Usage Details

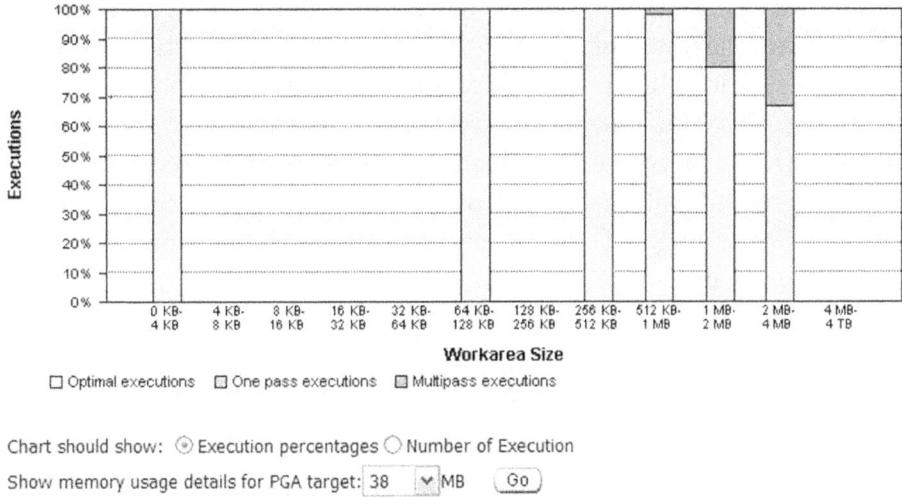

Figure 2.8: *PGA Memory Usage in Oracle 11g Enterprise Manager*

Memory usage for the PGA can be tuned as such by testing various settings in Oracle 11g Enterprise Manager. Next to be provided is an overview of the various components within the Oracle 11g SGA before the architecture for the PGA with Oracle 11g is covered.

Shared Pool

The shared pool is a key component of the Oracle SGA for Oracle 11g. As part of the Oracle 11g SGA, it contains the following caches within it:

- Library Cache
- Data Dictionary Cache
- Result Cache

The Library Cache

The library cache stores details for SQL and PL/SQL statements that are executed against the Oracle 11g database. In addition to the SQL statements, the library cache within the shared pool contains the execution plan and parse tree structures. In the event that the library cache buffer is sized too small, the parse trees and execution plans for SQL statements will be flushed out of the cache area, thereby requiring frequent reloading of SQL statements and causing performance degradation issues.

To monitor the memory configuration for the Oracle 11g library cache, the dynamic performance view *v$library_cache_memory* can be queried as shown below:

```
SQL> select lc_namespace, lc_inuse_memory_size, lc_freeable_memory_s
  2  from v$library_cache_memory;

LC_NAMESPACE    LC_INUSE_MEMORY_SIZE LC_FREEABLE_MEMORY_SIZE
--------------- -------------------- -----------------------
BODY                               7                       5
CLUSTER                            0                       0
INDEX                              0                       0
JAVA DATA                          0                       0
JAVA RESOURCE                      0                       0
JAVA SOURCE                        0                       0
OBJECT                             0                       0
OTHER/SYSTEM                       0                       0
PIPE                               0                       0
SQL AREA                           2                      33
TABLE/PROCEDURE                   17                       4
TRIGGER                            0                       0

12 rows selected.
```

In addition to the *v$library_cache_memory*, the dynamic performance view *v$librarycache* is useful for monitoring the library cache for Oracle 11g as shown in the example below.

```
SQL> desc v$librarycache

Name                                      Null?    Type
----------------------------------------- -------- ----------------
NAMESPACE                                          VARCHAR2(15)
GETS                                               NUMBER
GETHITS                                            NUMBER
GETHITRATIO                                        NUMBER
PINS                                               NUMBER
```

```
PINHITS                         NUMBER
PINHITRATIO                     NUMBER
RELOADS                         NUMBER
INVALIDATIONS                   NUMBER
DLM_LOCK_REQUESTS               NUMBER
DLM_PIN_REQUESTS                NUMBER
DLM_PIN_RELEASES                NUMBER
DLM_INVALIDATION_REQUESTS       NUMBER
DLM_INVALIDATIONS               NUMBER


SQL> select namespace, gets, pins, reloads, gethitratio, pinhitratio
     from v$librarycache;

NAMESPACE              GETS       PINS   RELOADS GETHITRATIO PINHITRATIO
---------------- ---------- ---------- ---------- ----------- -----------
SQL AREA              61114    5526459       1551 .651961907  .995038595
TABLE/PROCEDURE      326067    1299133       4257 .979053385  .987386203
BODY                   7957     888938         30 .875706925   .99881544
TRIGGER                5352     993863          5 .973281016  .999753487
INDEX                  5633       4825         80  .85087875  .683108808
CLUSTER                4380       1663          1 .996118721  .989176188
OBJECT                    0          0          0           1           1
PIPE                      0          0          0           1           1
JAVA SOURCE               0          0          0           1           1
JAVA RESOURCE             0          0          0           1           1
JAVA DATA                10        874          0          .7 .993135011

11 rows selected.
```

The Data Dictionary Cache

The second major cache area within the shared pool for Oracle 11g is the data dictionary cache. As a key buffer cache of the shared pool, the data dictionary cache houses the internal data structures for the Oracle database. When an Oracle database is first started, no data exists in the data dictionary cache. For this reason, the dictionary cache should be monitored and tuned only after the Oracle 11g database environment has been up and running for a period of time. One way to minimize contention issues on the data dictionary cache is to use Locally Managed Tablespaces (LMT) for Oracle 11g tablespaces instead of dictionary managed tablespaces. This will help reduced contention on the data dictionary cache.

Tuning the Shared Pool for Oracle 11g

Oracle 11g provides the *v$shared_pool_advice* dynamic performance view that can be used to obtain tuning advice for the shared pool as shown in the following example.

```
SQL> desc v$shared_pool_advice
```

```
Name                                      Null?    Type
----------------------------------------- -------- ----------
SHARED_POOL_SIZE_FOR_ESTIMATE                      NUMBER
SHARED_POOL_SIZE_FACTOR                            NUMBER
ESTD_LC_SIZE                                       NUMBER
ESTD_LC_MEMORY_OBJECTS                             NUMBER
ESTD_LC_TIME_SAVED                                 NUMBER
ESTD_LC_TIME_SAVED_FACTOR                          NUMBER
ESTD_LC_LOAD_TIME                                  NUMBER
ESTD_LC_LOAD_TIME_FACTOR                           NUMBER
ESTD_LC_MEMORY_OBJECT_HITS                         NUMBER
```

To obtain a truly useful value for sizing the shared pool for Oracle 11g, set the *statistics_level* parameter to either TYPICAL or ALL before querying the *v$shared_pool_advice* dynamic performance view.

So if one wants to look at recommended settings for the shared pool with Oracle 11g, issue the following query:

```
SQL> SELECT shared_pool_size_for_estimate "Size of Shared Pool in MB",
  2    shared_pool_size_factor "Size Factor",
  3    estd_lc_time_saved "Time Saved in sec"
  4  FROM v$shared_pool_advice;

Size of Shared Pool in MB Size Factor Time Saved in sec
------------------------- ----------- -----------------
                      136       .7727             17000
                      156       .8864             17009
                      176           1             17036
                      196      1.1136             17048
                      216      1.2273             17051
                      236      1.3409             17052
                      256      1.4545             17052
                      276      1.5682             17052
                      296      1.6818             17052
                      316      1.7955             17052
                      336      1.9091             17052

Size of Shared Pool in MB Size Factor Time Saved in sec
------------------------- ----------- -----------------
                      356      2.0227             17052

12 rows selected.
```

An interesting observation can be noted here in the output from the *v$shared_pool_advice* query in the above figure.

The performance benefit varies little between a shared pool size of 136MB to 156MB. Only a real performance benefit can be seen when the shared pool size has been increased to 236MB. Also of note is that increasing the shared pool size beyond 236MB yields no additional performance benefit for the shared pool performance with Oracle 11g. In fact, Oracle support notes on Metalink (Metalink Note #255409.1) advise against increasing the size of the shared pool to a large value as it may cause latch contention or fragmentation problems.

Another dynamic performance view, *v$rowcache*, may also assist tuning efforts for the shared pool memory cache regions. While hit ratios are no longer gospel as far as performance tuning results, they can be helpful when used as part of a comprehensive performance tuning assessment. In general, hit ratios should be above 95% for the library cache and data dictionary cache within the shared pool for Oracle 11g. Also, a performance report collected via the Oracle 11g ADDM (Automatic Database Diagnostic Monitor) and/or report from a recent snapshot with the Oracle 11g ADR (Automatic Diagnostic Repository) will yield outstanding performance issues with the shared pool cache areas.

Result Cache

The result cache is new to Oracle 11g and provides enhanced query performance for SQL and PL/SQL applications by caching the results of SQL queries into memory. The following Oracle 11g database initialization parameters affect the operation and function of the result cache for Oracle 11g:

- *client_result_cache_lag*
- *client_result_cache_size*
- *result_cache_max_result*
- *result_cache_max_size*
- *result_cache_mode*
- *result_cache_remote_expiration*

Database Buffer Cache

The database buffer cache is an integral part of the Oracle 11g SGA that provides the following tasks:

- Storage for data blocks that have been retrieved from data files

- Provides optimization boost for DML operations (updates)

- Managed via the LRU algorithm

Whenever a query is processed by Oracle 11g, the server process looks in the database buffer cache to locate any blocks that it needs. In the event that the block is not found in the database buffer cache, Oracle reads the block from the datafiles and then places a copy into the database buffer cache. The purpose of the LRU (Least Recently Used) algorithm is to age out buffers that are not accessed recently in order to free up space for new blocks in the database buffer cache.

To manage the database buffer cache, use Automatic Memory Management with Oracle 11g. Then the two database initialization parameters, *memory_target* and *memory_max_target*, will perform the automatic tuning sizing for the database buffer cache along with the other components of the SGA for Oracle 11g.

The database cache is composed of three different independent subcaches:

- *db_cache_size* is the default buffer cache for Oracle 11g

- *db_keep_cache_size* is for the KEEP buffer cache

- *db_recycle_ cache_size* is for the RECYCLE buffer cache

- *db_nk_ cache_size*

These subcaches can be dynamically resized using the *alter system* commands. Each buffer in the database buffer cache is equal in size to the size of an Oracle block which is determined by the *db_block_size* database initialization parameter.

In order to obtain the optimum size for each of these subcaches as well as the database buffer cache, the performance advisors in Oracle 11g Enterprise Manager can be used as well as the *v$db_cache_advice* dynamic performance view.

```
SQL> desc v$db_cache_advice

Name                                     Null?    Type
---------------------------------------- -------- ----------------
ID                                                NUMBER
NAME                                              VARCHAR2(20)
BLOCK_SIZE                                        NUMBER
ADVICE_STATUS                                     VARCHAR2(3)
SIZE_FOR_ESTIMATE                                 NUMBER
SIZE_FACTOR                                       NUMBER
BUFFERS_FOR_ESTIMATE                              NUMBER
ESTD_PHYSICAL_READ_FACTOR                         NUMBER
ESTD_PHYSICAL_READS                               NUMBER
ESTD_PHYSICAL_READ_TIME                           NUMBER
ESTD_PCT_OF_DB_TIME_FOR_READS                     NUMBER
ESTD_CLUSTER_READS                                NUMBER
ESTD_CLUSTER_READ_TIME                            NUMBER

SQL> alter system set db_cache_advice=on;

System altered.


SQL> alter system set db_cache_advice=READY;

column size_for_estimate        format 999,999,999,999
column buffers_for_estimate     format 999,999,999
column estd_physical_read_factor format 999.90
column estd_physical_reads      format 999,999,999

SELECT size_for_estimate, buffers_for_estimate
     , estd_physical_read_factor, estd_physical_reads
  FROM V$DB_CACHE_ADVICE
 WHERE name          = 'DEFAULT'
   AND block_size    = (SELECT value FROM V$PARAMETER
                        WHERE name = 'db_block_size')
   AND advice_status = 'ON';
```

| | | Estd Phys | Estd Phys | |
Cache Size (MB)	Buffers	Read Factor	Reads	
30	3,802	18.70	192,317,943	10% of Current Size
60	7,604	12.83	131,949,536	
91	11,406	7.38	75,865,861	
121	15,208	4.97	51,111,658	
152	19,010	3.64	37,460,786	
182	22,812	2.50	25,668,196	
212	26,614	1.74	17,850,847	
243	30,416	1.33	13,720,149	
273	34,218	1.13	11,583,180	
304	38,020	1.00	10,282,475	Current Size
334	41,822	.93	9,515,878	
364	45,624	.87	8,909,026	
395	49,426	.83	8,495,039	
424	53,228	.79	8,116,496	
456	57,030	.76	7,824,764	

```
486      60,832      .74    7,563,180
517      64,634      .71    7,311,729
547      68,436      .69    7,104,280
577      72,238      .67    6,895,122
608      76,040      .66    6,739,731    200% Size
```

The above example shows that at nearly twice the size of current
database buffer cache, one can obtain substantial performance
improvement over the number of physical reads that occur with the
Oracle 11g database.

Streams Pool

The Oracle 11g Streams Pool provides the following benefits within the
SGA:

- Stores buffered queue messages for Oracle Streams and Advanced
  Queuing

- Provides memory for Oracle Streams capture and apply processes

The Oracle 11g Streams Pool is configured via the *streams_pool_size*
database initialization parameter for Oracle 11g.

The dynamic performance view *v$streams_pool_advice* can be used to
gather details on how best to size the Streams pool for Oracle 11g or the
Oracle 11g Automatic Memory Management (AMM) can be used for
sizing the Streams pool. For example, to tune the Streams pool, query
the *v$streams_pool_advice* dynamic performance view for Oracle 11g as
shown in the following listing.

```
SQL> desc v$streams_pool_advice

 Name                                      Null?    Type
 ----------------------------------------- -------- ----------------
 STREAMS_POOL_SIZE_FOR_ESTIMATE                     NUMBER
 STREAMS_POOL_SIZE_FACTOR                           NUMBER
 ESTD_SPILL_COUNT                                   NUMBER
 ESTD_SPILL_TIME                                    NUMBER
 ESTD_UNSPILL_COUNT                                 NUMBER
 ESTD_UNSPILL_TIME                                  NUMBER

SQL> select estd_spill_time, estd_unspill_time, streams_pool_size_factor,
  2    streams_pool_size_factor
  3    from v$streams_pool_advice;


ESTD_SPILL_TIME ESTD_UNSPILL_TIME STREAMS_POOL_SIZE_FACTOR STREAMS_POOL_SIZE_FACTOR
--------------- ----------------- ------------------------------------------------ ---------------------------------
```

0	0	.2308	.2308
0	0	.3846	.3846
0	0	.5385	.5385

Large Pool

The large pool buffer is an important part of the Oracle 11g SGA that provides the following functions:

- Parallel Query performance management

- Recovery Manager (RMAN) backup and recovery operations

- Shared Server operations

It is recommended to use the Oracle 11g Automatic Shared Memory Management (ASMM) discussed earlier to size the SGA buffers, including the large pool. However, in the event that this is to be configured manually, Oracle recommends the following formula to size the large pool. For example, to size the large pool manually for RMAN operations, use the formula:

```
large_pool_size = num_of_allocated_channels * (16MB + (4 *
size_of_tape_buffer))
```

The large pool is set either using ASMM for Oracle 11g Automatic Memory Management (AMM) or by the database initialization parameter *large_pool_size*.

Redo Log Buffer

The Oracle 11g redo log buffer provides the following functions within the Oracle 11g SGA:

- Serves for assistance with database recovery tasks

- Records all changes made to database blocks

- Places changes recorded to redo entries for redo logs

The database initialization parameter *log_buffer* defines the default size of the redo log buffer within Oracle 11g.

Java Pool

The function of the Java pool buffer within the Oracle 11g SGA is to provide the following tasks:

- Parsing of Java code and scripts
- Installation tasks related to Java applications with Oracle 11g
- Java stored procedure code parsing

In order to tune the best size for the Java pool within Oracle 11g, either the AMM feature can be deployed or manual tuning can be conducted via the *v$javapool* and *v$java_pool_advice* dynamic performance views as shown in the following example listings:

```
SQL> desc v$javapool

Name                                      Null?    Type
----------------------------------------- -------- ---------------CATEGORY
VARCHAR2(16)
MEMUSED                                             NUMBER

SQL> select * from v$javapool;

CATEGORY          MEMUSED
----------------  ----------
                  8755260
```

The dynamic performance view *v$java_pool_advice* provides details for tuning the Java pool for different pool sizes. These sizes range from 10% of the current Java pool size all the way to up to 200% of the Java pool size.

```
SQL> desc v$java_pool_advice

Name                                      Null?    Type
----------------------------------------- -------- ---------------
.JAVA_POOL_SIZE_FOR_ESTIMATE                       NUMBER
JAVA_POOL_SIZE_FACTOR                              NUMBER
ESTD_LC_SIZE                                       NUMBER
ESTD_LC_MEMORY_OBJECTS                             NUMBER
ESTD_LC_TIME_SAVED                                 NUMBER
ESTD_LC_TIME_SAVED_FACTOR                          NUMBER
ESTD_LC_LOAD_TIME                                  NUMBER
ESTD_LC_LOAD_TIME_FACTOR                           NUMBER
ESTD_LC_MEMORY_OBJECT_HITS                         NUMBER
```

```
SQL> SELECT
estd_lc_load_time,java_pool_size_factor,java_pool_size_for_estimate
  from v$java_pool_advice;

ESTD_LC_LOAD_TIME JAVA_POOL_SIZE_FACTOR JAVA_POOL_SIZE_FOR_ESTIMATE
----------------- --------------------- ---------------------------
             2588                     1                          16
             2588                     2                          32
```

Now that the main buffers within the Oracle 11g SGA have been introduced, the section on the Oracle 11g SGA will be concluded by mentioning the other buffers that exist within the Oracle 11g SGA.

Other Components Within the Oracle 11g SGA

The additional components that may exist as optional memory structures within the Oracle 11g SGA include the flashback memory buffer, Streams pool, Java pool, and new to 11g, the ASM buffer cache. The flashback memory buffer area is used with the flashback features which were introduced in Oracle 10g such as the ability to perform flashback transaction query, flashback table, flashback database and flashback versions query. To view the contents of these additional memory buffers within Oracle 11g, issue the following query against the *v$sgastat* and *v$sga* dynamic performance views as was seen earlier in the chapter.

Oracle 11g introduces a new dynamic performance view called *v$memory_dynamic_components* that can be used to examine memory contents for 11g:

```
SQL> select component, current_size, max_size
  2  from v$memory_dynamic_components;

COMPONENT                   CURRENT_SIZE    MAX_SIZE
--------------------        ------------    ----------
shared pool                    121634816    121634816
large pool                       4194304      4194304
java pool                       12582912     12582912
streams pool                           0            0
SGA Target                     234881024    243269632
DEFAULT buffer cache            92274688    155189248
KEEP buffer cache                      0            0
RECYCLE buffer cache                   0            0
DEFAULT 2K buffer cache                0            0
DEFAULT 4K buffer cache                0            0
```

```
DEFAULT 8K buffer cache                  0            0

COMPONENT                         CURRENT_SIZE   MAX_SIZE
-------------------               ------------   ----------
DEFAULT 16K buffer cache                 0            0
DEFAULT 32K buffer cache                 0            0
Shared IO Pool                           0            0
PGA Target                        163577856    209715200
ASM Buffer Cache                         0            0

16 rows selected.
```

Inside the Oracle 11g Program Global Area (PGA)

The Oracle 11g PGA provides the following functions within the Oracle database:

- Stores data and control information for each user session

- Manages memory buffer for user processes connected to the database

Each user session contains its own PGA taken from the operating system free memory pool. As sessions have the need to use PGA memory, the Oracle 11g database will allocate these sessions' memory from the PGA until the total allocation of memory is equal to the *pga_aggregate_target* value set within the database. As sessions require additional memory from the PGA, Oracle will pull the memory from other sessions that no longer need the memory.

To query the contents of the current PGA settings within Oracle 11g, issue a request against the *v$pgastat* dynamic performance view as shown:

```
SQL> select * from v$pgastat;

NAME                              VALUE          UNIT
-------------------------------------------------------------
aggregate PGA target parameter    163577856      bytes
aggregate PGA auto target         80363520       bytes
global memory bound               32714752       bytes
total PGA inusen                  74283008       bytes

NAME                              VALUE          UNIT
-------------------------------------------------------------
total PGA allocated               156244992      bytes
maximum PGA allocated             240105472      bytes
total freeable PGA memory         9240576        bytes
process count                     30
```

```
max processes count                     41
PGA memory freed back to OS             273874944       bytes
total PGA used for auto workareas       0               bytes
maximum PGA used for auto workareas     7929856         bytes
total PGA used for manual workareas     0               bytes
maximum PGA used for manual workareas   270336          bytes
over allocation count                   0
bytes processed                         581040128       bytes
extra bytes read/written                0               bytes
cache hit percentage                    100 percent
recompute count (total)                 717

19 rows selected.
```

The following items from the *v$pgastat* query above warrant further examination:

- **Aggregate PGA target:** this is the setting for PGA total available memory

- **Aggregate PGA auto target:** this is the amount of memory managed automatically by Oracle 11g when the Automatic Shared Memory (AMM) method is deployed. The remainder is reserved for non-auto tuned settings such as with the stack space memory buffer.

- **Total PGA in use:** the current amount of PGA memory in use

- **Total PGA allocated:** refers to the amount of memory provided currently

- **Total freeable PGA memory:** is the amount of PGA memory that can be reallocated or given back to the operating system

- **Over allocation count:** refers to the number of times that Oracle 11g has to provide memory above the target amount. If this amount increases, it means that more target PGA memory needs to be allocated.

- **Cache Hit Percentage:** aim for a ratio of 100% as this indicates the number of times sessions can work in the PGA without the need to swap out memory to disk. If this ratio is below 90%, add more memory to the PGA to improve performance.

For tuning the PGA memory within Oracle 11g, either the memory advisors can be used as shown previously or automatic memory management can be deployed to tune the sizes of the PGA memory buffers via the *v$pga_target_advice* or query the new 11g dynamic performance view *v$memory_target_advice* as shown in the figure listed below.

```
SQL> select pga_target_for_estimate, pga_target_factor, estd_time
  2  from v$pga_target_advice;

PGA_TARGET_FOR_ESTIMATE PGA_TARGET_FACTOR   ESTD_TIME
----------------------- -----------------   ----------
               20447232              .125        8754
               40894464               .25        8754
               81788928                .5        8754
              122683392               .75        8754
              163577856                 1        8754
              196292608               1.2        8754
              229008384               1.4        8754
              261724160               1.6        8754
              294439936               1.8        8754
              327155712                 2        8754
              490733568                 3        8754
```

Tuning the size of the Oracle 11g PGA using the above view for *v$pga_target_advice* operates in a similar fashion to that of the SGA query (*v$sga_target_advice*) in that one needs to look at the pga_target_factor column and compare to the estd_time column from the query result to determine the best fit size for the PGA with Oracle 11g.

Another option is to experiment with the new 11g dynamic performance view *v$memory_target_advice* as shown below.

```
SQL> select * from v$memory_target_advice;


MEMORY_SIZE MEMORY_SIZE_FACTOR ESTD_DB_TIME ESTD_DB_TIME_FACTOR   VERSION
----------- ------------------ ------------ -------------------   ----------
        380                  1         2283                   1         3
        475               1.25         2284                   1         3
        570                1.5         2222               .9729         3
        665               1.75         2222               .9729         3
        760                  2         2222               .9729         3
```

So what can be ascertained from the output of the above query with *v$memory_target_advice* is that with a memory size between 570Mb and 665Mb, there is about the same performance estimate for the Oracle 11g database initialization *memory_target* parameter. This is beneficial because one can avoid wasting memory allocation by using 570Mb instead of the larger 760Mb maximum value available.

Semaphores and Oracle 11g

Semaphores are data structures within the operating system that function like signals for memory process communications. For Oracle, semaphores tell the Oracle processes when to stop, wait or start operations. In addition, semaphores tell Oracle processes when they are to resume processing. Each Oracle process has its own semaphore assigned to it.

For example, DBWR (Database Writer process) needs to flush the database buffer cache to write to the data files on disk. When it is time for DBWR to perform this task, DBWR's semaphore signals to DBWR to flush the data from the buffer out to disk. With System V implementations and variations of the UNIX and LINUX operating system, some of the key parameters that manage the use and allocation of semaphores with Oracle 11g exist in the following operating system level parameters:

- SEMMNS: number of semaphores in the operating system

- SEMMSL: size limit for a single semaphore set

- SEMMNI: number of semaphore set identifiers in the operating system

- SEMMNU: number of semaphore undo structures in the operating system

The output of semaphores can be viewed by using the *ipcs* command for UNIX and Linux platforms as will be observed in the following section on shared memory and Oracle 11g.

Mutexes and Oracle 11g

Mutexes are objects that exist within the operating system to provide access to shared memory structures. They are similar to latches, which will be covered in following chapters, as they are serialized mechanisms used to control access to shared data structures within the Oracle 11g SGA.

Serialization provides benefits via mutexes in that they are required to avoid having database objects being read during modification and to provide consistency as part of the relational database ACID (Atomicity, Consistency, Isolation and Durability) model.

Mutexes can be used and defined in various ways. Each data structure within Oracle which is under the protection of a mutex can also have its own mutex such as a parent cursor may have its own separate mutex as well as each child cursor can also have its own mutex. Structures within Oracle 11g can be protected by multiple mutexes so that each mutex will protect a different area of the database structure. While latches and mutexes are similar regarding both being serialization mechanisms and providing data protection, mutexes differ from latches in the following ways.

Mutexes are smaller and operate faster than latches because they contain fewer instructions than those in a latch get operation. Secondly, mutexes take up fewer memory resources and space than latches. Mutexes also provide less chance of contention within the database than latches do which means that mutexes provide greater protection of data structures and flexibility than latches. Another key feature of mutexes is that they can be referenced across many sessions concurrently by using shared mode. Mutexes also function in a dual role as both a serialization item similar to a latch and also as pin operator by preventing objects from aging out of the Oracle 11g memory buffers. Since both latches and mutexes are independent mechanisms, a process within Oracle can hold both a latch and mutex at the same time.

While mutexes have faster performance and less likelihood of contention issues than latches, they can still have wait events occur. For tuning mutex operations within Oracle 11g, examine the status with the *v$mutex_sleep* dynamic performance view. The *v$mutex_sleep* dynamic performance view shows a summary of sleeps and wait time for each *mutex_type*.

Another useful Oracle 11g dynamic performance view that can assist with mutex operations is *v$mutex_sleep_history* which shows which sessions are currently sleeping for a particular *mutex_type* and location. A useful query to examine the status of mutexes within Oracle 11g is shown in the example below:

```
SQL> desc v$mutex_sleep_history

Name                                       Null?    Type
-------------------------------------- -------- ----------------
MUTEX_IDENTIFIER                                    NUMBER
SLEEP_TIMESTAMP                                     TIMESTAMP(6)
MUTEX_TYPE                                          VARCHAR2(32)
GETS                                               NUMBER
SLEEPS                                             NUMBER
REQUESTING_SESSION                                 NUMBER
BLOCKING_SESSION                                   NUMBER
LOCATION                                           VARCHAR2(40)
MUTEX_VALUE                                         RAW(4)
P1                                                NUMBER
P1RAW                                             RAW(4)
P2                                                NUMBER
P3                                                NUMBER
P4                                                NUMBER
P5                                                VARCHAR2(64)


SQL> select mutex_type, gets, sleeps, mutex_value
  2  from v$mutex_sleep_history;

MUTEX_TYPE                               GETS     SLEEPS MUTEX_VA
-------------------------------- ---------- ---------- --------
Cursor Pin                               1083          9 00840000
Cursor Pin                                577          5 00840000
Cursor Pin                               1457         11 00850000
Cursor Pin                                721          6 00710000
Cursor Pin                              67443          4 009D0000
Cursor Pin                                  1         19 00820000
Cursor Pin                                  1         40 00850000
Cursor Pin                                987         19 009D0000
Cursor Pin                                651         13 009B0000
Cursor Pin                                693        110 00850000
Cursor Pin                                  9          3 007F0000
```

Wait Events and Mutexes for Oracle 11g

Mutex wait events fall into two categories:

- *cursor:mutex* shows all mutex waits on the parent cursor operations and statistics block operations

- *cursor:pin* events are mutex waits that occur whenever a cursor has been pinned within the database with the consequence that the mutex will be replaced by another object called the *latch:library* cache pin.

There are two primary wait events associated with mutexes within Oracle 11g: short duration and long duration events.

Short duration events with mutexes are rare. These wait events arise when any one process tries to update a mutex while it is in the middle of being changed by other processes. What will happen is that the waiting process will spin in wait state for the mutex to become available. An example would be for the *cursor:pin* S to be incremented at the same time when another process is updating the reference count for the shared cursor.

The second wait event associated with mutex and Oracle are long duration events. These occur whenever a process has to wait for other processes to complete their operations. For instance, the *cursor:mutex* X is being incremented at the same time as when a process wants exclusive access; however, the mutex is already being held in exclusive or shared mode by another process.

How Mutexes in Oracle 11g Differ from Operating System Mutexes

Oracle internal mutexes used for library cache cursor pinning are memory structures within the Oracle 11g SGA like latches yet smaller. Mutex allocation is performed via an all or nothing comparison swap operation and mutex release is performed via a decrement to the mutex value.

Mutexes within Oracle differ from operating system mutexes in that operating system mutexes reside in the operating system kernel space and use system calls to obtain access, whereas Oracle mutexes occupy space and reside within the Oracle SGA and do not require a system call. Rather, Oracle mutexes rely upon memory line updates.

In Oracle 11g, latches and mutexes are different mechanisms and managed via different modules within the Oracle kernel layer. Latches use the KSL* kernel layer modules and mutexes rely upon the KGX* for mutexes. A memory dump using oradebug will reveal mutex and latch structures in memory.

The primary performance benefit with mutexes over latches is that each mutex has a structure in each child cursor handle and the mutex can function as a cursor pin structure. In the event that a cursor is open or a session cursor cached, one would not be required to get the library cache latch in order to change the cursor pin status. Instead, one could modify the mutex refcount directly for the cursor.

Therefore, the mutex provides for better scalability over latches when it comes down to pinning and/or unpinning cursors since no library cache or library cache pin latching is necessary; hence, no contention for resources. However, library cache latches are still required to perform parsing operations. Whenever a mutex is enabled, cursor pins will not occur from within the *x$kglpn* output.

Now that an introduction to mutexes and semaphores for Oracle 11g has been provided, key architecture components for Windows and UNIX memory structures with Oracle will be reviewed.

Windows Memory and Threads and Oracle 11g

Windows differs from UNIX and Linux operating systems in the management of resources because it uses threads instead of shared memory segments and semaphores within Oracle 11g to manage memory usage.

Windows uses a virtual memory based system that combines physical memory along with a file system cache into a series of threads and processes. Each process or thread in the Windows architecture contains a linear flat 32 or 64-bit memory address space. As such, each process can view and access this memory space within an upper limit boundary.

The upper half regions between hexadecimal values of 0x80000000 through 0xFFFFFFFF of the virtual memory are reserved areas for system code which is accessed only by the process when it runs in privileged mode. The lower half between 0x00000000 through 0x7FFFFFFF is available to the process when it runs in user mode and user mode system services provide the communication to the processes for Oracle 11g within the Windows memory space. In earlier versions of 32-bit Windows operating systems, problems with memory allocation for the Oracle SGA arose due to a 4 GB memory ceiling limit in non 64-bit Windows operating systems. As a workaround, certain switches need to be set for the physical address area (PAE) to take advantage of larger memory on Windows based servers.

Windows divides up the physical and virtual memory into blocks called Memory Management Units (MMU) that go to the Windows Virtual Memory Manager (VMM), which then performs the memory address translation. Each Windows based server's physical MMU is broken up into a page frame that the processor numbers in a consecutive fashion with numbers up to the maximum physical memory available on the server for Windows. Page sizes vary depending on platform with Intel Windows based servers having 4096 bytes per page.

The Windows Server VMM deploys the following address resolution process of which each virtual address is split into the following components:

- Page Directory Entry/Offset (PDE)   bits 22 to 31

- Page Table Entry/Offset (PTE)   bits 12 to 21

- Page Offset   bits 0 to 11

Each process will then have its own private page directory along with a special type of hardware register to be used as a pointer to its memory address within the Windows operating system. Whenever the Windows server scheduler performs a switch between processes, the Windows operating system will copy the new process pointer into the memory register. The MMU translation mechanism makes use of the PDE offset from the virtual address in order to retrieve the contents from the page directory for the page frame number of the PTE. Finally, it then uses the PTE offset from the virtual address to retrieve to the page frame number of the code or data page required.

UNIX and Linux Shared Memory and Oracle 11g

The UNIX and LINUX operating systems allocate memory based on an interprocess communication model (IPC) to manage memory segments for Oracle database environments.

To obtain details on shared memory for UNIX and LINUX, make use of the *ipcs* command. Details on syntax are illustrated below from within the UNIX and LINUX man pages:

NAME

- *ipcs* : provide information on ipc facilities

SYNOPSIS

- *ipcs [-asmq] [-tclup]*
- *ipcs [-smq] -i id*
- *ipcs -h*

DESCRIPTION

- *ipcs* provides information on the ipc facilities for which the calling process has read access
- The -i option allows a specific resource ID to be specified. Only information on this id will be printed.

Resources may be specified as follows:

- -m   shared memory segments
- -q   message queues

In addition to the *ipcs* command, one can drill deeper into shared memory usage with Oracle 11g by using the *sysresv* command. The *sysresv*

---

command available in Linux can be used to view the currently allocated IPC resources for shared memory.

```
oracle@raclinux1 ~]$ sysresv

IPC Resources for ORACLE_SID "ORA11G":
Shared Memory:
ID              KEY
622606          0x83ed9a54
Semaphores:
ID              KEY
98304           0x521b2850
Oracle Instance alive for sid "ORA11G"
[oracle@raclinux1 ~]$
```

Now drill down to look at the shared memory segments for Linux by examination of the individual semaphores with the *ipcs* –m command.

```
[oracle@raclinux1 ~]$ ipcs -m

------ Shared Memory Segments --------
key        shmid      owner      perms      bytes      nattch     status
0x00000000 65536      oracle     600        393216     2          dest
0x00000000 98305      oracle     600        393216     2          dest
0x00000000 131074     oracle     777        393216     2          dest
0x00000000 196611     root       644        110592     2          dest
0x00000000 262148     oracle     600        393216     2          dest
0x00000000 294917     oracle     600        12288      2          dest
0x00000000 327686     oracle     600        393216     2          dest
0x00000000 360455     oracle     600        393216     2          dest
0x00000000 393224     oracle     600        393216     2          dest
0x00000000 425993     oracle     600        12288      2          dest
0x00000000 458762     oracle     600        393216     2          dest
0x00000000 491531     oracle     600        393216     2          dest
0x00000000 524300     oracle     600        393216     2          dest
0x00000000 557069     oracle     600        393216     2          dest
0x83ed9a54 622606     oracle     660        4096       0
```

Now do a check of the mapped memory segments for a single instance process for Oracle 11g by using the *pmap* command for Linux, shown next. This should provide details for SGA memory allocation for the single process.

```
[oracle@raclinux1 ~]$ pmap `pgrep -f lgwr`
4458:   ora_lgwr_ORA11G

0089d000      72K r-x--  /libnsl-2.3.4.so
008af000       8K rw---  /libnsl-2.3.4.so
008b1000       8K rw---    [ anon ]
0090a000      84K r-x--  /ld-2.3.4.so
0091f000       4K r----  /ld-2.3.4.so
00920000       4K rw---  /ld-2.3.4.so
00923000    1164K r-x--  /libc-2.3.4.so
20000000       4K r--s-  /ora_ORA11G_622606_0
31400000    4096K rw-s-  /ora_ORA11G_622606_69
```

```
31800000    4096K rw-s-    /ora_ORA11G_622606_70
31c00000    4096K rw-s-    /ora_ORA11G_622606_71
32000000    4096K rw-s-    /ora_ORA11G_622606_72
32400000    4096K rw-s-    /ora_ORA11G_622606_73
32800000    4096K rw-s-    /ora_ORA11G_622606_74
32c00000    4096K rw-s-    /ora_ORA11G_622606_75
33000000    4096K rw-s-    /ora_ORA11G_622606_76
33400000    4096K rw-s-    /ora_ORA11G_622606_77
33800000    4096K rw-s-    /ora_ORA11G_622606_78
33c00000    4096K rw-s-    /ora_ORA11G_622606_79
34000000    4096K rw-s-    /ora_ORA11G_622606_80
34400000    4096K rw-s-    /ora_ORA11G_622606_81
34800000    4096K rw-s-    /ora_ORA11G_622606_82
34c00000    4096K rw-s-    /ora_ORA11G_622606_83
35000000    4096K rw-s-    /ora_ORA11G_622606_84
35400000    4096K rw-s-    /ora_ORA11G_622606_85
35800000    4096K rw-s-    /ora_ORA11G_622606_86
b7fcd000     196K r-x--    /libskgxp11.so
b7ffe000       8K rw---    /libskgxp11.so
bfff1000      60K rwx--    [ stack ]
ffffe000       4K -----    [ anon ]
 total    536696K
```

The *pmap* command output for the LGWR process shows that Oracle 11g uses */dev/shm* for shared memory implementation. In fact, the SGA allocation files can be found by listing the contents of the */dev/shm* directory for Linux as shown in the figure listed below.

```
[oracle@raclinux1 ~]$ ls -l /dev/shm
total 247936

-rw-r----- 1 oracle oinstall 4194304 Oct 29 11:25 ora_ORA11G_622606_0
-rw-r----- 1 oracle oinstall 4194304 Oct 29 11:25 ora_ORA11G_622606_1
-rw-r----- 1 oracle oinstall       0 Oct 29 11:26 ora_ORA11G_622606_10
-rw-r----- 1 oracle oinstall       0 Oct 29 11:26 ora_ORA11G_622606_11
-rw-r----- 1 oracle oinstall       0 Oct 29 11:26 ora_ORA11G_622606_12
-rw-r----- 1 oracle oinstall       0 Oct 29 11:26 ora_ORA11G_622606_13
-rw-r----- 1 oracle oinstall       0 Oct 29 11:26 ora_ORA11G_622606_14
-rw-r----- 1 oracle oinstall       0 Oct 29 11:26 ora_ORA11G_622606_15
-rw-r----- 1 oracle oinstall       0 Oct 29 11:26 ora_ORA11G_622606_16
-rw-r----- 1 oracle oinstall       0 Oct 29 11:26 ora_ORA11G_622606_17
-rw-r----- 1 oracle oinstall       0 Oct 29 11:26 ora_ORA11G_622606_18
-rw-r----- 1 oracle oinstall       0 Oct 29 11:26 ora_ORA11G_622606_19
-rw-r----- 1 oracle oinstall       0 Oct 29 11:26 ora_ORA11G_622606_2
-rw-r----- 1 oracle oinstall       0 Oct 29 11:26 ora_ORA11G_622606_20
-rw-r----- 1 oracle oinstall       0 Oct 29 11:26 ora_ORA11G_622606_21
-rw-r----- 1 oracle oinstall       0 Oct 29 11:26 ora_ORA11G_622606_22
-rw-r----- 1 oracle oinstall       0 Oct 29 11:26 ora_ORA11G_622606_23
-rw-r----- 1 oracle oinstall       0 Oct 29 11:26 ora_ORA11G_622606_24
-rw-r----- 1 oracle oinstall       0 Oct 29 11:26 ora_ORA11G_622606_25
-rw-r----- 1 oracle oinstall       0 Oct 29 11:26 ora_ORA11G_622606_26
-rw-r----- 1 oracle oinstall       0 Oct 29 11:26 ora_ORA11G_622606_27
-rw-r----- 1 oracle oinstall       0 Oct 29 11:26 ora_ORA11G_622606_28
-rw-r----- 1 oracle oinstall       0 Oct 29 11:26 ora_ORA11G_622606_29
-rw-r----- 1 oracle oinstall       0 Oct 29 11:26 ora_ORA11G_622606_3
```

Now check the allocation of available space for shared memory under */dev/shm* for Linux:

```
[oracle@raclinux1 ~]$ df -k /dev/shm
```

```
Filesystem          1K-blocks      Used Available Use% Mounted on
--------------------------------------------------------------
none                  487452     237436    250016  49% /dev/shm
[oracle@raclinux1 ~]$
```

Of note here is that if the amount of space is not available for the
/dev/shm directory, the Oracle 11g Automatic Memory feature will fail
and generate the following error message:

```
ORA-00845: MEMORY_TARGET not supported on this system
```

One also will find a related error message written out to the Oracle 11g
alert.log for a database instance that has an improper sized */dev/shm* area:

```
Sat Nov 1 10:05:22 2008
Starting ORACLE instance (normal)
WARNING: You are trying to use the MEMORY_TARGET feature. This feature
requires the /dev/shm file system to be mounted for at least 847249408
bytes. /dev/shm is either not mounted or is mounted with available space
less than this size. Please fix this so that MEMORY_TARGET can work as
expected. Current available is 0 and used is 0 bytes.
memory_target needs larger /dev/shm
```

To resolve this issue, allocate more disk space to the */dev/shm* filesystem
mounted under *tmpfs* to have the shared memory allocation avoid
problems.

Also note that the PGA memory is mapped to */dev/zero* since it is not
allocated to shared memory. Oracle releases shared memory when the
instance is shutdown as can be seen from listing the contents of the
/dev/shm directory when the Oracle 11g instance has been shutdown as
in the example below.

```
SQL> shutdown immediate;

Database closed.
Database dismounted.
ORACLE instance shut down.

[oracle@raclinux1 ~]$ ls -l /dev/shm
total 0
[oracle@raclinux1 ~]$
```

When Oracle 11g database instance is started back up, the shared memory is allocated to the newly started Oracle 11g instance.

```
SQL> startup

ORACLE instance started.

Total System Global Area  397557760 bytes
Fixed Size                  1300184 bytes
Variable Size             234883368 bytes
Database Buffers          155189248 bytes
Redo Buffers                6184960 bytes
Database mounted.
Database opened.

SQL>

[oracle@raclinux1 ~]$ ls -l /dev/shm
total 237436
-rw-r-----  1 oracle oinstall 4194304 Nov  1 16:46 ora_ORA11G_950286_0
-rw-r-----  1 oracle oinstall 4194304 Nov  1 16:46 ora_ORA11G_950286_1
-rw-r-----  1 oracle oinstall       0 Nov  1 16:47 ora_ORA11G_950286_10
-rw-r-----  1 oracle oinstall       0 Nov  1 16:47 ora_ORA11G_950286_11
-rw-r-----  1 oracle oinstall       0 Nov  1 16:47 ora_ORA11G_950286_12
-rw-r-----  1 oracle oinstall       0 Nov  1 16:47 ora_ORA11G_950286_13
-rw-r-----  1 oracle oinstall       0 Nov  1 16:47 ora_ORA11G_950286_14
```

Stack Traces for Oracle 11g Shared Memory

Oracle provides a useful undocumented tool called oradebug that can be used to obtain memory stack dumps for shared memory. In addition, the *pstack* command available with Linux provides a stack dump for Oracle 11g processes and shared memory. Now use the following example to obtain a stack dump for the Oracle 11g SMON background process.

First to be used is the *pstack* command for Linux to dump the memory stack for the Oracle 11g SMON process:

```
[oracle@raclinux1 ~]$ ps -ef|grep smon

oracle    28774     1  0 16:47 ?        00:00:01 ora_smon_ORA11G
oracle    31798  4211  0 17:09 pts/2    00:00:00 grep smon

[oracle@raclinux1 ~]$ pstack 28774

#0  0x0090a7a2 in _dl_sysinfo_int80 () from /lib/ld-linux.so.2
#1  0x009eb2d4 in semtimedop () from /lib/tls/libc.so.6
#2  0x0e5571f7 in sskgpwwait ()
#3  0x0e556186 in skgpwwait ()
#4  0x0e2a431c in ksliwat ()
#5  0x0e2a3c89 in kslwaitctx. ()
#6  0x0e2a0fc9 in kslwait ()
```

```
#7   0x08697fb1 in ktmmon. ()
#8   0x08697d48 in ktmSmonMain ()
#9   0x08da1d49 in ksbrdp ()
#10  0x08e86b9c in opirip ()
#11  0x08985730 in opidrv ()
#12  0x08bf6b03 in sou2o ()
#13  0x0851a400 in opimai_real ()
#14  0x08bfa2d6 in ssthrdmain ()
#15  0x0851a2fc in main ()
```

Next to be viewed is the stack memory dump by using the *oradebug* command while logged into Oracle 11g as SYS:

```
SQL> oradebug setospid 28774

Oracle pid: 12, Unix process pid: 28774, image:
oracle@raclinux1.us.oracle.com (SMON)

SQL> oradebug short_stack
```

```
<-ksedsts()+285<-ksdxfstk()+22<-ksdxcb()+1599<-sspuser()+102<-
semtimedop()+36<-sskgpwwait()+211<-skgpwwait()+104<-ksliwat()+1256<-
kslwaitctx()+135<-kslwait()+329<-ktmmon()+591<-ktmSmonMain()+22<-
ksbrdp()+1209<-opirip()+548<-opidrv()+500<-sou2o()+91<-opimai_real()+238<-
ssthrdmain()+142<-main()+116<-__libc_start_main()+227<-_start()+33
```

As can be seen, obtaining memory stack dumps is essential to understanding Oracle 11g database internals.

Understanding the Oracle 11g Memory Call Stack

Oracle 11g memory call stacks can be cryptic to understand. Fortunately, Metalink Note #558671.1 provides insight into how to decipher the call stack that was generated earlier. To best understand the various flags and codes in the memory call stack, view the following chart.

```
Analysis of Call Stack:

Summary Stack   (to Full stack)   (to Function List)
-----------------------------------------------------
ksedst            # KSE: dump the call stack
ksedmp            # KSE: dump the process state
ksddoa            # Debug support Do an Action
ksdpcg            # KSD: Post and check event in the specified event group
ksdpec            #KSD:  Post   Event   and   Check   trigger   conditionPGOSF70_ksfpec104
kgesev            KGE: Signal Error code (with Va_list)
ksesec0           # IGNORE: Signal an error
kpoblng
kpobsv
kpobii
kpobav
opibvg
opiexe            opiexe - ORACLE Program Interface EXEcute
opipls            opipls.c — contains opi bundled call executor and support routines
opiodr            OPIODR: ORACLE coderequestdriver-routethecurrentrequest PGOSF163_rpidrus
skgmstack         skgmstack - call specified function with extra STACK space
```

```
rpidru          RPI: setup memory for the recursive session (unclear)
rpiswu2         RPI: SWitch User in recursive sql
rpidrv          RPI: Recursive Program Interface DRiVer


Summary Stack   (to Full stack)   (to Function List)
-------------------------------------------------------
psddr0          Null pointer definitions for ttcdrv callback and context.Used in psddrv.
psdnal          ARGSUSED */
pevm_EXECC
pfrinstr_EXECC
pfrrun_no_tool
pfrrun          PSDEVN: PL/SQL Interpreter Main Instruction Loop
plsql_run
peicnt          PL/SQL controlled Execution
kkxexe          KKX: execute plsql
opiexe          opiexe - ORACLE Program Interface EXEcute
kpoal8          kpoal8.c - Kernel Programmatic Oracle ALl Version 8
opiodr          OPIODR: ORACLE code request driver - route the current request
ttcpip          TTCPIP: Two Task Common PIPe read/write
opitsk          opitsk - Two Task Oracle Side Function Dispatcher
opiino          opiino - ORACLE Program Interface INitialize Opi
opiodr          OPIODR: ORACLE code request driver - route the current request
opidrv          # opidrv - ORACLE Program Interface DRiVer (IGNORE)
sou2o           # Main Oracle executable entry point
opimai_real
main            # Standard executable entry point
```

Tracing Shared Memory for Oracle 11g

In addition to the *pstack* and *pmap* commands for Linux, another way to
trace Oracle shared memory is to use the oradebug *ipc* command.

```
SQL> oradebug setmypid

Statement processed.

SQL> oradebug unlimit

Statement processed.

SQL> oradebug ipc

Information written to trace file.
```

Look at the shared memory generated to the trace file as shown below
from the oradebug *ipc* command.

```
Processing Oradebug command 'ipc'

Dump of unix-generic skgm context
-------------------------------
areaflags          000000f7
realmflags         0000000f
mapsize            00000800
protectsize        00001000
lcmsize            00001000
seglen             00400000
largestsize   0000000080000000
smallestsize  0000000000400000
```

```
stacklimit          0xbe07f24c
stackdir                  -1
mode                     660
magic                acc01ade Handle:              0xb7fdd058
`/u01/app/oracle/product/11.1.0/11gORA11G' Dump of unix-generic realm handle
`/u01/app/oracle/product/11.1.0/11gORA11G', flags = 00000000  Area #0 `Fixed
Size' containing Subareas 0-0
  Total size 000000000013d6d8 Minimum Subarea size 00000000

   Area  Subarea     Shmid     Stable Addr       Actual Addr
      0        0    950286 0x00000020000000 0x00000020000000
                           Subarea size     Segment size
                           000000000013e000 0000000018000000
  Area #1 `Variable Size' containing Subareas 4-4
   Total size 0000000017400000 Minimum Subarea size 00400000
   Area  Subarea     Shmid     Stable Addr       Actual Addr
      1        4    950286 0x00000020800000 0x00000020800000
                           Subarea size     Segment size
```

To dump the contents of the SGA memory for Oracle 11g, proceed with the oradebug *dumpsga* command:

```
SQL> oradebug setmypid

Statement processed.

SQL> oradebug unlimit

Statement processed.

SQL> oradebug dumpsga

Statement processed.
```

The trace file from oradebug shows the contents of the SGA memory buffers:

```
----- Fixed Areas Dump (level=2) -----
----- Dump of the Fixed SGA -----
ksmsgft ksmsgf_ [20000000, 20001000) = 00000000 00000000 00000000 00000000 ...
Dump of memory from 0x20000010 to 0x20001000
20000010 00000000 00000000 00000000 00000000  [................]
  Repeat 254 times
kywmr * kywmrsga_ [20001000, 20001004) = 37834020
ksllt kywmll_ [20001004, 20001068) = 00000000 00000000 00000000 00000000 ...
Dump of memory from 0x20001014 to 0x20001068
20001010          00000000 00000000 00000000       [............]
20001020 00000000 00000000 00000000 00000000  [................]
```

Summary

In this chapter, a detailed explanation for the Oracle 11g Memory structures has been provided. The following topics about how Oracle 11g memory operates were discussed:

- Essential new features Oracle 11g memory management

- Oracle 11g SGA memory structures

- Oracle 11g PGA memory structures

- UNIX memory management for Oracle 11g

- Windows memory architecture for Oracle 11g

- Tips for tuning and sizing Oracle 11g Memory

In the next couple of chapters, how Oracle 11g handles locking and latching activities with a focus on transaction management and tuning will be examined. Furthermore, exploration of the interaction between locking and latching with Oracle 11g memory structures to provide a "best practices" methodology for tuning and solving problems that involve Oracle locks and latches will occur.

Oracle Internals: Locks and Oracle 11g

CHAPTER

3

Introduction

In the previous chapter, the Oracle 11g memory structures and how they interact with the operating system were covered in great detail. Now database locking structures will be examined in terms of how they provide database concurrency with Oracle. The following topics will be presented on Oracle 11g locking:

- Locks and Oracle 11g

- Lock management and escalation with Oracle 11g

- Lock management in an Oracle 11g RAC environment

- Enhancements to locks with Oracle 11g

- Tips for resolving lock issues with Oracle 11g

- Avoiding deadlock conditions with Oracle 11g

First to be introduced are the concepts and architecture for how Oracle 11g locks operate within the relational database model for concurrency.

What Are Locks?

Oracle locks have been around a long time since the inception of the first major database release with the Oracle database environment. What is the purpose of a lock within the Oracle database? Locks function as the primary mechanism to provide for data concurrency and data consistency within the database. It allows for multiple users to access the data simultaneously while providing a consistent view of data including any changes made by each user's transaction and that of other user transactions made to and against the data within Oracle 11g.

Furthermore, locks prevent errors in read and write consistency as part of the relational database ACID model. The database ACID model refers to Atomic, Consistency, Isolation, and Durability. To further explain what ACID means in terms of Oracle and other relational database models, the following explanation illustrates.

Atomicity:

For each transaction within the Oracle database, all of the units of work for a transaction must either be all or nothing. In other words, the transaction must be completed or else it must be undone or rolled back. Undo and rollback provide these functions with transactions in concert with locking and latching mechanisms.

Consistency:

Every transaction is required to preserve the integrity constraints which function as part of the declared consistency rules within the Oracle database. Database constraints are the business rules that provide for consistency.

Isolation:

This means that multiple transactions cannot interfere with one another at the same time. Results that are performed in flight, i.e. uncommitted transactions, are not visible to other transactions until a commit phase is executed and completed. Locks provide the mechanism for the isolation phase within the ACID model for Oracle database transactions. For example, if Sally user locks table A with an exclusive lock, then user Bill will not be able to update the rows in that table until Sally has completed her transaction on that table. If locks did not exist within Oracle, there would be many problems with phantom reads and writes. This concurrency control ensures that all transactions within Oracle are executed safely and according to these rules so that no committed transactions are lost while in the event of a rollback undo operation to abort transactions.

Durability:

Durability is provided for by the Oracle database engine so that completed transactions are maintained and not lost in the future. Oracle protects against lost transactions by use of committed transactions stored within the undo/rollback segments and undo tablespaces within the Oracle 11g database engine.

Database Isolation Levels and Serialization for Transactions

Before this chapter delves into a detailed explanation of how locks work within Oracle 11g, it would be beneficial to quickly review a few basics on how transactions operate within the relational database model.

In terms of how database isolation levels function, the ANSI/ISO SQL standard (SQL92) breaks these down into four levels of transaction isolation. Each isolation level contains various degrees of impact on transaction processing. The isolation levels are explained in terms of the following three phenomena that must be prevented between concurrently executing transactions:

1. Dirty reads: dirty reads occur when a transaction reads data that has been written by another transaction that has not yet been committed

2. Fuzzy or non-repeatable reads: fuzzy reads occur when a database transaction re-reads data it has already read and then finds that another committed transaction has modified or deleted the same data.

3. Phantom reads: phantom reads occur when a transaction in Oracle re-executes a query that returns the rows that satisfy a particular search and discovers that another committed transaction has already inserted additional rows that meet the condition.

The database standard for SQL92 expounds these four levels of isolation as shown in the following table.

Isolation Level	Dirty Read	Nonrepeatable Read	Phantom Read
Read uncommitted	Possible	Possible	Possible
Read committed	Not possible	Possible	Possible
Repeatable read	Not possible	Not possible	Possible
Serializable	Not possible	Not possible	Not possible

Table 3.1: *Read Phenomena per Isolation Level*

The Oracle database uses the read committed and serializable isolation levels in addition to a read-only mode. By default, Oracle uses the Read committed isolation level for database transactions. Next to be examined are how locks operate within Oracle 11g.

Since Oracle is a database system that permits hundreds, if not thousands, of multiple users to access data, it requires a method to lock data in order to resolve problems associated with data concurrency, consistency, and integrity. Here is where locks enter the picture.

Database locks are mechanisms that prevent errors from occurring that could cause dire consequences during user interaction between transactions accessing the same particular resource within Oracle. As such, these resources contain two basic types of data locks for user objects such as tables and data and system objects which are the hidden underlying data structures within the database engine such as the Oracle 11g data dictionary and memory.

For all purposes of explanation, the Oracle database will automatically obtain the necessary locks when SQL statements are executed by users. This process is hidden from users so that they are able to perform tasks without manual intervention. By default, Oracle will use the lowest possible level of restriction to provide for the highest rate of data concurrency while also providing perfect data integrity. In addition, users have the ability to lock data manually within Oracle 11g based on the nature of the application design.

As was mentioned earlier, locks function to protect data integrity and consistency within the Oracle database environment. Locks operate both implicitly when SQL statements are executed by users as well as explicitly when user application design dictates that locking be performed in such a manner. Explicit locking prevents the resource from being shared by other users so that a particular application user can modify data without interference.

Share locks allow resources to be shared based on the nature of the operation performed. Multiple transactions can obtain a shared lock on the same resource within Oracle 11g. Table 3.2 on page 91 provides a truth logic table that illustrates the interaction between various lock modes within Oracle.

The following section will explain each mode of table lock from least restrictive to most restrictive. It will also describe the actions that cause the transaction to acquire a table lock in that mode and which actions are permitted and prohibited in other transactions by a lock in that mode.

How Locks Operate within Oracle 11g

Now that a background on data concurrency has been provided with respect to Oracle 11g, move on to how locking mechanisms function with Oracle.

The Oracle database automatically uses different types of locks to control concurrent access to data and to prevent destructive interaction between users. The Oracle database automatically locks a resource on behalf of a transaction to prevent other transactions from doing something when also requiring exclusive access to the same resource. The lock is released automatically when some event occurs so that the transaction no longer requires the resource.

Throughout its operation, Oracle will acquire specific types of locks at different levels of restrictiveness depending on the resource being locked and the operation being performed.

The next section will explain what the three main types of locks are within Oracle and how they function.

Types of Locks within Oracle 11g

Oracle 11g provides the following three main kinds of locks:

- DML locks
- DDL locks
- Internal locks and latches

First to be explained is how DML locks function within Oracle 11g.

DML Locks

DML locks or data locks guarantee the integrity of data being accessed concurrently by multiple users. DML locks help to prevent damage caused by interference from simultaneous conflicting DML or DDL operations. By default, DML statements acquire both table-level locks and row-level locks.

The reference for each type of lock or lock mode is the abbreviation used in the Locks Monitor from Oracle 11g Enterprise Manager (OEM). For example, OEM might display TM for any table lock within Oracle 11g rather than show an indicator for the mode of table lock (RS or SRX).

Row Locks (TX)

Row-level locks serve a primary function to prevent multiple transactions from modifying the same row. Whenever a transaction needs to modify a row, a row lock is acquired by Oracle.

There is no hard limit on the exact number of row locks held by a statement or transaction. Also, unlike other database platforms, Oracle will never escalate a lock from the row level to a coarser granular level. This row locking ability provides the DBA with the finest granular level of locking possible and, as such, provides the best possible data concurrency and performance for transactions.

The mixing of multiple concurrency levels of control and row level locking means that users face contention for data only whenever the same rows are accessed at the same time. Furthermore, readers of data will never have to wait for writers of the same data rows. Writers of data are not required to wait for readers of these same data rows except in the case of when a *select...for update* is used.

Writers will only wait on other writers if they try to update the same rows at the same point in time. In a few special cases, readers of data may need to wait for writers of the same data. For example, concerning certain unique issues with pending transactions in distributed database environments with Oracle.

Transactions will acquire exclusive row locks for individual rows that are using modified *insert*, *update*, and *delete* statements and also for the *select* with the *for update* clause.

Modified rows are always locked in exclusive mode with Oracle so that other transactions do not modify the row until the transaction which holds the lock issues a commit or is rolled back. In the event that the Oracle database transaction does fail to complete successfully due to an instance failure, then Oracle database block level recovery will make a row available before the entire transaction is recovered. The Oracle database provides the mechanism by which row locks acquire automatically for the DML statements mentioned above.

Whenever a transaction obtains row locks for a row, it also acquires a table lock for the corresponding table. Table locks prevent conflicts with DDL operations that would cause an override of data changes in the current transaction.

Table Locks (TM)

What are table locks in Oracle? Table locks perform concurrency control for simultaneous DDL operations so that a table is not dropped in the middle of a DML operation, for example. When Oracle issues a DDL or DML statement on a table, a table lock is then acquired. As a rule, table locks do not affect concurrency of DML operations. Locks can be acquired at both the table and sub-partition level with partitioned tables in Oracle 11g.

A transaction acquires a table lock when a table is modified in the following DML statements: *insert*, *update*, *delete*, *select* with the *for update* clause, and *lock table*. These DML operations require table locks for two purposes: to reserve DML access to the table on behalf of a transaction and to prevent DDL operations that would conflict with the transaction. Any table lock prevents the acquisition of an exclusive DDL lock on the same table, and thereby prevents DDL operations that require such locks. For example, a table cannot be altered or dropped if an uncommitted transaction holds a table lock for it.

A table lock can be held in any of several modes: row share (RS), row exclusive (RX), share (S), share row exclusive (SRX), and exclusive (X). The restrictiveness of a table lock's mode determines the modes in which other table locks on the same table can be obtained and held.

Transaction Locks (TX)

Transaction locks (TX) lock are acquired and based on the actions that a transaction performs within the Oracle database. For instance, whenever a transaction initiates its first change, a new transaction lock is acquired and held until the transaction completes its unit of work by either a commit or rollback action. These types of locks within Oracle are used mainly as a queuing mechanism so that other sessions can wait for the transaction to complete. The lock name (ID1 and ID2) of the TX lock reflects the transaction ID of the active transaction.

The following chart provides a breakdown for how locks operate with various database operations.

SQL Statement	Table Lock Mode	RS	RX	S	SRX	X
SELECT...FROM table...	None	Y	Y	Y	Y	Y
INSERT INTO table ...	RX	Y	Y	N	N	N
UPDATE table ...	RX	Y*	Y*	N	N	N
DELETE FROM table ...	RX	Y*	Y*	N	N	N
SELECT ... FROM table FOR UPDATE OF ...	RX	Y*	Y*	N	N	N
LOCK TABLE .... IN ROW SHARE MODE	RS	Y	Y	Y	Y	N
LOCK TABLE ...... IN ROW EXCLUSIVE MODE	RX	Y	Y	N	N	N
LOCK TABLE ..... IN SHARE MODE	S	Y	N	Y	N	N
LOCK TABLE ..... IN SHARE ROW EXCLUSIVE MODE	SRX	Y	N	N	N	N
LOCK TABLE .... IN EXCLUSIVE MODE	X	N	N	N	N	N

Table 3.2: *Summary of Table Locks within Oracle 11g*

RS: Row Share

RX: Row eXclusive

S: Share

SRX: Share Row eXclusive

X: eXclusive

*Yes, if there are no conflicting row locks being held by other transactions. Otherwise, waits will occur.

One way to better understand how locks work within the Oracle database environment is to query the underlying *v$* dynamic performance views as listed below:

```
SQL> select table_name from dict
  2  where table_name like 'V$LOCK%';

TABLE_NAME
------------------------------
V$LOCK
V$LOCKED_OBJECT
V$LOCKS_WITH_COLLISIONS
V$LOCK_ACTIVITY
V$LOCK_ELEMENT
V$LOCK_TYPE

6 rows selected.
```

Of particular interest would be *v$lock* and *v$lock_type* which provide a nice summary of the locks held currently within the Oracle database. For instance, obtain a list of the various locks currently active along with a description of each lock type with the following query:

```
select name, type, description
from v$lock_type
```

NAME	TYPE	DESCRIPTION
WLM Plan Operations	WM	Synchronizes new WLM Plan activation
Cross-Instance Call	CI	Coordinates cross-instance function invocations
Process Startup	PR	Synchronizes process startup
GES Deadlock Test	AK	Lock used for internal testing
GES Internal	DI	Coordinates Global Enqueue deadlock detection
GES Resource Remastering	RM	Coordinates Global Enqueue Service resource remastering
Parameter	PE	Synchronizes system parameter updates
Global Parameter	PG	Synchronizes global system parameter updates
File Object	FP	Synchronizes various File Object(FOB) operations
Block Repair/Resilvering	RE	Synchronizes block repair/mirror resilvering operations
Scheduler	KM	Synchronizes various Resource Manager operations
Scheduler Plan	KT	Synchronizes accesses to the current Resource Manager plan
Calibration	CA	Lock used by IO Calibration
KSV slave startup	PV	Synchronizes slave start_shut
File Mapping	FM	Synchronizes access to global file mapping state
Internal Test	XY	Lock used for internal testing
Service Operations	AS	Synchronizes new service activation
Property Lock	PD	Serializes property update
Rolling Migration	RU	Serialized rolling migration operations
ksz synch nodes	MX	Used to synchronize storage server info across all
System Change Number instances	SC	Coordinates system change number generation on multiple

---

Controlfile Transaction	CF	Synchronizes accesses to the controlfile
Suspend Writes	SW	Coordinates the 'alter system suspend' operation
Database Suspend	DS	Prevents a database suspend during LMON reconfiguration
Tablespace Checkpoint tablespace checkpoint	TC	Lock held to guarantee uniqueness of a
Buffer Cache PreWarm buffers	PW	Coordinates Direct Loads with Prewarmed cache
Multiple Object Reuse	RO	Coordinates flushing of multiple objects
Multiple Object Checkpoint	KO	Coordinates checkpointing of multiple objects
LNS archiving log	WR	Coordinates access to logs by Async LNS and ARCH/FG
LogWriter Standby databases	WS	Used by LogWriter to coordinate communication to standby
Being Written Redo Log logs	WL	Coordinates access to redo log files and archive
Redo Log Nab Computation during recovery	RN	Coordinates nab computations of online logs
Datafile Online in RAC is brought online in RAC	DF	Enqueue held by foreground or DBWR when a datafile
Instance State	IS	Enqueue used to synchronize instance state changes
File Set / Dictionary Check operations or synchronize dictionary check	FS	Enqueue used to synchronize recovery and file
Database Mount/Open database mount/open with other operations	DM	Enqueue held by foreground or DBWR to synchronize
Resilver / Repair datablock is repaired from mirror	RP	Enqueue held when resilvering is needed or when
Redo Thread indicate mounted or open status	RT	Thread locks held by LGWR, DBW0, and RVWR to
Kick Instance to Switch Logs force a log switch	KK	Lock held by open redo thread, used by other instances to
Instance Recovery	IR	Synchronizes instance recovery
Media Recovery of datafiles	MR	Lock used to coordinate media recovery with other uses
Backup/Restore other operations to wait for it	BR	Lock held by a backup/restore operation to allow
NID operations to wait for it	ID	Lock held by a NID operation to allow other
LogMiner prevents multiple instances from preparing the same LogMiner session	MN	Synchronizes updates to the LogMiner dictionary and
Transportable Tablespace tablespaces	PL	Coordinates plug-in operation of transportable
LogicalStandby	SB	Synchronizes Logical Standby metadata operations
Quiesce / Force Logging force logging	XR	Lock held during database quiesce or for database
Block Change Tracking various purposes	CT	A general class of locks used by change tracking for
Reclaimable Space operations to wait for it	RS	Lock held by a space reclaimable operation to allow other

Flashback database log	FL	Synchronize access to flashback database log
Flashback Database	FD	Coordinate flashback database
Flashback Writer	FW	Coordinate RVWR on multiple instances
DML	TM	Synchronizes accesses to an object
Space Transaction managed tablespaces	ST	Synchronizes space management activities in dictionary-
Instance Undo tablespaces	TA	Serializes operations on undo segments and undo
Transaction to wait for it	TX	Lock held by a transaction to allow other transactions
Cross-Instance Transaction instances to finish	TW	Lock held by one instance to wait for transactions on all
Undo Segment	US	Lock held to perform DDL on the undo segment
Kti blr lock	IM	Serializes block recovery for an IMU txn
KTF map table enqueue mapping table	TD	Serializes updates and inserts to the SMON_SCN_TIME
KTF broadcast	TE	Serializes broadcasts for flushes to SMON_SCN_TIME
KTCN REG enq	CN	Enqueue held for registrations for change notifications
KTUCLO Master Slave enq	CO	Enqueue held for determining Master Slaves
KTFA Recovery	FE	Flashback archive Enqueue to serialize recovery
Temporary File	TF	Serializes dropping of a temporary file
Default Temporary Tablespace table space and user creation	DT	Serializes changing the default temporary
Segment High Water Mark inserts	HW	Lock used to broker the high water mark during parallel
Temporary Segment	TS	Serializes accesses to temp segments
Format Block blocks in auto segment space managed tablespaces	FB	Ensures that only one process can format data
Sort Segment parallel DML operations aren't prematurely cleaned up	SS	Ensures that sort segments created during
Shrink Segment	SK	Serialize shrink of a segment
In memory Dispenser	DW	Serialize in memory dispenser operations
SaveUndo Segment	SU	Serializes access to SaveUndo Segment
Tablespace	TT	Serializes DDL operations on tablespaces
SMON Serialization	SM	Lock to check SMON global work in RAC
KTSJ Slave Task Cancel process	SJ	Serializes cancelling task executed by slave
Sequence Cache replenish the sequence cache	SQ	Lock to ensure that only one process can
Sequence Ordering RAC mode	SV	Lock to ensure ordered sequence allocation in
Direct Loader High Water Mark during parallel inserts	HV	Lock used to broker the high water mark
Direct Loader Index Creation	DL	Lock to prevent index DDL during direct load
Hash Queue	HQ	Synchronizes the creation of new queue IDs

Types of Locks within Oracle 11g

Queue Page	HP	Synchronizes accesses to queue pages
LOB KSI LOCK	KL	KSI lock for buffer cache and wgc concurrency
Write gather local enqueue	WG	Long term lock on wgc file state
Serialize Lock request	SL	Request serialization to LCK0
Row Cache cache objects	Q	Coordinates updates and accesses to row
Diana Versioning (PL/SQL intermediate representation)	DV	Synchronizes access to lower-version Diana
Shared Object Manager)	SO	Synchronizes access to Shared Object(PL/SQL Shared Object
Library Cache Lock 3	V	Synchronizes accesses to library cache objects
Library Cache Lock 2	E	Synchronizes accesses to library cache objects
Library Cache Lock 1	L	Synchronizes accesses to library cache objects
Library Cache Pin 3 objects	Y	Synchronizes accesses to the contents of library cache
Library Cache Pin 2 library cache objects	G	Synchronizes accesses to the contents of
Library Cache Pin 1 library cache objects	N	Synchronizes accesses to the contents of
Library Cache Invalidation instances	IV	Synchronizes library cache object invalidations across
Materialized View Flags flags in detail tables	RW	Lock used when creating or reading materialized view
Outline Cache	OC	Synchronizes write accesses to the outline cache
Outline Name	OL	Synchronizes accesses to a particular outline name
Cursor compiling	CU	Recovers cursors in case of death while
Edition Lock	AE	Prevent Dropping an edition in use
Password File	PF	Synchronizes accesses to the password file
User Name during use	UN	Protects a user name from being dropped
Label Security structures	IL	Synchronizes accesses to internal label data
Label Security cache	CL	Synchronizes accesses to label cache and label tables
Master Key	MK	Serializes enc$ access
Encryption Wallet	OW	Serializes wallet initialization and access
Audit index file file	AU	Lock held to synchronize access XML to audit index
Distributed Transaction	DX	Serializes tightly coupled distributed transaction branches
Distributed Recovery	DR	Serializes the active distributed recovery operation
Global Transaction Branch	BB	2PC distributed transaction branch across RAC instances
Job Queue Date slave processes	JD	Synchronizes dates between job queue coordinator and
Job Queue single job	JQ	Lock to prevent multiple instances from running a

Online DDLs	OD	Lock to prevent concurrent online DDLs
DbsDriver logging attributes	DB	Synchronizes modification of database wide supplemental
Materialized View Log DDL statements	MD	Lock held during materialized view log DDL
Materialized View Refresh Log log	MS	Lock held during materialized view refresh to setup MV
Remote PX Process Spawn Status creation status	PI	Communicates remote Parallel Execution Server Process
PX Process Reservation synchronization	PS	Parallel Execution Server Process reservation and
KSXA Test Affinity Dictionary	AY	Affinity Dictionary test affinity synchronization
Temp Object	TO	synchronizes DDL and DML operations on a temp object
In-Mem Temp Table Meta Creation	IT	Synchronizes accesses to a temp object's metadata
BLOOM FILTER parallel statement	BF	Synchronize access to a bloom filter in a
Result Cache: Enqueue	RC	Accessing a result in the result-set cache
Kupp Process Startup	KP	Synchronizes kupp process startup
Synchronized Replication operations	SR	Coordinates replication / streams
Streams Table Instantiation instantiations	SI	Prevents multiple streams table
File Group	ZG	Coordinates file group operations
Internal	IA	
Materialized View operations (like refresh, alter) to prevent materialized view	JI	Lock held during materialized view concurrent operations on the same
Alter Tablespace	AT	Serializes 'alter tablespace' operations
User-defined	UL	Lock used by user applications
Cleanup query cache registrations registrations	CQ	Serializes access to cleanup client query cache
Session Migration	SE	Lock used by transparent session migration
Queue table enqueue	TQ	Synchronizes access to queue table
LDAP Parameter	DP	Synchronizes access to LDAP parameters
AQ Notification Mail Host Host for AQ e-mail notifications	MH	Lock used for recovery when setting Mail
AQ Notification Mail Port Port for AQ e-mail notifications	ML	Lock used for recovery when setting Mail
AQ Notification Proxy notifications	PH	Lock used for recovery when setting Proxy for AQ HTTP
AQ Notification Sender for AQ e-mail notifications	SF	Lock used for recovery when setting Sender
AQ Notification No-Proxy Domains for AQ HTTP notifications	XH	Lock used for recovery when setting No Proxy
AQ Notification Watermark for memory usage in AQ notifications	WA	Lock used for recovery when setting Watermark

Data Guard Broker	RF	Synchronizes broker lock operation involving lock value
Analytic Workspace	AW	Synchronizes access to Analytic Workspace resources
Analytic Workspace Generation	AG	Synchronizes generation use of a particular workspace
MultiWriter Object Access	AO	Synchronizes access to objects and scalar variables
OLAPI Histories resources	OQ	Synchronizes access to olapi history
INSTANCE LOCK instance	IZ	Protects the lock name space used by the
ASM Enqueue	AM	ASM instance general-purpose enqueue
ASM Freezing Cache Lock	FZ	Freezes ASM Cache for a diskgroup
ASM Instance Enqueue	CM	ASM instance and gate enqueue
ASM Extent Relocation Enqueue	XQ	ASM extent relocation
ASM Disk AU Lock disk AU	AD	Synchronizes accesses to a specific ASM
ASM Disk Online Lock recovery	DO	Synchronizes disk onlines and their
ASM Extent Fault Lock the same extent chunk	XL	Keep multiple processes from faulting in
ASM Disk Group Modification	DG	Synchronizes accesses to ASM disk groups
ASM Local Disk Group groups	DD	Synchronizes local accesses to ASM disk
ASM Disk Header	HD	Serializes accesses to ASM SGA data structures
ASM RBAL doorbell notification	DQ	Inter-RBAL process metadata invalidation
Diskgroup number generator	DN	Serializes Group number generations
ASM Group Block lock reconfiguration	XB	Prevents client diskgroup use during storage
ASM File Access Lock	FA	Synchronizes accesses to open ASM files
ASM Extent Relocation Lock	RX	Synchronizes relocating ASM extents
ASM Relocation Lock relocation	AR	Protects locked extent pointers during ASM file
Disk Group Recovery previous recovery	FR	local enqueue to serialize with PMON cleanup of a
ACD Relocation Gate Enqueue	FG	ACD relocation serialization
Disk Group Redo Generation	FT	controls the privilege to generate redo in a thread
Disk Group Chunk Mount	FC	controls access to an ACD chunk
ACD Xtnt Info CIC	FX	serialize ACD relocation CIC
ASM Rollback Recovery	RB	Serializes ASM rollback recovery operations
ASM Partnership and Status Table	PT	Gates inter-node synchronization of ASM PST metadata
ASM PST Signaling	PM	Signals inter-instance access to ASM PST metadata
ASM Cached Attributes	KE	Synchronization of ASM cached attributes
ASM Attributes Enqueue	KQ	Single Inst Sync of ASM attributes

AVD DG Number Lock	AV	AVD DG unique enqueue
AWR Flush snapshots	WF	This enqueue is used to serialize the flushing of
AWR Purge baselines	WP	This enqueue handles concurrency between purging and
DBFUS DB Feature Usage and High Water Mark Statistics	FU	This enqueue is used to serialize the capture of the
MWIN Schedule the manageability schedules with the Maintenance Window	MW	This enqueue is used to serialize the calibration of
SQL Tuning Base Existence Cache	TB	Synchronizes writes to the SQL Tuning Base Existence Cache
Active Session History Flushing	SH	To prevent multiple concurrent flushers
Advisor Framework to an advisor task	AF	This enqueue is used to serialize access
MMON restricted session restricted sessions	MO	Serialize MMON operations for
Log Lock	TL	Serializes threshold log table read and update
Threshold Chain	TH	Serializes threshold in-memory chain access
Auto Task Serialization from being spawned	TK	Prevents more than one AutoTask Background Slave
Workload Capture and Replay	RR	Prevents concurrent invokers of DBMS_WORKLOAD_*
Job Scheduler	JS	Synchronizes accesses to the job cache

187 rows selected.

As can be seen, there are over 180 types of locks that exist within the Oracle 11g database! Understanding locking within Oracle 11g provides insight into the database internal operations. Next to be covered is how lock management and escalation affect transactions in terms of the Oracle 11g database.

Lock Management and Escalation

Lock escalation occurs when numerous locks are held at one level of granularity, such as rows, and a database raises the locks to a higher level of granularity, like table. For example, if a single user locks many rows in a table, some databases automatically escalate the user's row locks to a single table. The number of locks is reduced, but the restrictiveness of what is being locked is increased.

Unlike other database products such as IBM DB2 and Microsoft SQL Server, Oracle never escalates locks. Lock escalation greatly increases the

---

likelihood of deadlocks. Imagine the situation where the system is trying to escalate locks on behalf of transaction T1 but cannot because of the locks held by transaction T2. A deadlock is created if transaction T2 also requires lock escalation of the same data before it can proceed.

Now some tips will be provided on how to manage locking issues with clustered Oracle 11g RAC environments.

Lock Management for Oracle RAC Environments

Oracle Real Application Cluster (RAC) environments introduce a special case of how locking activity is managed quite differently than single instance Oracle 11g environments. Since Oracle 11g RAC involves multiple instances that share a common database on shared storage, the *gv$* dynamic performance views can be used to monitor the status for locking activities and to resolve lock conflicts within a RAC environment.

Locking Mechanism for Oracle 11g RAC

Database resources within Oracle 11g, such as tables and rows, are represented by enqueues. Enqueues are a special type of lock within Oracle that places a request for a resource into a queue. These can be locked in various modes such as shared or exclusive lock modes. Concurrent locking requests may enter a conflict based upon lock compatibility rules. Enqueue lock resources are accessed externally by querying the *gv$resource* dynamic performance view. Lock requests can be viewed by query of the *gv$lock* dynamic performance view. Next, how locking functions with Oracle 11g RAC environments will be illustrated by a review of common lock conflict types and example.

Locking Conflict Types

Within Oracle environments, lock conflicts are composed of the following two basic types:

- Local locking conflicts (block level)

- Global lock conflicts (block level)

Local lock conflicts are limited to conflicting sessions connected to the same instance which may also apply to a single instance within RAC environments. In the *v$lock* dynamic performance view, the column for BLOCK contains the value of 1 for blocking lock (session).

Global locking conflict (block) occurs when conflicting sessions are connected to different instances for RAC environments only. With RAC environments for Oracle 11g, the *v$lock* column BLOCK will contain a value of 2 to mark potential conflicts. The value will always appear as 2 for RAC environments unless there is a local conflict present.

The first task is to use a script to display all sessions that are holding or requesting locking of resources for a particular session. Waiting sessions have a non-zero value for the column gv$lock.request. Resources are identified by the TYPE, ID1, and ID2 columns in the dynamic performance view for *gv$lock*.

How to Locate the Root Blocker with Lock Problems

The following query provides the code sample along with the query to execute to determine the root blockers causing the lock problems. The solution is to first locate and kill the root blockers. Usually the row with the highest CTIME value, e.g. row L1, will be the starting point for determine the root blocker.

Make sure that there is not another row with the same SID as that found in the L1 column, then kill the root blocker value in L1 column. Another option is to kill the oldest blocking session, which should have the highest CTIME value.

Detecting Object of Locking Conflict

Typically, problematic conflicts happen with DML Locks (transaction - TX and table - TM lock types) and sometimes it is important to find out

---

the subject of the conflict such as the need to fix the application design error to prevent these conflicts.

Object names for the TM locks can be easily identified by matching the column value for v$lock.ID1 to the column value for *dba_objects.object_id*.

We need to find a way to determine where the row is waiting for in the session waiting to match the TX request to the TM lock on the table name. It is possible to make an educated guess of where the lock problem exists by looking at the CTIME column values.

For simplicity, *gv$lock* is referred as view but actually this is synonym for the view *gv$_lock* (the same applies to *v$lock*).

```
prompt CTIME is in Seconds
set linesize 120
col BLOCK format 9
col LMODE format 9
col INST_ID format 9
col REQUEST format 9
col SID format 999999
SELECT INST_ID, SID, TYPE, ID1, ID2, LMODE, REQUEST, CTIME, BLOCK
FROM GV$LOCK WHERE (ID1,ID2,TYPE) IN
(SELECT ID1,ID2,TYPE FROM GV$LOCK WHERE request>0);
```

The following script sample output displayed next in the table gives two independent lock conflicts.

It can be noted that the oldest conflict in the below case (sid 64 vs 38) is not the same root cause since session 38 is blocked by session 67.

INST_ID	SID	TYPE	ID1	ID2	LMODE	REQUEST	CTIME	BLOCK
2	212	TX	1114116	1399221	6	0	308	2
1	248	TX	1114116	1399221	0	6	304	0
42	67	TX	6225949	1244199	6	0	26	2
1	38	TX	6225949	1244199	0	6	23	0
2	64	TX	131103	2270514	0	6	117	0
1	38	TX	131103	2270514	6	0	171	2

Table 3.3: *Blocking Sessions and Lock Escalation Issues for Oracle 11g*

Another method to locate the source of locking issues within Oracle 11g is to use the graphical interface available with Oracle 11g Enterprise Manager (OEM). While the author is not a big fan of GUI tools and prefers command line scripts and SQL*Plus, OEM has improved dramatically from previous incarnations. The following figure provides the main screen to monitor locking activity within OEM:

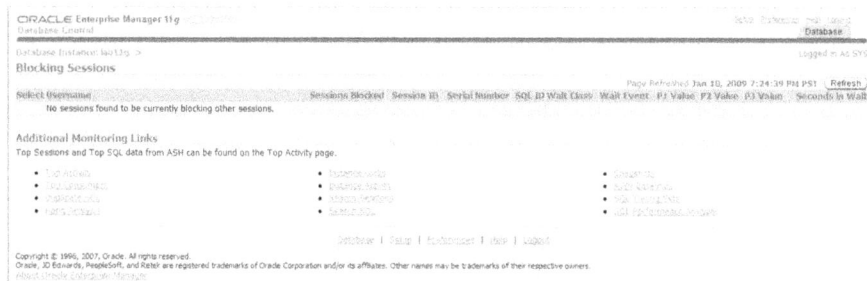

Figure 3.1: *Using Oracle 11g Enterprise Manager (OEM) to View Locking*

Within Oracle 11g, OEM also allows one to view the instance locks held for both single instance and RAC environments as shown in the following example.

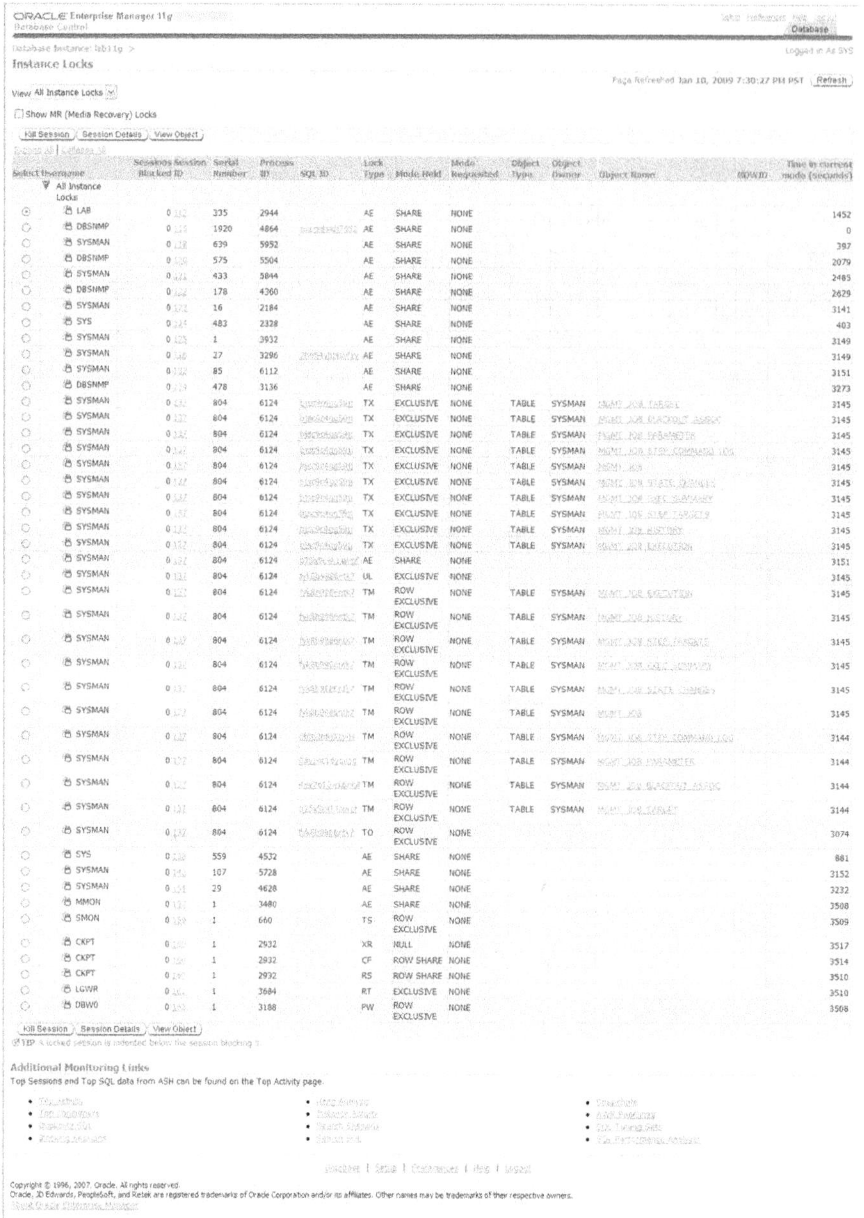

Figure 3.2: *Instance Locks within Oracle 11g via OEM Database Control*

One can also obtain more detailed information on lock conditions within Oracle 11g RAC environments by querying all result sets from the *gv$lock* dynamic view as shown below:

```
SQL> desc gv$lock
```

Name	Null?	Type
INST_ID		NUMBER
ADDR		RAW(4)
KADDR		RAW(4)
SID		NUMBER
TYPE		VARCHAR2(2)
ID1		NUMBER
ID2		NUMBER
LMODE		NUMBER
REQUEST		NUMBER
CTIME		NUMBER
BLOCK		NUMBER

```
SQL> select * from gv$lock;
```

INST_ID	ADDR	KADDR	SID	TYPE	ID1	ID2	LMODE	REQUEST	CTIME	BLOCK
1	3736701C	37367048	116	AE	99	0	4	0	102027	0
1	37366C08	37366C34	126	AE	99	0	4	0	978125	0
1	37366AAC	37366AD8	141	AE	99	0	4	0	2424366	0
1	37366CF0	37366D1C	157	AE	99	0	4	0	3241512	0
1	37367090	373670BC	158	TS	3	1	3	0	3241526	0
1	37366A38	37366A64	160	RS	25	1	2	0	3241548	0
1	373669C4	373669F0	160	CF	0	0	2	0	3241552	0
1	37366950	3736697C	160	XR	4	0	1	0	3241558	0
1	37366FA8	37366FD4	161	MR	201	0	4	0	3241534	0
1	37366F34	37366F60	161	MR	5	0	4	0	3241534	0
1	37366EC0	37366EEC	161	MR	4	0	4	0	3241534	0
1	37366E4C	37366E78	161	MR	3	0	4	0	3241534	0
1	37366DD8	37366E04	161	MR	2	0	4	0	3241534	0
1	37366D64	37366D90	161	MR	1	0	4	0	3241534	0
1	37366B94	37366BC0	162	RT	1	0	6	0	3241548	0
1	373672D4	37367300	167	KT	11187	0	4	0	9408	0

```
16 rows selected.
SQL>
```

Enhancements to Lock Management with Oracle 11g

Oracle 11g provides many additional new features for locking activities to improve database concurrency with Oracle 11g applications and databases. For example, 11g now allows DDL commands to wait for DML locks. The new serializing features help to prevent locking problems as part of the enhanced 11g new features for database lock serialization. In addition, tables can be locked explicitly within Oracle. Now examine how 11g allows one to better serialize locks.

Serializing Locks with Oracle 11g

The Oracle database 11g now allows DDL commands to wait for DML locks. The time that DDL commands wait for DML locks can be limited by setting the *ddl_lock_timeout* parameter at the system or at session level. The default initialization parameter value is set to 0 which is the NOWAIT condition for locking with DDL operations. Also of note is that this parameter records time in seconds.

The *ddl_lock_timeout* parameter in Oracle 11g Release 1 has a range of values from 0 (NOWAIT) up to 1000000. If this parameter is set to the maximum value of 1000000, it will allow the DDL statement to wait for an extremely long time. In fact, up to 11.5 days for the DML locking to occur within the 11g database environment!

In the event that the lock is not acquired upon expiration of the timeout set by the *ddl_lock_timeout* parameter, design logic should be incorporated into the application to correctly address lock timeouts.

Locking Tables Explicitly

As seen earlier, Oracle 11g DDL commands are required to hold exclusive locks on internal structures. If these internal locks are unavailable when DDL commands are issued, the consequence will be that the DDL commands will fail even though they may have succeeded if they had been sent only a few seconds later. The WAIT option allows a DDL command to wait for its locks for a specified period of time before failing.

The *lock table* command has new syntax that lets the DBA specify the maximum number of seconds the statement should wait to obtain a DML lock on the table. For instance, the following Oracle 11g syntax to perform these options would be as follows:

```
LOCK TABLE … IN {lock_mode} MODE [NOWAIT | WAIT {integer_value}
```

If the database return control is desired without a wait period, use the NOWAIT clause for the *lock table* command.

In the following example, there is a table that the DBA does not want to lock for any longer than necessary.

```
SQL> LOCK TABLE LAB.NOWAITING IN EXCLUSIVE MODE NOWAIT;

Table(s) Locked.
```

Now if the DBA tries to lock this same table owned by the lab user schema account, there will be an error message that the resource is busy as indicated by the below example:

```
C:\>sqlplus lab/lab

SQL*Plus: Release 11.1.0.6.0 - Production on Sat Jan 10 19:06:15 2009

Copyright (c) 1982, 2007, Oracle.  All rights reserved.

SQL> lock table nowaiting in share mode nowait;
lock table nowaiting in share mode nowait
*
ERROR at line 1:
ORA-00054: resource busy and acquire with NOWAIT specified or timeout
expired
```

As shown here, if the particular table, partition, or table sub-partition is already locked by another user such as SYS in the example above, then Oracle 11g will generate the ORA-0054: Resource Busy error message.

Enhancements to Lock Management with Oracle 11g

Use the WAIT clause to allow Oracle to lock tables with the *lock table* statement so that it will wait for the number of seconds in the command to acquire the DML lock. In the event that one does not specify an option for NOWAIT or WAIT, then Oracle will wait forever until the table is available, lock the object, and finally return control back to the user. When the database is executing DDL statements concurrently with DML statements, timeouts and deadlocks may occur from time to time on rare occasions. Oracle 11g has an automatic detection mechanism for such timeouts and deadlocks. If a deadlock or deadly embrace condition occurs, an error message is written to the alert log and Oracle returns the error message for the deadlock. As will soon be covered, there are some ways to resolve these conditions.

Sharing Locks in Oracle 11g

Oracle 11g has made further enhancements to locking features. Some of the changes are that the following DDL commands will no longer acquire exclusive locks (X) as was the case for previous database releases of Oracle, but rather shared exclusive locks (SX):

- *create index online*

- *create materialized view log*

- *alter table enable constraint novalidate*

In many busy environments that deploy Oracle 11g, exclusive locks during heavy DML operations may cause major performance degradation and could lead to excessive waits. The new feature that distributes the sharing of lock management of database resources eliminates many performance issues for online index and materialized view operations.

Useful Tips and Tricks for Locking Problems

The majority of locking issues within Oracle are the result of application design within database applications. One root cause of such lock contention problems lies in a basic misunderstanding of the Oracle locking model. Developers often assume incorrectly that database locking is the same across different platforms. For instance, a new Oracle developer who is used to writing database applications in Microsoft SQL Server may use the same design approach with Oracle database applications that he/she used with SQL Server. This causes most of the locking issues. The solution is simple: educate the development staff on how Oracle database locking works.

If a lock related hang scenario is encountered, the following SQL statements are useful to help isolate the waiters and blockers involved with locking problems.

Show all sessions waiting for any lock:

```
select event,p1,p2,p3 from v$session_wait
  where wait_time=0 and event='enqueue';
```

Show sessions waiting for a TX lock:

```
select * from v$lock where type='TX' and request>0;
```

Show sessions holding a TX lock:

```
select * from v$lock where type='TX' and lmode>0;
```

Of course, one can also view lock activity from the Oracle 11g Enterprise Manager (OEM) database or Grid control application as mentioned earlier. Next to be covered are some issues regarding lock contention as related to use of interested transaction lists at the Oracle 11g database block level.

Oracle 11g Database Waits: Insufficient ITL Slots

Oracle keeps track of rows that are locked per transaction in a storage area at the top of each data block called the Interested Transaction List (ITL). Two parameters, *initrans* and *maxtrans,* control the number of ITL slots in any block for an object within Oracle 11g.

Iitrans contains the total number of slots initially created in an Oracle database block when it is first used. The *maxtrans* parameter sets the

---

upper bound for the total number of entries allowed within the interested transaction list for the block. As such, each transaction that plans to modify a database block will require a new slot in the ITL list contained within the block. The *maxtrans* parameter also sets the upper limit for the number of concurrent transactions that may be active at any single point in time within an Oracle database block.

The *initrans* parameter also grants the minimum concurrency set per block. If the value is greater for *initrans* but less than the values available for *maxtrans* for transactions that are active concurrently within the same block, then the ITL list will be further extended. However, space must be available within the database block for the ITL list to be expanded.

If there are no more free ITL lists available, then the requesting session will wait on one of the active transaction locks to complete its transaction. How ITL works with 11g database locking can be investigated by using the following example:

Session 1:

```
SQL> update txns set txt='Garbage' where num=1;

1 row updated.
```

Session 2:

```
SQL> update lab.txns set txt='Junkers' where num=2;

1 row updated.
```

Now examine the locks held, if any:

```
SQL> select sid, type, id1, id2, lmode, request
  2  from v$lock
  3  where type='TX';


SID TY          ID1         ID2       LMODE     REQUEST
---------- --   ----------  ----------  ----------  ----------
       137  TX      589844         821           6           0
       134  TX      196613         705           6           0
       138  TX      393217         702           6           0
```

If there was a lock issue, the request column would display a value and the correlated SID column would be the session waiting for the lock.

One can check the ITL waits by querying the *v$segment_statistics* dynamic performance view as shown in the following example.

```
SQL> desc v$segment_statistics

Name                                     Null?    Type
---------------------------------------- -------- ---------------

OWNER                                             VARCHAR2(30)
OBJECT_NAME                                       VARCHAR2(30)
SUBOBJECT_NAME                                    VARCHAR2(30)
TABLESPACE_NAME                                   VARCHAR2(30)
TS#                                               NUMBER
OBJ#                                              NUMBER
DATAOBJ#                                          NUMBER
OBJECT_TYPE                                       VARCHAR2(18)
STATISTIC_NAME                                    VARCHAR2(64)
STATISTIC#                                        NUMBER
VALUE                                             NUMBER

SQL> select t.owner, t.object_name, t.object_type, t.statistic_name, t.value

  2  from v$segment_statistics t
  3  where t.statistic_name='ITL waits'
  4  and t.value>0;

no rows selected
```

If there were any ITL related waits, the above query would return the details.

Avoiding Deadlock Conditions

A deadlock can occur whenever multiple users are in a waiting pattern for data locked by each other. Deadlocks prevent some transactions from continuing to work. In the event of deadlock, Oracle writes the message and error in the form of an ORA-60 error to the Oracle 11g *alert.log* file. The following diagram illustrates the perfect storm condition that causes a deadlock or "deadly embrace" to occur within Oracle 11g.

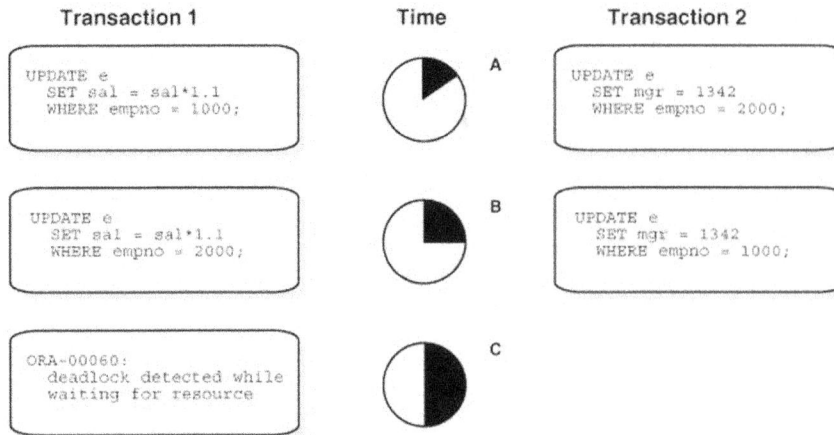

Figure 3.3: *Deadlock Condition with Oracle 11g Transactions*

Deadlock problems have a similar root cause as that found with basic locking issues with Oracle which is the result of poor database application design. To resolve deadlock conditions with Oracle, the DBA needs to work together with the developer and software engineering team to modify or rewrite the database application code so that such deadlocks do not reoccur.

Lock Contention Issues and Solutions

After the database administrator has exhausted possibilities to visit the design of the database application with the development team, the next step is to perform further analysis to solve lock contention issues.

Oftentimes, the lock issue is the result of a zombie batch process or hung database session which has placed an exclusive lock on a specific row or table, thereby blocking access to the data from other users. The simple solution to this type of problem is to identify the particular user and session causing the blocking condition and then to contact the user so that the session can be killed using the *alter system kill session 'sid,serial#' immediate* command from within SQL*Plus. In the previous section, numerous locking scenarios and potential solutions were covered.

Summary

In this chapter, the following topics about the new database locking with Oracle 11g have been explained:

- Concepts for Oracle database locks with Oracle 11g

- Oracle database locking operations within Oracle 11g

- Tips for solving locking problems with Oracle 11g

In the next chapter, latches which function similar to locks, but in a different way, will be visited.

Oracle Internals: Latches

In the previous chapter, detailed coverage was provided on how locks and concurrency function in Oracle 11g. The focus of this chapter will be to complement topics from locking with an examination of how latches operate in Oracle 11g. The various types of latches as well as differences between how latches function in a single instance Oracle 11g database as opposed to an Oracle 11g RAC clustered multiple instance environment will be covered. This chapter begins by offering a solid introduction to latches and how they exist within an Oracle 11g database.

What are Latches?

Latches are a close cousin to lock mechanisms in Oracle that provide concurrency functions and protect data integrity for Oracle data structures. Latches are a type of locking device that are quickly acquired and released. They prevent multiple processes from running the same application code in the database more than once at the same time, thus making available a serialization mechanism to provide data integrity for transaction management with Oracle database environments.

Cleanup procedures are associated with latches that are brought into play in case a process fails while holding a particular latch. Another benefit of latches within Oracle is that they help to prevent deadlocks from occurring within the Oracle database environment. Latches are the lightweight serialization mechanisms that are held and quickly released for shorter durations of time as opposed to locks which are held for longer durations of time within Oracle. Just as one would lock a door with a deadbolt heavy-duty lock to prevent entry into one's home, use a lock to protect long running transactions. Conversely, when one just wants to close the door for a short period of time, latch a transaction to keep it protected for a briefer period of time than a lock would do.

With each latch is an associated level that functions as such whenever a process within the operating system acquires a latch that determines how the latch affects the process. The level associated with a latch helps to prevent deadlocks within the Oracle database. Once a process acquires a latch at a certain level, it cannot then acquire another latch at a level that is equal or less than that level unless the latch uses the NOWAIT function.

So how are latches implemented within Oracle? Actually, latches are operating system-dependent, meaning that the specific operating system determines many of the characteristics of how a latch will behave with Oracle. For example, UNIX implementations affect latch operation for Oracle differently than Windows platforms. Later in the chapter how latches differ from enqueues and locks within Oracle will be covered. Next, take a closer look at how latches behave within Oracle 11g.

How Do Latches Work with Oracle 11g?

Latches consist of several key components as lightweight serialization mechanisms that protect access to data structures and transactions within the Oracle database. They consist of a spin count and level that is associated with each latch. Each time a latch is requested by a process in Oracle, it obtains either one of two latch request modes. The first latch request mode is called willing-to-wait. In a willing-to-wait request mode for the latch, the process that requests the latch will loop, wait and attempt another request until the latch is obtained. Some key examples of willing-to-wait type latches would be shared pool and library cache latches.

The second request mode for latches is called the no-wait mode. In no-wait mode, when the process requests a latch and if no latches are available for the process, then instead of waiting on the latch, another latch will be requested rather than waiting. The server process will only wait when all requests have failed in no-wait request mode for the latch. Redo copy latch is a type of latch that uses the no-wait request mode.

Whenever a process acquires a latch where memory data structures are accessed in the Oracle SGA (System Global Area) for Oracle 11g, it continues to hold the latch for the entire time period that it works with that memory structure. After the process has finished working with the memory structure in the Oracle 11g SGA, the latch will then be dropped. Each set of data structures within the Oracle SGA is protected by a specific latch that is identified by its latch name. In order to implement latches, Oracle uses a set of instructions such as TEST and SET in order to manage latch operations with the Oracle database environment. System processes within the operating system level wait until the latch is released before they execute a part of the code identified with the latch in question. Some examples of this would be redo allocation latches and archive control latches.

Because Oracle uses atomic instructions to manage how latches are set and freed up to processes, the operating system ensures that only one process will have access to a particular latch at one time. Due to the fact that this is only a single instruction, latches operate a lot faster than locks.

The short duration of latches are held briefly. Latches provide the safety net to block concurrent access to shared data structures within Oracle SGA memory. Without latches, memory regions in the Oracle SGA could very well become corrupted, thus causing dangerous corruption within the Oracle database environment. Latches are the failsafe mechanism to protect these memory structures within Oracle.

Oracle has a built-in mechanism for latch cleanup in the event that a latch holder fails abnormally while holding the latch. The Oracle PMON process performs this latch cleanup for failed processes with latches. Now the various types of latches that exist within Oracle 11g and how they behave within Oracle applications will be introduced.

Types of Latches within Oracle 11g

Oracle 11g has many types of latches and an entire explanation would fill a volume of encyclopedias. Hence, coverage will be provided about only the key latch types and how they function within an Oracle database environment. Each memory data structure within the Oracle 11g SGA has a latch associated with it. For example, the redo buffer has a redo latch and the buffer cache has a latch buffer cache associated with it.

The latches within Oracle can be broken down into short and long wait latches. Short wait latches are such that processes dependent on them do not have a long period to wait before acquiring the latch. Waiters spin in CPU usage for short-term latches for a brief period before latch acquisition or being freed. The process will then grab onto the latch and perform its tasks. On the other hand, long wait latches are held for long periods of time. As a consequence, processes that seek to acquire these types of long wait latches go to sleep and wake up to retry an attempt to acquire the latch rather than spinning CPU resources to acquire the resource. This helps to avoid excessive usage of memory and CPU resources since the process sleeps before attempting to gain access to the long-term latch rather than spinning CPU cycles. As soon as the long-term latch is free, waiters post the available latch as free so that the processes can acquire the latch. An example of a long-term latch would be the library cache latch family as the time to search the hash chain for SQL statements is often time consuming. Oracle 11g has a hidden parameter called *latch_wait_posting* that affects behavior of long and short-term latches within Oracle.

> **Warning:** Do not mess with changing undocumented and hidden parameters, especially in a production environment, unless guidance is provided by Oracle support. Changing settings for these undocumented parameters can introduce unexpected and potentially dangerous affects in Oracle 11g.

Cache Buffer Chain Latch Family

The first main type of latch that will be detailed for Oracle 11g is called the buffer cache latch. The buffer cache latch family consists of two types of latches: the cache buffers chain latch and the other is the cache buffers LRU chain latch. First, take a look at the cache buffers chain latch. Cache buffers chain latches are acquired at the moment in time when a data block within the Oracle 11g buffer cache is accessed by a process within Oracle. Usually latch contention for these buffer caches is due to poor disk I/O configuration. Reducing contention with these latches involves tuning the logical I/O for the associated SQL statements as well as the disk subsystem.

Another factor for latch contention with buffers chain latches could possibly be hot block contention. Oracle Metalink Note # 163424.1 has some useful tips on tuning and identifying hot blocks within the Oracle database environment.

The other buffer cache latch type is the cache buffers LRU chain latch. Whenever a new block enters the Oracle buffer cache within the SGA, this latch is acquired to allow block management in the Oracle SGA. Also, the latch is acquired when buffers are written back to disk such as when a scan is performed to move the LRU or least recently used chain of dirty blocks to flush out to disk from the buffer cache.

Library Cache Latch

Library cache latches function to protect all cached SQL statements as well as the associated object definitions contained within the library cache region in the shared pool of the Oracle 11g SGA. Whenever new statements are added to the library cache area, this type of latch must be acquired by Oracle as part of the operation. Oracle scans the library cache area during the parse phase for matching SQL statements. If one is not found, then Oracle will complete the task, obtain the library cache latch for the SQL statement and then insert it into the library cache area for future usage by the Oracle database.

There is a hidden Oracle database initialization parameter called *kgl_latch_count* which controls behavior in terms of the number of library cache latches created within the Oracle database. By default, this value should not be changed as it is sufficiently set in most cases. In the event that there should be a library cache contention issue and no other recourse is available to resolve the contention with the library cache latch, this value can be increased.

By the way, the default value for *kgl_latch_count* is set to the following prime number plus value of the database initialization parameter for *cpu_count*. The maximum allowable value for *kgl_latch_count* is no greater than 66 according to Oracle support per Bug # 1381824. Now move on to learning more about shared pool latches within Oracle 11g.

Shared Pool Latches

Shared pool latches provide the essential function of protecting crucial operations within the memory management tasks of allocating and freeing up memory resources within the shared pool region of the Oracle 11g SGA. As most senior DBAs are aware of with respect to performance tuning of Oracle database environments, SQL statements that rely on literal expressions can peg memory in the shared pool, thereby adversely affecting performance of the Oracle database. This limits database throughput and the ability to scale out for critical applications and, as such, literal SQL statements can be quite expensive.

Before Oracle 9i, there was just a single shared pool latch provided by the instance to manage these operations. With 9i and later releases of Oracle, multiple child latches were introduced to manage shared pool activities to reduce latch contention problems.

Redo Log Buffer Latches

Redo log buffer latches can be broken down into two main types of latches: redo allocation latches and redo copy latches. Redo allocation latches serve the critical purpose of providing a method to allocate space within the redo log buffer within Oracle 11g. This latch must be acquired first before entries can be made in the redo log buffer. Also of note is that if a new redo log entry is to be made that is larger than the value provided by the database initialization parameter for Oracle 11g of *log_small_entry_max_size*, the session making the request will acquire a redo allocation latch so that it may copy the entry into the redo log buffer immediately while maintaining this latch.

On the other hand, if the log entry in question is smaller than the value for the *log_small_entry_max_size* database initialization parameter for 11g, then the session will drop the redo allocation latch and instead it will acquire the second type of redo latch, the redo copy latch, so that it may copy the data into the redo log buffer. Another purpose of the redo allocation latch is that it manages the allocation of space for redo within the redo log buffer. One redo allocation latch is granted per Oracle 11g instance. The redo copy latch writes redo log records into the redo log buffer.

Row Cache Objects Latch

A correlated latch to the shared pool latch is the row cache objects latch. The purpose of this latch is to provide data protection for user processes that access the cached data dictionary area within Oracle 11g.

Exploring Latches with Dynamic Performance Views

Within the Oracle 11g data dictionary there are many *v$* and *dba_* dynamic performance views that can provide the DBA with additional details on latch behavior. First, one can perform a describe against *v$latch* from within SQL*Plus to obtain the dynamic performance view definition as shown in the following example.

```
SQL> desc v$latch

Name                                   Null?    Type
-------------------------------------- -------- ----------------
ADDR                                            RAW(4)
LATCH#                                          NUMBER
LEVEL#                                          NUMBER
NAME                                            VARCHAR2(64)
HASH                                            NUMBER
GETS                                            NUMBER
MISSES                                          NUMBER
SLEEPS                                          NUMBER
IMMEDIATE_GETS                                  NUMBER
IMMEDIATE_MISSES                                NUMBER
WAITERS_WOKEN                                   NUMBER
WAITS_HOLDING_LATCH                             NUMBER
SPIN_GETS                                       NUMBER
SLEEP1                                          NUMBER
SLEEP2                                          NUMBER
SLEEP3                                          NUMBER
SLEEP4                                          NUMBER
SLEEP5                                          NUMBER
SLEEP6                                          NUMBER
SLEEP7                                          NUMBER
SLEEP8                                          NUMBER
SLEEP9                                          NUMBER
SLEEP10                                         NUMBER
SLEEP11                                         NUMBER
WAIT_TIME                                       NUMBER
```

An explanation of *v$latch* is warranted next to better understand how latches behave within Oracle 11g. The gets column shows the total number of successful willing-to-wait requests for the latch. The misses column shows the total number of times that the initial willing-to-wait request failed. The sleeps column describes the total number of times that the process waited for a requested latch after the initial willing-to-wait request. Later to be examined is how to determine root cause of latch contention issues by using tools within Oracle 11g including these dynamic performance views for latches within Oracle. Next to be covered is another useful view to find the listing for all latches in Oracle 11g.

The following query against the dict table provides this comprehensive listing:

```
SQL> select table_name from dict where table_name like '%LATCH%';

TABLE_NAME
------------------------------
DBA_HIST_LATCH
DBA_HIST_LATCH_CHILDREN
DBA_HIST_LATCH_MISSES_SUMMARY
DBA_HIST_LATCH_NAME
DBA_HIST_LATCH_PARENT
V$LATCH
V$LATCHHOLDER
V$LATCHNAME
V$LATCH_CHILDREN
V$LATCH_MISSES
V$LATCH_PARENT
V$LOGMNR_LATCH
GV$LATCH
GV$LATCHHOLDER
GV$LATCHNAME
GV$LATCH_CHILDREN
GV$LATCH_MISSES
GV$LATCH_PARENT
GV$LOGMNR_LATCH
GV$DLM_LATCH
V$DLM_LATCH

21 rows selected.
```

Of particular note for Oracle 11g RAC environments are the *gv$* performance views such as *gv$dlm_latch* and *gv$latch* which provide cluster-wide latch activity details for Oracle 11g RAC environments.

For example, the following sample query against the *gv$dlm_latch* dynamic performance view provides a gold mine of latch information for an Oracle 11g RAC clustered environment.

```
SQL> desc gv$dlm_latch

Name                                      Null?    Type
----------------------------------------- -------- ----------------
INST_ID                                            NUMBER
ADDR                                               RAW(4)
```

```
LATCH#                              NUMBER
LEVEL#                              NUMBER
NAME                                VARCHAR2(64)
GETS                                NUMBER
MISSES                              NUMBER
SLEEPS                              NUMBER
IMMEDIATE_GETS                      NUMBER
IMMEDIATE_MISSES                    NUMBER
WAITERS_WOKEN                       NUMBER
WAITS_HOLDING_LATCH                 NUMBER
SPIN_GETS                           NUMBER
SLEEP1                              NUMBER
SLEEP2                              NUMBER
SLEEP3                              NUMBER
SLEEP4                              NUMBER
SLEEP5                              NUMBER
SLEEP6                              NUMBER
SLEEP7                              NUMBER
SLEEP8                              NUMBER
SLEEP9                              NUMBER
SLEEP10                             NUMBER
SLEEP11                             NUMBER
WAIT_TIME                           NUMBER
```

Next, the dynamic performance view for the Oracle 11g RAC cluster on Linux can be queried using this sample query:

```
SQL> col inst_id format 9999
SQL> col level# format 999
SQL> select inst_id, name, level#, spin_gets, wait_time from gv$dlm_latch

INST_ID NAME                          LEVEL#  SPIN_GETS  WAIT_TIME
------- ----------------------------- ------  ---------- ----------
      1 ges process table freelist       4          0          0
      1 ges process parent latch         2          0          0
      1 ges process hash list            2          0          0
      1 ges resource table freelist      3          0          0
      1 ges caches resource lists        2          0          0
      1 ges resource hash list           1          0          0
      1 ges resource scan list           3          0          0
      1 ges s-lock bitvec freelist       6          0          0
      1 ges enqueue table freelist       5          0          0
      1 ges timeout list                 3          0          0
      1 ges deadlock list                3          0          0
      1 ges statistic table              1          0          0
      1 ges synchronous data             3          0          0
      1 ges domain table                 3          0          0
      1 ges group table                  5          0          0
      1 gcs resource hash                4          0          0
      1 gcs opaque info freelist         5          0          0
      1 gcs resource freelist            5          0          0
      1 gcs resource scan list           6          0          0
      1 gcs resource validate list       8          0          0
      1 gcs domain validate latch        3          0          0
      1 gcs shadows freelist             5          0          0
      1 gcs commit scn state             8          0          0
```

```
  1 gcs remastering latch            5              0              0
  1 gcs partitioned table hash       6              0              0
  1 gcs pcm hashed value bucket hash 6              0              0
  1 gcs remaster request queue       1              0              0
  1 ges value block free list        5              0              0

28 rows selected.
```

In the previous query, of note is that for Oracle 11g RAC environments, the *gv$* dynamic performance views are being used versus the *v$* dynamic performance views to obtain cluster-wide latch information for RAC environments with Oracle. Oracle 11g has special latches and locks associated with it that perform inter-instance communication and data block transmission in terms of Oracle RAC cache fusion. These latches and locks are based on GCS (global cache services) and GES (global enqueue services). Detailed coverage of RAC is unfortunately outside the scope of this chapter, but dozens of fine books and papers are available that provide further information on RAC and Cache Fusion for Oracle 11g.

Now continue the research into gathering latch information with Oracle 11g. Since *v$latch* by itself will not provide comprehensive latch information, join this view with *v$latchname* and *v$latchholder* to grab a more complete picture of how latches currently behave within the Oracle 11g database environment.

Below is a useful query to view system wide latch information for Oracle 11g followed by the output results.

```
select c.name, a.addr, a.gets, a.misses, a.sleeps,
 a.immediate_gets, a.immediate_misses, b.pid
 from v$latch a, v$latchholder b, v$latchname c
 where a.addr=b.laddr(+)
 and a.latch#=c.latch#
  order by a.latch#
/


NAME

ADDR      GETS     MISSES    SLEEPS IMMEDIATE_GETS IMMEDIATE_MISSES     PID
--------- -------- --------- -------------- ----------------- ----------
PC and Classifier lists for WLM

20001004   0        0          0              0                 0

event range base latch
```

```
20006108     0         0         0         0              0

post/wait queue

2000616C    244        0         0        136             0


NAME
ADDR       GETS    MISSES     SLEEPS IMMEDIATE_GETS IMMEDIATE_MISSES        PID
---------- ---------- ---------- -------------- ---------------- ----------
hot latch diags

200061D0     0         0         0         0              0

test excl. non-parent 10

20006234     0         0         0         0              0

test excl. parent 10

20006298     1         0         0         0              0

test excl. parent2 10

200062FC     1         0         0         0              0
```

The *dba_hist_latch* view provides information on latch behavior with respect to waits and latch misses within Oracle 11g as shown below.

```
SQL> desc dba_hist_latch

Name                                      Null?      Type
-----------------------------------------  --------   ---------------
 SNAP_ID                                   NOT NULL   NUMBER
 DBID                                      NOT NULL   NUMBER
 INSTANCE_NUMBER                           NOT NULL   NUMBER
 LATCH_HASH                                NOT NULL   NUMBER
 LATCH_NAME                                NOT NULL   VARCHAR2(64)
 LEVEL#                                               NUMBER
 GETS                                                 NUMBER
 MISSES                                               NUMBER
 SLEEPS                                               NUMBER
 IMMEDIATE_GETS                                       NUMBER
 IMMEDIATE_MISSES                                     NUMBER
 SPIN_GETS                                            NUMBER
 SLEEP1                                               NUMBER
 SLEEP2                                               NUMBER
 SLEEP3                                               NUMBER
 SLEEP4                                               NUMBER
 WAIT_TIME                                            NUMBER
```

In addition, *v$latchname* provides a comprehensive listing of all latches available in the Oracle 11g database environment. Each latch is associated with a specific latch number and hash value.

```
SQL> col name format a50
SQL> select name, latch#, hash from v$latchname;
```

```
NAME                                             LATCH#         HASH
------------------------------------------------ ----------    -----
PC and Classifier lists for WLM                       0    3839880517
event range base latch                                1    2713425810
NAME                                             LATCH#         HASH
------------------------------------------------ ----------    -----
post/wait queue                                       2     823771719
hot latch diags                                       3    1435869216
test excl. non-parent 10                              4      62285240
test excl. parent 10                                  5    2851750944
test excl. parent2 10                                 6     496096266
test shared non-parent 10                             7     141753558
test excl. non-parent lmax                            8     810409585
process allocation                                    9    2600548697
session allocation                                   10     896287525
session switching                                    11    1492598149
process group creation                               12     527658566
session idle bit                                     13    2155272050
client/application info                              14     773918085
longop free list parent                             15     853437045
ksuosstats global area                              16    4289843503
ksupkttest latch                                     17    1143481739
cached attr list                                     18    1152940740
ksim membership request latch                        19    3846407325
object stats modification                            20    3370897971
kss move lock                                         21    3265392135
```

To find a listing of all latches for an Oracle 11g RAC environment, query the *gv$latchname* dynamic performance view as shown in the example below:

```
SQL> desc gv$latchname

 Name                                     Null?     Type
 ---------------------------------------- --------  ----------------
 INST_ID                                            NUMBER
 LATCH#                                             NUMBER
 NAME                                               VARCHAR2(64)
 HASH                                               NUMBER

SQL> select inst_id, name, latch# from gv$latchname;

INST_ID NAME                                               LATCH#
------- -------------------------------------------------- ------
      1 JS broadcast drop buf latch                           484
      1 JS broadcast kill buf latch                           485
      1 JS broadcast load blnc latch                          486
      1 JS broadcast autostart latch                          487
      1 JS broadcast LW Job latch                             488
      1 JS mem alloc latch                                    489
      1 JS slv state obj latch                                490
      1 JS queue state obj latch                              491
      1 JS queue access latch                                 492
      1 JS Sh mem access                                       493
      1 PL/SQL warning settings                               494
      1 dbkea msgq latch                                       495

496 rows selected.
```

Now that a sneak peek into latches has been given, examine how latches differ from locks within Oracle 11g.

How Latches Differ From Locks

As was mentioned earlier in the chapter, latches differ from locks within Oracle in terms of duration with respect to restricting access to data structures for transactions and processes with the database. Latches are short term in length of operation and locks are long duration in restricting access to Oracle data structures. As such, latches are lightweight serialization and locks are the heavy duty long-running serialization mechanism. However, latches are strict compared to locks in terms of restricting access to data structures within Oracle.

While locks permit shared and concurrent access, latches allow access to only a single process at a time and prevent other processes within Oracle from accessing that process while a latch is held by the process. Latches affect only data structures within the Oracle SGA, whereas locks apply to Oracle transactions. As such, latches affect a more limited scope compared to locks. Latches also fulfill a single purpose which is to grant exclusive access to Oracle memory structures. Therefore, they control access to the SGA memory data structures for single operations in contrast to locks, which serve dual purposes.

Unlike latches, locks and enqueues function to allow multiple processes to share resources when lock modes are compatible as well as to enforce data integrity by restricting access to resources based on lock modes in place for transactions. Latches are limited serialization mechanisms that are non-transactional and only for memory resources in the SGA for Oracle, as mentioned earlier, whereas locks are application driven and control access to database transactions. Latches also differ from locks in that they can be requested in only two modes: no-wait and willing-to-wait, while locks have six different request modes: null, row share, row exclusive, share row exclusive, share, or exclusive.

Another key difference between latches and locks within Oracle lies in terms of scope of process, memory and transaction management. Latches are visible only to the local instance in memory as opposed to locks, which maintain information within the Oracle database and are visible to all of the instances that have access to the database. As such, locks operate at the database level versus latches, which are based at the instance level in Oracle memory.

Yet another difference between latches and locks can be explained in how complex both mechanisms are within Oracle. Latches use simple instructions, such as simple CPU-based OS instructions, and are based on operating system implementations while locks are heavy weight mechanisms that use a series of complex instructions in terms of context switching.

In addition to the above, differences between latches and locks can explain using duration of operation. Latches are simple, short-lived mechanisms that last in microseconds versus longer held running locks that can last for hours based on the lock mode and transaction held by the lock in question.

Furthermore, locks operate based on a queuing methodology in that for every Oracle process that fails to obtain a lock, the request for the process is placed into a queue and serviced in order unless NOWAIT is specified in the lock request. Latches, on the other hand, do not use any type of queuing mechanism except for the latch wait list latch which does use a queue as part of its algorithm. For instance, when a specific process within Oracle falls into sleep mode and fails to acquire a latch, the request will not be queued up and serviced in order.

In other words, latches are on a first-come, first grab basis in terms of allocation and management. Because of the way that latches operate within Oracle, they are not affected by deadlocks. Locks, on the other hand, are affected by deadlock conditions. Whenever a deadlock occurs that involves a lock, Oracle generates a trace file with the deadlock error message in the alert log file. Latch waiters, on the other hand, use either timers to wake up and retry or will spin before retry access to the latch.

Tips for Latch Contention Issues with Oracle 11g

Latch contention issues are a frequent source of pain to even veteran Oracle database administrators. This chapter will explain the root cause methods to investigate latch contention issues within Oracle 11g along with some tips and tricks to remediate these performance issues. First stop is to look at the holistic cause of database problems within Oracle 11g.

A prudent step is to examine the performance of the disk I/O subsystem and system environment. If the disk subsystem of the Storage Area Network (SAN) or Network Attached Storage (NAS) is poorly configured, latch performance will suffer greatly. Since time is valuable to busy DBAs, often one has to perform ad hoc reactive tuning to resolve outstanding crisis situations such as delayed report processing from an Oracle 11i Financials application.

One useful method is to run either a fresh STATSPACK or ADDM report within Oracle 11g to look at the symptoms before drilling down deeper into $v\$$ and $x\$$ views. This means it is best to not mistake the forest for the trees, and these performance tools are available either from within Oracle 11g Database Control, Grid Control or via the trusty and venerable SQL*Plus command line. An example follows that shows how to generate the details for performance with the Oracle 11g Automatic Workload Repository (AWR) and Automatic Diagnostic Database Monitor (ADDM).

```
SQL> @?/rdbms/admin/addmrpt.sql

Current Instance
~~~~~~~~~~~~~~~~~

   DB Id     DB Name      Inst Num Instance
----------- ------------ -------- ------------
 1837423851 SD11G               1 sd11g

Instances in this Workload Repository schema
~~~~~~~~~~~~~~~~~~~~~~~~~~~~~~~~~~~~~~~~~~~~~~
```

```
    DB Id     Inst Num DB Name      Instance     Host
------------  -------- ------------  ------------ -------------
* 1837423851         1 SD11G         sd11g        raclinux1.us
                                                  .oracle.com

Using 1837423851 for database Id
Using            1 for instance number

Analysis Period
---------------
AWR snapshot range from 32 to 51.
Time period starts at 28-MAR-09 11.34.42 AM
Time period ends at 29-MAR-09 08.00.36 PM

Analysis Target
---------------
Database 'SD11G' with DB ID 1837423851.
Database version 11.1.0.6.0.
ADDM performed an analysis of instance sd11g, numbered 1 and hosted at
raclinux1.us.oracle.com.

Activity During the Analysis Period
-----------------------------------
Total database time was 773 seconds.
The average number of active sessions was .01.

Summary of Findings
-------------------
    Description            Active Sessions      Recommendations
                           Percent of Activity
    -------------------    -------------------  ---------------
1   Top SQL by DB Time     0 | 32.39            5
2   CPU Usage              0 | 26.77            4
3   PL/SQL Execution       0 | 10.11            1
4   Undersized SGA         0 | 8.67             1
5   "Scheduler" Wait Class 0 | 3.44             0
```

With each major release of Oracle, new enhancements are added to improve the instrumentation for performance analysis. In Oracle 11g, many new features have been added to tune Oracle RAC performance such as that with the interconnect. Disk performance is also provided by Oracle 11g AWR and ADDM which is a useful place to understand system-wide tuning in addition to standard operating system utilities such as *iostat* and *sar* for Linux and UNIX environments. Now compare the previous ADDM report information on latch issues with the correlated report from AWR.

```
SQL> @?/rdbms/admin/awrrpt.sql

Current Instance
~~~~~~~~~~~~~~~~
```

```
     DB Id    DB Name      Inst Num Instance
----------- ------------- -------- ------------
 1837423851 SD11G             1 sd11g


Load Profile           Per Second    Per Transaction  Per Exec  Per Call
~~~~~~~~~~~~           ---------------  ---------------  --------- ---------
       DB Time(s):           197.9              5.4       0.44      0.29
        DB CPU(s):             1.0              0.0       0.00      0.00
        Redo size:       475,434.9         12,915.9
    Logical reads:        77,351.4          2,101.4
    Block changes:         3,052.1             82.9
   Physical reads:           415.3             11.3
  Physical writes:            88.5              2.4
       User calls:           690.9             18.8
          Parses:            364.2              9.9
      Hard parses:             7.4              0.2
  W/A MB processed:     9,575,197.4        260,124.9
           Logons:             2.3              0.1
         Executes:           450.0             12.2
        Rollbacks:            26.2              0.7
     Transactions:            36.8

Instance Efficiency Percentages (Target 100%)
~~~~~~~~~~~~~~~~~~~~~~~~~~~~~~~~~~~~~~~~~~~~~~~~~
            Buffer Nowait %:   99.99       Redo NoWait %:    99.98
            Buffer  Hit   %:   99.71    In-memory Sort %:   100.00
            Library Hit   %:   95.93        Soft Parse %:    97.96
         Execute to Parse %:   19.07        Latch Hit  %:   100.00
  Parse CPU to Parse Elapsd %:  0.00      % Non-Parse CPU:   96.60

  Shared Pool Statistics     Begin     End
                             ------    ------
            Memory Usage %:   85.80     85.89
   % SQL with executions>1:   86.61     69.15
   % Memory for SQL w/exec>1:  87.97     82.29
```

Of particular interest to the above AWR/ADDM report would be to examine the instance efficiency percentages for the *latch hit %* which should be above 90%. Anything below 90% for any of these hit ratios could possibly reference performance issues within the database for latch activity. Continuing with the review of the AWR performance report from the test Oracle 11g RAC cluster, also look at the foreground events to find possible latching issues as shown below.

```
Top 5 Timed Foreground Events
~~~~~~~~~~~~~~~~~~~~~~~~~~~~~~~
                                                        Avg
                                                        wait   % DB
Event                         Waits       Time(s)       (ms)   time  Wait Class
----------------------------  -----------  -----------  ------ ----- ----------
SQL*Net more data from client  2,356,277   5,983,083     2539   96.9 Network
library cache lock                64,592      46,352      718     .8 Concurrenc
DB CPU                                        32,024             .5
db file sequential read        1,279,125      17,880       14     .3 User I/O
enq: JI - contention              13,666      10,898      797     .2
```

In the above report, there is a possible lock issue with library cache. One solution would be to examine the SQL statements referenced in the report summary and look for tuning opportunities for the SQL in the library cache that could be a source of these contention issues. After exhausting tuning possibilities from ADDM, AWR, and system wide tuning, the next step for addressing latch and lock contention issues would be to delve into the *v$* dynamic performance views for latching operations.

So what exactly causes latch contention within Oracle? Recall from earlier in the chapter that whenever a latch is busy and currently in use within Oracle, any process that requests access to the latch will spin before attempting to gain access to the latch. If the latch is still unavailable, the process will keep spinning and using up valuable CPU resources, thus causing a performance problem. Within Oracle 11g, there is a hidden parameter called *spin_count* that sets the number of times that the process will spin\in a loop before giving up and going to sleep. What happens is that the initial sleep period is one centisecond on the first spin count. Each subsequent spin count is doubled until the *spin_count* threshold is reached, at which the process must relinquish CPU resources and sleep. So, how does one identify latch contention issues within Oracle 11g outside of using ADDM and AWR reports? Simple. Query the dynamic performance views shown below:

- *v$latch*

- *v$latchholder*

- *v$latchname*

For *v$latch*, there is a unique value for each type of latch within Oracle 11g. Latch request details are provided in this dynamic performance view as well. So examine the values for gets, misses and sleeps for each latch so that one can determine where the latch problem is to be found.

```
SQL> desc v$latch_parent;

Name                                      Null?    Type
----------------------------------------- -------- ----------------
ADDR                                               RAW(4)
LATCH#                                             NUMBER
```

```
LEVEL#                                          NUMBER
NAME                                            VARCHAR2(64)
HASH                                            NUMBER
GETS                                            NUMBER
MISSES                                          NUMBER
SLEEPS                                          NUMBER
IMMEDIATE_GETS                                  NUMBER
IMMEDIATE_MISSES                                NUMBER
WAITERS_WOKEN                                   NUMBER
WAITS_HOLDING_LATCH                             NUMBER
SPIN_GETS                                       NUMBER
SLEEP1                                          NUMBER
SLEEP2                                          NUMBER
SLEEP3                                          NUMBER
SLEEP4                                          NUMBER
SLEEP5                                          NUMBER
SLEEP6                                          NUMBER
SLEEP7                                          NUMBER
SLEEP8                                          NUMBER
SLEEP9                                          NUMBER
SLEEP10                                         NUMBER
SLEEP11                                         NUMBER
WAIT_TIME                                       NUMBER


SQL> desc v$latch_children

Name                                     Null?    Type
---------------------------------------- -------- ----------------
ADDR                                              RAW(4)
LATCH#                                            NUMBER
CHILD#                                            NUMBER
LEVEL#                                            NUMBER
NAME                                              VARCHAR2(64)
HASH                                              NUMBER
GETS                                              NUMBER
MISSES                                            NUMBER
SLEEPS                                            NUMBER
IMMEDIATE_GETS                                    NUMBER
IMMEDIATE_MISSES                                  NUMBER
WAITERS_WOKEN                                     NUMBER
WAITS_HOLDING_LATCH                               NUMBER
SPIN_GETS                                         NUMBER
SLEEP1                                            NUMBER
SLEEP2                                            NUMBER
SLEEP3                                            NUMBER
SLEEP4                                            NUMBER
SLEEP5                                            NUMBER
SLEEP6                                            NUMBER
SLEEP7                                            NUMBER
SLEEP8                                            NUMBER
SLEEP9                                            NUMBER
SLEEP10                                           NUMBER
SLEEP11                                           NUMBER
WAIT_TIME                                         NUMBER
```

One key item to examine is the latch cache hit ratio metric. While the Wait Class model has been a hot method used by Oracle performance analysts in recent years over the old hit ratio model, the latch hit ratio can provide a useful addition to the big picture of tuning in addition to the wait event tuning model. Oracle support provides a DBA with a nice clean formula to calculate this latch hit ratio as shown below.

- Willing-to-Wait Hit Ratio = (gets – misses)/gets

- No-Wait Hit Ratio = (immediate_gets – immediate_misses)/immediate_gets

The ratio should be as close as possible to 1. If the latch hit ratio is not close to 1, then the latch in question requires further tuning analysis.

Tuning Latch Contention Issues for LRU Chain Latches

Usually latch contention issues for LRU chain latches pertain to an inadequately sized buffer cache for the Oracle 11g SGA. Fortunately, the solution is fairly simple. The size of the buffer cache can be increased which should alleviate the latch contention issue for the LRU chain latches. Oracle 11g has two database initialization parameters that affect the buffer cache within Oracle: *db_block_size* and *db_block_buffers*.

Unfortunately, only *db_block_buffers* can be changed without recreating the database. While mixed results have been recorded for tuning the database block size via *db_block_size*, in actuality for most Oracle environments, the default value of 8k block size is sufficient. Also of note is to exercise caution and extensive testing when tuning the setting for *db_block_buffers* since simply increasing the size will not guarantee a performance boost for the buffer cache. Especially with full table scans that do not rely on the buffer cache, it would be a foolish exercise and potentially risky to set it to a large value.

Another option for tuning LRU chain buffer cache latches would be to add multiple buffer pools in order to reduce latch contention with the buffer cache LRU chain latches. Additional cache buffer LRU chain latches can also be created by modifying the database initialization parameter for *db_block_lru_latches*. A further option under the guidance of Oracle support would be to increase the value of the hidden parameter for *db_block_hash_buckets* to optimize this latch performance within Oracle 11g.

Tuning Shared Pool Latches

The majority of performance problems associated with shared pool latches are due to poorly written SQL, PL/SQL and other database application code. One method that has been proven to alleviate these latch contention issues with the shared pool latch is to avoid literals in SQL code and replace them with efficient application code. For example, hard parses are best avoided and developers should write SQL code that executes multiple times with fewer parses. Another option in concert with tuning SQL code is to adjust the size of the shared pool and possible use of shared server option with Oracle database applications.

Additional Tips for Tuning Oracle 11g Latches

Recall that earlier it was mentioned how the *spin_count* parameter controls the number of times a particular process within Oracle will attempt to obtain a latch before going into sleep mode. In other words, there is a feedback-control loop process that it goes through in order to acquire a latch within Oracle 11g. With single CPU systems, the process will release the CPU resource and go to sleep for a brief period of time before waking up and trying to acquire the latch. However, with SMP based systems that contain multiple CPUs, the possibility exists that the process holding the latch in question is already operating on one of the other CPUs in the multi-processor server and could release the latch in the next few cycles of processing time.

What this means is that overall database performance with respect to latch issues and SMP systems can be optimized by adjusting the value for the *spin_count* database initialization parameter within Oracle. For instance, if a high value is set for *spin_count*, the latch could be obtained sooner rather than later by the process. The converse side of setting *spin_count* to a higher setting has a potential impact of using up more CPU time because the process must keep spinning up CPU cycles and thus, using up more CPU resources to get the latch.

Another option in the event that CPU resources are spiking and at peak capacity is to decrease the *spin_count* parameter to a lower value for Oracle 11g. By lowering the value for *spin_count*, the process has less chance of sleeping between attempts to acquire the latch. This would have the effect of conserving CPU resources on the server with respect to latch activity for Oracle 11g. However, tuning the *spin_count* value is largely trial and error and should only be attempted with test environments at first to avoid impact with production environments.

Summary

In this chapter, the following topics about latches were covered and how they behave within Oracle 11g:

- Concepts and features for latches with Oracle 11g

- Useful scripts and dynamic performance views for latch operations

- Differences between latches and locks

- Performance tuning of latch issues for Oracle 11g

In the next chapter, hidden and undocumented Oracle 11g database parameters will be investigated and ways to best take advantage of these undocumented parameters to optimize database performance for Oracle 11g will be offered.

Hidden Parameters in Oracle 11g

The previous chapters have shown how Oracle 11g concurrency operates with locking and latches. The focus on this chapter will be to provide insight into the world of undocumented and hidden database parameters. As such, the following themes for undocumented and hidden database parameters for Oracle 11g will be touched upon:

- Purpose of hidden parameters for Oracle 11g

- How to locate the hidden parameters for Oracle 11g

- Explanation of some key hidden parameters for Oracle 11g

Purpose of Hidden Parameters for Oracle 11g

Undocumented parameters have always existed ever since the first release of the Oracle database software. The primary purpose of these hidden and undocumented database parameters has been to provide internal support engineers and development teams at Oracle with a method to resolve unforeseen issues that are not addressed by the core functionality within the Oracle database engine. In Oracle 11g, many of the new features are controlled behind the scenes via these hidden parameter settings.

How to Locate Hidden Parameters for Oracle 11g

The following warning bears repeating before advancing into the topic of these undocumented and hidden parameters for Oracle 11g:

> **Caution!** Do not change these hidden and undocumented parameters in a production or mission critical environment without the guidance of Oracle support! Data loss may result if these parameters are changed without supervision from Oracle support.

These hidden and undocumented parameters are hidden for a very good reason, only to be adjusted under the watchful eye of an advanced Oracle support engineer in emergency conditions. For educational purposes, one may play around with these in a sandbox environment to obtain a deeper understanding of Oracle 11g internals. Do not mess with these in production unless there is an Oracle support engineer involved or there may be the risk of data loss and other undesirable consequences.

Since these are not documented by Oracle, there needs to be a way to locate these hidden parameters for 11g along with their definitions. There are over 1600 hidden database parameters for Oracle 11g! With each new release, Oracle adds hundreds more new undocumented parameters. The following query reveals these hidden parameters for Oracle 11g.

```
SQL> spool hidden11g.log
SQL> col ksppinm format a39
SQL> col ksppdesc format a39
SQL>
SQL>  select ksppinm, ksppdesc
2     from x$ksppi
3     where substr(ksppinm,1,1)='_'
4   /
```

One can then view the hundreds of hidden parameters for Oracle 11g along with the brief description generated by the output from the *x$ksppi* view as shown in the following figure which has been shortened for sake of discussion.

```
KSPPINM                              KSPPDESC
-------------------------------------  --------------------------------------
_ior_serialize_fault                 inject fault in the ior serialize code
_inject_startup_fault                inject fault in the startup code
_latch_recovery_alignment            align latch recovery structures
_spin_count                          Amount to spin waiting for a latch
_latch_miss_stat_sid                 Sid of process for which to collect
                                     latch stats

_max_sleep_holding_latch             max time to sleep while holding a latch
_max_exponential_sleep               max sleep during exponential backoff
_other_wait_threshold                threshold wait percentage for event
                                     wait class Other

_other_wait_event_exclusion          exclude event names from _other_wait_
                                     threshold calculations
_use_vector_post                     use vector post
_latch_class_0                       latch class 0
_latch_class_1                       latch class 1
_latch_class_2                       latch class 2
_latch_class_3                       latch class 3
_latch_class_4                       latch class 4
_latch_class_5                       latch class 5
_latch_class_6                       latch class 6
_latch_class_7                       latch class 7
_latch_classes                       latch classes override
_ultrafast_latch_statistics          maintain fast-path statistics for ultra
                                     fast latches
_enable_reliable_latch_waits         Enable reliable latch waits
_wait_breakup_time_csecs             Wait breakup time (in centiseconds)
_wait_breakup_threshold_csecs        Wait breakup threshold (in centiseconds
                                     )
_disable_wait_stack                  Disable wait stack
_session_idle_bit_latches            one latch per session or a latch per
                                     group of sessions

_ksu_diag_kill_time                  number of seconds ksuitm waits before
                                     killing diag

_ksuitm_dont_kill_dumper             delay inst. Termination to allow 131econd131
                                     ses to dump

_disable_image_check                 Disable Oracle executable image
                                     checking

_longops_enabled                     longops stats enabled
_test_ksusigskip                     test the function ksusigskip
_disable_kcbhxor_osd                 disable kcbhIxor OSD functionality
_disable_system_state                disable system state dump
_session_wait_history                enable session wait history collection
_session_idle_check_interval         Resource Manager session idle limit
                                     check interval in seconds

_pkt_enable                          enable progressive kill test
_pkt_start                           start progressive kill test instrumention

_pkt_pmon_interval                   PMON process clean-up interval (cs)
_dead_process_scan_interval          PMON dead process scan interval
_collapse_wait_history               collapse wait history
_short_stack_timeout_ms              short stack timeout in ms
_sga_early_trace                     sga early trace event

_kill_session_dump                   Process dump on kill session immediate
_logout_storm_rate                   number of processes that can logout in
                                     a second

_logout_storm_timeout                timeout in centi-seconds for time to
                                     wait between retries

_logout_storm_retrycnt               maximum retry count for logouts


KSPPINM                              KSPPDESC
-------------------------------------  --------------------------------------
_ksuitm_addon_trccmd                 command to execute when dead processes
                                     do not go away
```

Purpose of Hidden Parameters for Oracle 11g

```
_timeout_actions_enabled              enables or disables KSU timeout actions
_idle_session_kill_enabled            enables or disables resource manager
                                      session idle limit checks

_disable_vktm                         disable vktm process
_disable_highres_ticks                disable high-res tick counter
_disable_sec_ticks                    disable low-res (sec) counter
_timer_precision                      VKTM sleep time in milli-sec
_iorm_tout                            IORM scheduler timeout value in msec
__oracle_base                         ORACLE_BASE
_single_process                       run without detached processes

_dbg_proc_startup                     debug process startup
_static_backgrounds                   static backgrounds
_enqueue_deadlock_time_sec            requests with timeout <= this will not
                                      have deadlock detection

_number_cached_attributes             maximum number of cached attributes per
                                      instance

_kss_quiet                            if TRUE access violations during kss
                                      dumps are not recorded

_oradebug_force                       force target processes to execute orade
                                      bug commands?

_ksdxdocmd_default_timeout_ms         default timeout for internal oradebug
                                      commands

_ksdxdocmd_enabled                    if TRUE ksdxdocmd* invocations are
                                      enabled

_watchpoint_on                        is the watchpointing feature turned on?
_ksdxw_num_sgw                        number of watchpoints to be shared by
                                      all processes

_ksdxw_num_pgw                        number of watchpoints on a per-process
                                      basis

_ksdxw_stack_depth                    number of PCs to collect in the stack
                                      when watchpoint is hit

_ksdxw_cini_flg                       ksdxw context initialization flag
_ksdxw_nbufs                          ksdxw number of buffers in buffered
                                      mode

_enable_shared_pool_durations         temporary to disable/enable kgh policy
_NUMA_pool_size                       aggregate size in bytes of NUMA pool
_enable_NUMA_optimization             Enable NUMA specific optimizations
_use_ism                              Enable Shared Page Tables - ISM
_lock_sga_areas                       Lock specified areas of the SGA in
                                      physical memory

_NUMA_instance_mapping                Set of nodes that this instance should
                                      run on

_simulator_upper_bound_multiple       upper bound multiple of pool size
_simulator_pin_inval_maxcnt           maximum count of invalid chunks on pin
                                      list

_simulator_lru_rebalance_thresh       LRU list rebalance threshold (count)
_simulator_lru_rebalance_sizthr       LRU list rebalance threshold (size)
_simulator_bucket_mindelta            LRU bucket minimum delta
_simulator_lru_scan_count             LRU scan count
_simulator_internal_bound             simulator internal bound percent
_simulator_reserved_obj_count         simulator reserved object count
_simulator_reserved_heap_count        simulator reserved heap count

_simulator_sampling_factor            sampling factor for the simulator
_realfree_heap_max_size               minimum max total heap size, in Kbytes
_realfree_heap_pagesize_hint          hint for real-free page size in bytes
KSPPINM                               KSPPDESC
-------------------------------       -------------------------------------
_realfree_heap_mode                   mode flags for real-free heap
_use_realfree_heap                    use real-free based allocator for PGA m
                                      Emory
```

```
_pga_large_extent_size                PGA large extent size
_uga_cga_large_extent_size            UGA/CGA large extent size
_total_large_extent_memory            Total memory for allocating large
                                      extents

_use_ism_for_pga                      Use ISM for allocating large extents
_private_memory_address               Start address of large extent memory
                                      segment

_mem_annotation_sh_lev                shared memory annotation collection
                                      level

_mem_annotation_pr_lev                private memory annotation collection
                                      level

_mem_annotation_scale                 memory annotation pre-allocation
                                      scaling

_mem_annotation_store                 memory annotation in-memory store
_4031_dump_bitvec                     bitvec to specify dumps prior to 4031
                                      error

_4031_max_dumps                       Maximum number of 4031 dumps for this
                                      process

_4031_dump_interval                   Dump 4031 error once for each n-second

_4031_sga_dump_interval               Dump 4031 SGA heapdump error once for
                                      each n-second interval

_4031_sga_max_dumps                   Maximum number of SGA heapdumps
_mem_std_extent_size                  standard extent size for fixed-size-
                                      extent heaps

_kgsb_threshold_size                  threshold size for base allocator
_endprot_chunk_comment                chunk comment for selective overrun
                                      protection

_endprot_heap_comment                 heap comment for selective overrun
                                      protection

_endprot_subheaps                     selective overrun protection for
                                      subheaps

_sga_locking                          sga granule locking state
__shared_pool_size                    Actual size in bytes of shared pool
__large_pool_size                     Actual size in bytes of large pool

__java_pool_size                      Actual size in bytes of java pool
__streams_pool_size                   Actual size in bytes of streams pool
_large_pool_min_alloc                 minimum allocation size in bytes for
                                      the large allocation pool

_shared_pool_reserved_pct             percentage memory of the shared pool
                                      allocated for the reserved area

_shared_pool_reserved_min_alloc       minimum allocation size in bytes for
                                      reserved area of shared pool
_kghdsidx_count                       max kghdsidx count
_test_param_1                         test parmeter 1 - integer
_test_param_2                         test parameter 2 - string
_test_param_3                         test parameter 3 - string
_test_param_4                         test parameter 4 - string list
_test_param_5                         test parmeter 5 - deprecated integer
_test_param_6                         test parmeter 6 - size (ub8)
_disable_instance_params_check        disable instance type check for ksp

_parameter_table_block_size           parameter table block size
_ksb_disable_diagpid                  disable the call to ksb_diagpid
_high_priority_processes              High Priority Process Name Mask

KSPPINM                               KSPPDESC
------------------------------------- -------------------------------------
_os_sched_high_priority               OS high priority level
_ksb_restart_clean_time               process uptime for restarts
_ksb_restart_policy_times             process restart policy times in seconds
_ksd_test_param                       KSD test parameter
```

```
_kse_die_timeout                        amount of time a dying process is spared
                                        by PMON (in centi-secs)

_stack_guard_level                      stack guard level
_kse_pc_table_size                      kse pc table cache size
_kse_signature_entries                  number of entries in the kse stack
                                        signature cache

_kse_signature_limit                    number of stack frames to cache per kse
                                        signature

_kse_snap_ring_size                     ring buffer to debug internal error 170
                                        90

_messages                               message queue resources - dependent on
                                        # processes & # buffers

_enqueue_locks                          locks for managed enqueues

_enqueue_resources                      resources for enqueues
_enqueue_hash                           enqueue hash table length
_enqueue_debug_multi_instance           debug enqueue multi instance
_enqueue_hash_chain_latches             enqueue hash chain latches
_ksi_trace                              KSI trace string of lock type(s)
_ksi_trace_bucket                       memory tracing: use ksi-private or rdbm
                                        s-shared bucket

_ksi_trace_bucket_size                  size of the KSI trace bucket

_trace_processes                        enable KST tracing in process
_trace_events                           trace events enabled at startup

_trace_buffers                          trace buffer sizes per process
_trace_dump_static_only                 if TRUE filter trace dumps to always lo
                                        134econ dlls

_trace_dump_all_procs                   if TRUE on error buckets of all processes
                                        will be dumped to the current trace
                                        file

_trace_dump_cur_proc_only               if TRUE on error just dump our process
                                        bucket

_trace_dump_client_buckets              if TRUE dump client (ie. Non-kst)
                                        buckets

_nchar_imp_cnv                          NLS allow Implicit Conversion between C
                                        HAR and NCHAR

_disable_file_locks                     disable file locks for control, data,
                                        redo log files

_ksfd_verify_write                      verify asynchronous writes issued
                                        through ksfd

_disable_odm                            disable odm feature
_enable_list_io                         Enable List I/O
_omf                                    enable/disable OMF
_aiowait_timeouts                       Number of aiowait timeouts before error
                                        is reported

_io_shared_pool_size                    Size of I/O buffer pool from SGA
_max_io_size                            Maximum I/O size in bytes for 134econd134134ne
                                        l file accesses

_io_statistics                          if TRUE, ksfd I/O statistics are
                                        collected

KSPPINM                                 KSPPDESC
--------------------------------------- ---------------------------------------
_db_file_direct_io_count                Sequential I/O buf size
_ioslave_issue_count                    Ios issued before completion check
_ioslave_batch_count                    Per attempt Ios picked
_io_slaves_disabled                     Do not use I/O slaves
_lgwr_io_slaves                         LGWR I/O slaves
_arch_io_slaves                         ARCH I/O slaves
_backup_disk_io_slaves                  BACKUP Disk I/O slaves
_fg_iorm_slaves                         ForeGround I/O slaves for IORM
```

```
_backup_io_pool_size                      memory to reserve from the large pool
_high_server_threshold                    high server thresholds
_low_server_threshold                     low server thresholds
_max_temp_overhead                        max tempspc overhead
_yield_check_interval                     interval to check whether actses should
                                          Yield

_resource_manager_always_off              disable the resource manager always
_resource_manager_always_on               enable the resource manager always
_io_resource_manager_always_on            io resource manager always on
_max_small_io                             IORM:max number of small I/O's to issue

_max_large_io                             IORM:max number of large I/O's to issue
_auto_assign_cg_for_sessions              auto assign CGs for sessions
_ksr_unit_test_processes                  number of ksr unit test processes
_ksv_spawn_control_all                    control all spawning of background
                                          slaves

_ksv_max_spawn_fail_limit                 bg slave spawn failure limit
_ksv_pool_wait_timeout                    bg slave pool wait limit
_ksv_pool_hang_kill_to                    bg slave pool terminate timeout
_ksvppktmode                              ksv internal pkt test
_first_spare_parameter                    first spare parameter - integer

_second_spare_parameter                   second spare parameter - integer
_third_spare_parameter                    third spare parameter - integer
_fourth_spare_parameter                   fourth spare parameter - string
_fifth_spare_parameter                    fifth spare parameter - string
_sixth_spare_parameter                    sixth spare parameter - string list
_seventh_spare_parameter                  seventh spare parameter - string list
_ksxp_ping_enable                         disable dynamic loadin of lib skgxp
_ksxp_ping_polling_time                   max. arrays for ipc statistics
_ksxp_disable_dynamic_loading             disable dynamic loadin of lib skgxp
_skgxp_udp_use_tcb                        disable use of high speek timer
_ksxp_skgxp_library_path                  over-ride default location of lib skgxp

_ksxp_skgxp_compat_library_path           over-ride default location of lib skgxp
                                          compat

_ksxp_disable_ipc_stats                   disable ipc statistics
_ksxp_max_stats_bkts                      max. arrays for ipc statistics
_ksxp_init_stats_bkts                     initial number arrays for ipc statistics

_ksxp_stats_mem_lmt                       limit ipc statistics memory. This parameter
                                          is a percentage value

_ksxp_send_timeout                        set timeout for sends queued with the
                                          inter-instance IPC

_ksxp_diagmode                            set to OFF to disable automatic slowsend
                                          diagnostics

_skgxp_reaping                            tune skgxp OSD reaping limit
_ksxp_reaping                             tune ksxp layer reaping limit
_skgxp_udp_hiwat_warn                     ach hiwat mark warning interval
_skgxp_udp_ach_reaping_time               time in minutes before idle ach's are
                                          reaped

_skgxp_udp_timed_wait_seconds             time in seconds before timed wait is
                                          invoked

_skgxp_udp_timed_wait_buffering           diagnostic log buffering space (in bytes)
                                          for timed wait (0 means unbuffered


KSPPINM                                   KSPPDESC
----------------------------------------- -----------------------------------------
_skgxp_udp_keep_alive_ping_timer_secs     connection idle time in seconds before
                                          keep alive is initiated. Min: 30 sec
                                          max: 1800 sec default: 300 sec

_disable_duplex_link                      Turn off connection duplexing
_diag_diagnostics                         Turn off diag diagnostics
_disable_interface_checking               disable interface checking at startup
_skgxp_udp_interface_detection_time_sec   time in seconds between interface
                                          detection checks
```

```
_skgxp_udp_lmp_on                            enable UDP long message protection
_skgxp_udp_lmp_mtusize                       MTU size for UDP LMP testing
_skgxp_udp_enable_dynamic_credit_mgmt        Enables dynamic credit management
_skgxp_udp_ack_delay                         Enables delayed acks
_ksxp_testing                                KSXP test parameter

_ksxp_reporting_process                      reporting process for KSXP
_ksxp_unit_test_byte_transformation          enable byte transformation unit test
_ksmd_protect_mode                           KSMD protect mode for catching stale
                                             access

_ksmg_granule_size                           granule size in bytes
_ksmg_granule_locking_status                 granule locking status
_ksmg_lock_check_interval                    timeout action interval in minutes
_ksmg_lock_reacquire_count                   repeat count for acquisition of locks
_filemap_dir                                 FILEMAP directory

_object_statistics                           enable the object level statistics
                                             collection

_object_stats_max_entries                    Maximum number of entries to be tracked
                                             per stat

_enable_rlb                                  enable RLB metrics processing
_enable_midtier_affinity                     enable midtier affinity metrics
                                             processing

_midtier_affinity_timeout                    default timeout for midtier affinity
                                             processing

_midtier_affinity_clusterwait_threshold      cluster wait threshold to enter
                                             secondary

_midtier_affinity_goodness_threshold         goodness gradient threshold to dissolve
                                             affinity

_disable_health_check                        Disable Health Check
_accept_versions                             List of parameters for rolling
                                             operation

_hang_analysis_num_call_stacks               hang analysis num call stacks
_local_hang_analysis_interval_secs           the interval at which local hang
                                             analysis is run

_deadlock_resolution_level                   automatic deadlock resolution level
_deadlock_resolution_incidents_enabled       create incidents during deadlock
                                             resolution

_deadlock_resolution_min_wait_timeout_s      the minimum wait timeout required for
ecs                                          deadlock resolution

_deadlock_resolution_signal_process_thr      the amount of time given to process a
esh_secs                                     deadlock resolution signal

_heur_deadlock_resolution_secs               the heuristic wait time per node for
                                             deadlock resolution

_deadlock_diagnostic_level                   automatic deadlock resolution

_blocking_sess_graph_cache_size              blocking session graph cache size in
                                             bytes

_kspol_tac_timeout                           timeouts for TAC registerd by kspol
_disable_12751                               disable policy timeout error (ORA-12751)

KSPPINM                                      KSPPDESC
-------------------------------------------  -------------------------------------------
_diskmon_pipe_name                           DiSKMon skgznp pipe name
_ksmb_debug                                  ksmb debug flags
_diag_daemon                                 start DIAG daemon
_dump_system_state_scope                     scope of sysstate dump during instance
                                             termination

_dump_trace_scope                            scope of trace dump during a process
                                             crash

_dump_interval_limit                         trace dump time interval limit (in seconds)
```

```
_dump_max_limit                            max number of dump within dump interval
_diag_dump_timeout                         timeout parameter for SYNC dump
_hang_detection                            Hang Management detection interval
_hang_resolution                           Hang Management hang resolution
_hm_analysis_output_disk                   if TRUE the hang manager outputs hang
                                           analysis results to disk

_hm_analysis_oradebug_node_dump_level      the oradebug node dump level for hang
                                           manager hang analysis

_hm_analysis_oradebug_sys_dump_level       the oradebug system state level for hang
                                           manager hang analysis

_global_hang_analysis_interval_secs        the interval at which global hang analysis
                                           is run

_hm_verification_interval                  the hang manager verification interval
_hm_log_incidents                          Hang Manager incident logging
_trace_navigation_scope                    enabling trace navigation linking
_max_protocol_support                      Max occurrence protocols supported in a
                                           process

_lm_lms                                    number of background gcs server processes
                                           to start

_lm_dynamic_lms                            dynamic lms invocation
_lm_max_lms                                max. number of background global cache
                                           server processes

_lm_activate_lms_threshold                 threshold value to activate an additional
                                           lms

_lm_lmd_waittime                           default wait time for lmd in centiseconds

_lm_lms_waittime                           default wait time for lms in centiseconds

_lm_procs                                  number of client processes configured
                                           for cluster database

_lm_ress                                   number of resources configured for cluster
                                           database

_lm_locks                                  number of enqueues configured for cluster
                                           database

_lm_master_weight                          master resource weight for this instance

_active_standby_fast_reconfiguration       if TRUE optimize dlm reconfiguration for
                                           active/standby OPS

_lm_enq_rcfg                               if TRUE enables enqueue reconfiguration

_lm_asm_enq_hashing                        if TRUE makes ASM use enqueue master
                                           hashing for fusion locks

_lm_xids                                   number of transaction IDs configured for
                                           cluster database

_lm_res_part                               number of resource partition configured
                                           for gcs

KSPPINM                                    KSPPDESC
-----------------------------------------  --------------------------------------
_lm_drm_window                             dynamic remastering bucket window size
_lm_drm_max_requests                       dynamic remastering maximum affinity re
                                           quests processed together

_lm_drm_xlatch                             dynamic remastering forced exclusive
                                           latches

_lm_contiguous_res_count                   number of contiguous blocks that will
                                           hash to the same HV bucket

_lm_num_pt_buckets                         number of buckets in the object secondary
                                           hash table
```

Purpose of Hidden Parameters for Oracle 11g   **137**

```
_lm_num_pt_latches                      number of latches in the object secondary
                                        hash table

_lm_node_join_opt                       cluster database node join optimization
                                        in reconfig

_lm_non_fault_tolerant                  disable cluster database fault-tolerance
                                        mode

_lm_cache_res_cleanup                   percentage of cached resources should be
                                        cleanup

_lm_cache_res_type                      cache resource: string of lock types(s)
_lm_cache_lvl0_cleanup                  how often to cleanup level 0 cache res
                                        (in sec)

_ogms_home                              GMS home directory

_lm_sync_timeout                        Synchronization timeout for DLM reconfig-
                                        uration steps

_lm_ticket_active_sendback              Flow control ticket active sendback
                                        threshold

_lm_rcfg_timeout                        Reconfiguration timeout
_lm_enq_lock_freelist                   Number of ges enqueue element freelist
_lm_enqueue_freelist                    Number of enqueue freelist
_lm_dd_interval                         dd time interval in seconds
_lm_dd_scan_interval                    dd scan interval in seconds

_lm_dd_search_cnt                       number of dd search per token get
_lm_dd_max_search_time                  max dd search time per token
_dlmtrace                               Trace string of global enqueue type(s)
_lm_tx_delta                            TX lock localization delta
_lm_proc_freeze_timeout                 reconfiguration: process freeze timeout
_lm_validate_resource_type              if TRUE enables resource name 138econd138138nen

_lm_file_affinity                       mapping between file id and master
                                        instance number

_lm_share_lock_opt                      if TRUE enables share lock optimization
_lm_res_hash_bucket                     number of resource hash buckets

_ges_diagnostics                        if TRUE enables GES diagnostics
_fair_remote_cvt                        if TRUE enables fair remote convert
_lm_rcvr_hang_check_frequency           receiver hang check frequency in seconds

_lm_rcvr_hang_allow_time                receiver hang allow time in seconds
_lm_rcvr_hang_kill                      to kill receiver hang
_lm_lmon_nowait_latch                   if TRUE makes lmon get nowait latches
                                        with timeout loop

_ges_dd_debug                           if 1 or higher enables GES deadlock
                                        detection debug diagnostics

_lm_global_posts                        if TRUE delivers global posts to remote
                                        nodes

_rcfg_parallel_replay                   if TRUE enables parallel replay and
                                        cleanup at reconfiguration

KSPPINM                                 KSPPDESC
--------------------------------------- ---------------------------------------
_parallel_replay_msg_limit              Number of messages for each round of
                                        parallel replay

_rcfg_parallel_fixwrite                 if TRUE enables parallel fixwrite at
                                        reconfiguration

_parallel_fixwrite_bucket               Number of buckets for each round of fix
                                        Write

_rcfg_parallel_verify                   if TRUE enables parallel verify at
                                        reconfiguration

_dump_rcvr_ipc                          if TRUE enables IPC dump at instance
                                        eviction time
```

```
_ges_health_check                        if greater than 0 enables GES system
                                         health check

_kill_enqueue_blocker                    if greater than 0 enables killing enqueue
                                         blocker

_lm_psrcfg                               enable pseudo reconfiguration
_gcs_testing                             GCS testing parameter

_lm_better_ddvictim                      GES better deadlock victim
_lm_msg_batch_size                       GES batch message size
_lm_tickets                              GES messaging tickets
_lm_msg_cleanup_interval                 GES message buffer cleanup interval time

_lm_idle_connection_check                GES idle connection check
_lm_idle_connection_check_interval       GES idle connection check interval time
_lm_idle_connection_kill                 GES idle connection kill
_lm_send_mode                            GES send mode
_lm_postevent_buffer_size                postevent buffer size

_lm_send_queue_length                    GES send queue maximum length
_lm_send_queue_batching                  GES send queue message batching
_lm_process_batching                     GES implicit process batching for IPC
                                         messages

_lm_sq_batch_factor                      GES send queue minimum batching factor
_lm_sq_batch_type                        GES send queue batching mechanism
_lm_sq_batch_waittick                    GES send queue batching wait time in tick

_lm_sendproxy_reserve                    GES percentage of send proxy reserve of
                                         send tickets

_lm_checksum_batch_msg                   GES checksum batch messages
_abort_recovery_on_join                  if TRUE, abort recovery on join reconfig-
                                         urations

_send_ast_to_foreground                  if TRUE, send ast message to foreground
_reliable_block_sends                    if TRUE, block sends across
                                         are reliable

_blocks_per_cache_server                 number of consecutive blocks per global
                                         cache server

_object_reuse_bast                       if 1 or higher, handle object reuse
_send_close_with_block                   if TRUE, send close with block even with
                                         direct sends
_gcs_fast_reconfig                       if TRUE, enable fast reconfiguration for
                                         gcs locks

_cr_grant_global_role                    if TRUE, grant lock for CR requests when
                                         block is in global role

_cr_grant_local_role                     turn 3-way CR grants off, make it
                                         automatic, or turn it on

_skip_assume_msg                         if TRUE, skip assume message for 139econd139
                                         ns at the master

KSPPINM                                  KSPPDESC
---------------------------------------  ---------------------------------------
_gcs_resources                           number of gcs resources to be allocated
_gcs_latches                             number of gcs resource hash latches to
                                         be allocated per LMS process

_gcs_process_in_recovery                 if TRUE, process gcs requests during
                                         instance recovery

_scatter_gcs_resources                   if TRUE, gcs resources are scattered
                                         uniformly across sub pools

_gcs_res_per_bucket                      number of gcs resource per hash bucket
_gcs_shadow_locks                        number of pcm shadow locks to be allocated

_scatter_gcs_shadows                     if TRUE, gcs shadows are scattered
                                         uniformly across sub pools

_side_channel_batch_size                 number of messages to batch in a side
                                         channel message (DFS)
```

```
_side_channel_batch_timeout            timeout before shipping out the batched
                                       side channel messages in seconds

_side_channel_batch_timeout_ms         timeout before shipping out the batched
                                       side channel messages in milliseconds

_master_direct_sends                   direct sends for messages from master
                                       (DFS)

_cgs_send_timeout                      CGS send timeout value
_imr_active                            Activate Instance Membership Recovery
                                       feature

_imr_max_reconfig_delay                Maximum Reconfiguration delay (seconds)
_imr_splitbrain_res_wait               Maximum wait for split-brain resolution
                                       (seconds)

_imr_disk_voting_interval              Maximum wait for IMR disk voting (second
                                       ds)

_imr_systemload_check                  Perform the system load check during IMR

_imr_device_type                       Type of device to be used by IMR
_imr_highload_threshold                IMR system highload threshold
_imr_evicted_member_kill               IMR issue evicted member kill after a
                                       wait

_imr_evicted_member_kill_wait          IMR evicted member kill wait time in
                                       seconds

_imr_avoid_double_voting               Avoid device voting for CSS reconfig
                                       during IMR

_cluster_library                       cluster library selection
_cgs_reconfig_timeout                  CGS reconfiguration timeout interval
_cgs_tickets                           CGS messaging tickets
_lm_dynamic_load                       dynamic load adjustment
_notify_crs                            notify cluster ready services of
                                       startup and shutdown

_kill_diagnostics_timeout              timeout delay in seconds before killing
                                       enqueue blocker

__sga_target                           Actual size of SGA
_disable_streams_pool_auto_tuning      disable streams pool auto tuning
_memory_management_tracing             trace memory management activity

_memory_sanity_check                   partial granule sanity check

_init_granule_interval                 number of granules to process for defer
                                       red cache

_shared_pool_max_size                  shared pool maximum size when auto SGA
                                       enabled

KSPPINM                                KSPPDESC
-------------------------------------  -------------------------------------
_shared_pool_minsize_on                shared pool minimum size when auto SGA
                                       enabled

_streams_pool_max_size                 streams pool maximum size when auto SGA
                                       enabled

_simulate_mem_transfer                 simulate auto memory sga/pga transfers

_memory_nocancel_defsgareq             do not cancel deferred sga reqs with
                                       auto-memory

_memory_broker_stat_interval           memory broker statistics gathering
                                       interval for auto sga

_automemory_broker_interval            memory broker statistics gathering
                                       interval for auto memory

_memory_broker_shrink_heaps            memory broker allow policy to shrink
                                       shared pool
```

```
_memory_broker_shrink_java_heaps          memory broker allow policy to shrink
                                          java pool

_memory_broker_shrink_streams_pool        memory broker allow policy to shrink
                                          streams pool

_memory_broker_shrink_timeout             memory broker policy to timeout shrink
                                          shared/java pool

_memory_broker_log_stat_entries           memory broker num stat entries

_memory_broker_marginal_utility_sp        Marginal Utility threshold pct for sp
_memory_broker_marginal_utility_bc        Marginal Utility threshold pct for bc
_disable_latch_free_SCN_writes_via_32ca   disable latch-free SCN writes using 32-
s                                         bit compare & swap

_disable_latch_free_SCN_writes_via_64ca   disable latch-free SCN writes using 64-
s                                         bit compare & swap

_controlfile_enqueue_timeout              control file enqueue timeout in seconds
_controlfile_enqueue_holding_time         control file enqueue max holding time in
                                          seconds

_controlfile_update_check                 controlfile update sanity check
_controlfile_enqueue_dump                 dump the system states after controlfile
                                          enqueue timeout

_controlfile_block_size                   control file block size in bytes
_controlfile_section_init_size            control file initial section size
_controlfile_section_max_expand           control file max expansion rate
_kill_controlfile_enqueue_blocker         enable killing controlfile enqueue blocker
                                          on timeout

_db_block_buffers                         Number of database blocks cached in
                                          memory: hidden parameter

_db_block_cache_protect                   protect database blocks (true only when
                                          debugging)

_db_block_cache_protect_internal          protect database blocks (for strictly
                                          internal use only)

_dbwr_tracing                             Enable dbwriter tracing
_tsenc_tracing                            Enable TS encryption tracing

_disable_multiple_block_sizes             disable multiple block size support (for
                                          debugging)

_db_fast_obj_truncate                     enable fast object truncate
_db_fast_obj_ckpt                         enable fast object checkpoint
_enable_obj_queues                        enable object queues
_db_obj_enable_ksr                        enable ksr in object checkpoint/reuse
_small_table_threshold                    threshold level of table size for direct
                                          reads

1627 rows selected.
```

It would be impossible to explain the purpose and function of all hidden parameters for Oracle 11g since such a Herculean task would fill volumes of documentation. Furthermore, the exact purpose and comprehensive details are internal knowledge to Oracle and only product developers, Oracle internal consultants and managers within Oracle corporation have access to this information. Suffice it to say, many notes on Oracle Metalink support will reference a hidden parameter in the event that a bug is addressed or a support issue needs to be resolved. Therefore, it is useful to be familiar with the most common hidden parameters that will be covered in the following section.

Explanation of Key Hidden Parameters for Oracle 11g

With the Oracle 11g release, there are many new hidden parameters that maintain a great deal of the functionality for the myriad of new features that come with 11g as shown below. For example, the following hidden parameters are new to Oracle 11g and support many new features:

- *diag_adr_enabled*
- *diag_adr_auto_purge*
- *prop_old_enabled*
- *diag_hm_rc_enabled*

New Features for 11g and Hidden Parameters

Every new feature within Oracle 11g has a hidden and undocumented parameter associated with it that contains the critical settings for the internal operations of the functionality within the Oracle database. The Oracle 11g Automatic Diagnostic Repository (ADR) contains the following key hidden parameters:

- *_diag_adr_test_param*
- *_diag_adr_enabled*
- *_diag_adr_auto_purge*

The *diag_adr_test_param* is a hidden 11g parameter that serves as a testing parameter to verify operation of the 11g ADR diagnostic features.

Another key hidden 11g parameter for the ADR new feature with Oracle is *diag_adr_enabled*. This parameter either enables or disables the operation of the 11g ADR feature.

Finally, there is the *diag_adr_auto_purge* parameter for Oracle 11g which allows one to enable or disable the 11g ADR Memory Monitor

(MMON) background process behavior with respect to the ADR operations.

Oracle 11g Hidden Parameters for 11g Data Recovery Advisor (DRA)

The Oracle 11g Data Recovery Advisor (DRA) is an exciting new feature that is new to 11g for backup and recovery functionality. The following hidden parameters perform the behind-the-scenes add-on functions as part of the DRA with Oracle 11g:

- *dra_enable_offline_dictionary*
- *dra_bmr_number_threshold*
- *dra_bmr_percent_threshold*

The hidden parameter *dra_enable_offline_dictionary* enables the periodic creation for offline dictionary objects associated with the Data Recovery Advisor. The other two hidden 11g parameters pertain to block media recovery (BMR) tasks as performed with database backup and recovery operations by the Data Recovery Advisor within Oracle 11g. As for the hidden parameter *dra_bmr_number_threshold*, this parameter relates to the maximum amount of block media recovery tasks that can be performed on a file during recovery. The other hidden parameter for the Data Recovery Advisor, *dra_bmr_percent_threshold,* measures the largest percentage of blocks in a file during recovery tasks performed by the DRA for Oracle 11g.

Hang Detection Parameters for the 11g Health Monitor (HM) System

As part of the self-healing and tuning new features for 11g, Oracle has provided the health monitor (HM) suite of tools and hidden parameters listed next.

- *_hang_detection*
- *_hang_resolution*
- *_hm_analysis_output_disk*
- *_hm_analysis_oradebug_node_dump_level*

- *_hm_analysis_oradebug_sys_dump_level*

- *_diag_hm_rc_enabled*

- *_diag_hm_tc_enabled*

The hidden 11g parameter *hang_detection* provides for an interval to detect hang conditions as part of the health monitor tasks. For hang resolution, there is the 11g hidden parameter *hang_resolution*. The *hm_analysis_output_disk* is a hidden 11g parameter which generates a return code of TRUE if the hang manager outputs hangs within the Oracle database. For Oradebug dump activity, there are also two 11g hidden parameters. The first 11g hidden parameter that coordinates Oradebug node dump level output for hang manager analysis is *hm_analysis_oradebug_node_dump_level*. Another hidden parameter for 11g related tasks with conjunction to Oradebug system level traces is the *hm_analysis_oradebug_sys_dump_level* parameter which allows the 11g hang manager to output system state level information with the Oradebug utility.

For the health monitor (HM) checks performed by the Oracle 11g health checkers, there are a couple of new undocumented 11g database parameters: *diag_hm_rc_enabled* and *diag_hm_tc_enabled*. The parameter *diag_hm_rc_enabled* performs the task of either enabling or disabling the health monitor checks for diagnosis of 11g database health conditions. There is also a partner hidden 11g parameter called *diag_hm_tc_enabled* that allows one to either enable or disable the test or dummy checks performed by the 11g health monitor system within Oracle.

Summary

In this chapter, insight has been given on the following topics regarding undocumented parameters for Oracle 11g database:

- Purpose of 11g hidden database parameters

- Hidden initialization database parameters Oracle 11g

- New features for 11g and hidden parameters

In the following chapters, coverage will be provided about the mystery surrounding Oracle 11g *v$* dynamic performance views as well as *x$* tables. Also, the chapters will dig deeper into Oracle 11g database internals so that the reader can understand how to diagnose, tune, and resolve complex Oracle database problems using these undocumented and hidden Oracle 11g features.

Exploring New *v$* Tables in Oracle 11g

The previous chapter explained how Oracle 11g hidden parameters encapsulate many of the new underlying features within the Oracle database engine. The journey will continue into Oracle database internals by exploring the power of *v$* dynamic performance views available with Oracle 11g. As such, these following themes for the new *v$* dynamic performance views for Oracle 11g will be touched upon:

- New features for the *v$* tables and Oracle 11g data dictionary

- Investigating Oracle 11g database internals with the *v$* views

- Scripts and tips for *v$* and data dictionary with Oracle 11g

New Features for the *v$* Tables and Oracle 11g Data Dictionary

As mentioned in previous chapters, Oracle 11g provides an entire new set of amazing new features such as Real Application Testing (RAT), Flashback Data Archives and Total Recall, and the Oracle Data Recovery Advisor. While these are available via the graphical user friendly interface in Oracle Enterprise Manager, the Oracle expert will wisely turn to the command line power of *v$* views accessible only from within the text based SQL*Plus interface for Oracle 11g. First, examine the purpose and origins of these *v$* dynamic performance views in the Oracle 11g data dictionary.

Purpose of *v$* Views for Oracle 11g

The Oracle *v$* dynamic performance views have always existed ever since the first major release of the Oracle database software. The primary purpose of these hidden and undocumented database parameters has been to provide internal support for engineers and development teams at Oracle with a method to resolve unforeseen issues that are not addressed by the core functionality within the Oracle database engine. In Oracle 11g, many of the new features are controlled behind the scenes via these hidden parameter settings.

The *v$* views are created by the *catalog.sql* script as part of the Oracle 11g database installation process. As of Oracle 11g, there are approximately 484 different *v$* views. To understand how rapidly these dynamic *v$* performance views have been added across different Oracle database releases, examine the following table.

Oracle Version/Release	V$ Views	X$ Tables
6	23	Unknown
7	72	126
8	185	271
9	259	394
10	372	613
11	484	798

Table 6.1: *Quantity of v$ Views and x$ Tables per Oracle Database Release*

Of interest to the reader is that *v$* dynamic performance views are technically created with the format *v_$* within the data dictionary. The *v$* views referenced by SQL*Loader are created during installation by the *catldr.sql* script. The hard coded definitions for the *v$* views can be obtained by querying the view called *v$fixed_view_definition* table.

To provide a clear walkthrough of the *v$* dynamic performance views for Oracle 11g, the views will be summarized into various categories for 11g to better assist the Oracle DBA professional.

Categories for Oracle 11g Database Administration with v$ Views

With hundreds of *v$* views in the Oracle 11g database, it is believed that by separating these into various categories, it will prove easier for the database professional to understand and select the useful *v$* dynamic performance views to best assist them in database administration tasks. One way to differentiate the Oracle beginner from the true Oracle expert is to ask the Oracle database practitioner if he or she knows the core *v$* dynamic performance views and how to access them from the SQL*Plus interface. If the DBA candidate or professional shrugs and gives a coy reply that "I only know how to use the Oracle Enterprise Manager (OEM) GUI", then he or she most likely is really a database baby sitter (DBBS) and not a true Oracle guru.

In fact, I recall one time when I interviewed years ago for a midlevel Oracle DBA position and the senior DBA asked me if I knew any of the key *v$* and *x$* tables! Fortunately, I was able to reply affirmatively with such key *v$* tables such as *v$database* and *v$instance* which should be within every seasoned Oracle DBA's vocabulary.

General Oracle 11g Database Administration

One key task of the Oracle database professional is to perform daily monitoring to ensure that the database environment is healthy for Oracle 11g. The following key *v$* dynamic views allow the DBA to quickly drill down into the Oracle 11g database engine to quickly assess the database status.

```
V$DATABASE
V$INSTANCE
V$OPTION
V$LICENSE
V$CONTROLFILE
V$TABLESPACE
V$DATAFILE
V$LOG
V$LOGFILE
V$ARCHIVED_LOG
V$TEMPFILE
```

Oracle 11g New Features

The follow *v$* views are used by the new 11g result cache:

```
V$RESULT_CACHE_STATISTICS
V$RESULT_CACHE_MEMORY
V$RESULT_CACHE_OBJECTS
V$RESULT_CACHE_DEPENDENCY
V$CLIENT_RESULT_CACHE_STATS
```

The Oracle 11g RAT suite includes database replay and the following *v$* view provides details on usage and status for this key new 11g feature with Oracle.

```
V$WORKLOAD_REPLAY_THREAD
```

For the new 11g feature for the Incident Repair component of the 11g ADR, there are the following *v$* views:

```
V$IR_FAILURE
V$IR_REPAIR
V$IR_MANUAL_CHECKLIST
V$IR_FAILURE_SET
```

The 11g health monitor (HM) is linked to the following *v$* views listed below:

```
V$HM_CHECK
V$HM_CHECK_PARAM
V$HM_RUN
V$HM_FINDING
V$HM_RECOMMENDATION
V$HM_INFO
```

V$ Views- Oracle 11g NFS New Features

Oracle 11g provides a new feature to setup NFS based files within Oracle 11g. The following *v$* views provide the details for NFS configuration within Oracle 11g.

```
V$NFS_CLIENTS
V$NFS_OPEN_FILES
V$NFS_LOCKS
V$IOSTAT_NETWORK
```

Oracle 11g Backup and Recovery

Backup and Recovery is the most important function of the serious Oracle DBA and can mean the difference between life and death in terms of corporate safety and job security. The following *v$* views provide details for Oracle 11g Backup and Recovery.

```
V$RMAN_BACKUP_SUBJOB_DETAILS
V$RMAN_BACKUP_JOB_DETAILS
V$BACKUP_SET_DETAILS
V$BACKUP_PIECE_DETAILS
V$BACKUP_COPY_DETAILS
$BACKUP
V$RECOVERY_STATUS
V$RECOVERY_FILE_STATUS
V$BACKUP_SET
V$BACKUP_PIECE
V$BACKUP_DATAFILE
V$BACKUP_REDOLOG
V$BACKUP_CORRUPTION
V$BACKUP_DEVICE
V$BACKUP_SPFILE
V$BACKUP_SYNC_IO
V$BACKUP_ASYNC_IO
V$RECOVER_FILE
V$RMAN_STATUS
V$RMAN_OUTPUT
V$BACKUP_DATAFILE_DETAILS
V$BACKUP_CONTROLFILE_DETAILS
V$BACKUP_ARCHIVELOG_DETAILS
V$BACKUP_SPFILE_DETAILS
V$BACKUP_DATAFILE_SUMMARY
V$BACKUP_CONTROLFILE_SUMMARY
V$BACKUP_ARCHIVELOG_SUMMARY
V$BACKUP_SPFILE_SUMMARY
V$BACKUP_SET_SUMMARY
V$RECOVERY_PROGRESS
V$RMAN_BACKUP_TYPE
V$RMAN_CONFIGURATION
```

Oracle 11g RAC and ASM, Oracle 11g Data Guard and 11g Streams

Oracle 11g RAC and ASM provide highly available robust architectures for performance, service and reliability as part of the Oracle Maximum Availability Architecture (MAA). The following *v$* views provide details on these key HA technologies.

11g Data Guard

```
V$DATAGUARD_CONFIG
V$DATAGUARD_STATUS
V$MANAGED_STANDBY
```

```
V$LOGSTDBY
V$LOGSTDBY_STATS
V$LOGSTDBY_TRANSACTION
V$LOGSTDBY_PROCESS
V$LOGSTDBY_PROGRESS
V$LOGSTDBY_STATE
```

11g Streams

```
V$STREAMS_APPLY_COORDINATOR
V$STREAMS_APPLY_SERVER
V$STREAMS_APPLY_READER
V$STREAMS_CAPTURE
V$STREAMS_TRANSACTION
V$STREAMS_MESSAGE_TRACKING
```

11g RAC

```
V$CLUSTER_INTERCONNECTS
V$CONFIGURED_INTERCONNECTS
V$DYNAMIC_REMASTER_STATS
V$DLM_MISC
V$DLM_LATCH
V$DLM_CONVERT_LOCAL
V$DLM_CONVERT_REMOTE
V$GES_ENQUEUE
V$GES_BLOCKING_ENQUEUE
V$DLM_ALL_LOCKS
V$DLM_LOCKS
V$DLM_RESS
V$GLOBAL_BLOCKED_LOCKS
```

11g ASM

```
V$ASM_TEMPLATE
V$ASM_ALIAS
V$ASM_FILE
V$ASM_CLIENT
V$ASM_DISKGROUP
V$ASM_DISKGROUP_STAT
V$ASM_DISK
V$ASM_DISK_STAT
$ASM_DISK_IOSTAT
V$ASM_OPERATION
V$ASM_ATTRIBUTE
```

Performance Tuning Oracle 11g

Performance tuning is a complex task that daunts many Oracle DBAs. It is as much an art as a science. While GUI tools such as Oracle Enterprise Manager and Quest TOAD provide a nice slick graphical interface, to dig into the internal nuts and bolts of database performance, the serious Oracle performance analyst relies on reports generated by *v$* dynamic performance views from within the Oracle 11g data dictionary. The following *v$* views provide insight into database tuning for Oracle 11g.

Wait Events for 11g

```
V$SESSION
V$WAITCLASSMETRIC
V$WAITCLASSMETRIC_HISTORY
V$WAITSTAT
V$WAIT_CHAINS
```

Oracle 11g Concurrency and SQL Tuning

```
V$LOCK
V$SQL
V$SQLAREA
V$SESSTAT
V$MYSTAT
V$SESS_IO
V$SYSSTAT
V$STATNAME
V$OSSTAT
V$ACTIVE_SESSION_HISTORY
V$ACTIVE_SESS_POOL_MTH
V$SESSION_WAIT
V$SESSION_WAIT_CLASS
V$SYSTEM_WAIT_CLASS
V$TRANSACTION
V$LOCKED_OBJECT
V$LATCH
V$LATCH_CHILDREN
V$LATCH_PARENT
V$LATCHNAME
V$LATCHHOLDER
V$LATCH_MISSES
V$ENQUEUE_LOCK
V$TRANSACTION_ENQUEUE
V$SYS_OPTIMIZER_ENV
V$SES_OPTIMIZER_ENV
V$SQL_OPTIMIZER_ENV
V$SQL_PLAN
V$SQL_PLAN_STATISTICS
V$SQL_PLAN_STATISTICS_ALL
```

Oracle 11g Memory Tuning

```
V$SGA
V$SGASTAT
V$SGAINFO
V$SGA_CURRENT_RESIZE_OPS
V$SGA_RESIZE_OPS
```

```
V$SGA_DYNAMIC_COMPONENTS
V$SGA_DYNAMIC_FREE_MEMORY
V$PGASTAT
V$SQL_WORKAREA_HISTOGRAM
V$PGA_TARGET_ADVICE_HISTOGRAM
V$PGA_TARGET_ADVICE
V$MEMORY_CURRENT_RESIZE_OPS
V$MEMORY_RESIZE_OPS
V$MEMORY_DYNAMIC_COMPONENTS
V$LIBRARY_CACHE_MEMORY
V$SHARED_POOL_ADVICE
V$JAVA_LIBRARY_CACHE_MEMORY
V$JAVA_POOL_ADVICE
V$STREAMS_POOL_ADVICE
```

Next, a useful way to generate the complete listing for all Oracle 11g *v$* dynamic performance views within the Oracle database environment will be shown.

Comprehensive Listing of Oracle 11g Dynamic *v$* Performance Views

With each new major release and version of Oracle, dozens if not hundreds of new dynamic performance *v$* views are added. For instance, in Oracle 10gR2, there are 398 dynamic performance *v$* views. In Oracle 11gR1 there are now 484 dynamic performance *v$* views which means that between 10gR2 and 11gR1, there are 86 new *v$* views in 11gR1.

So how does one find out what all of the dynamic performance views are within Oracle 11g? Well, one needs a query such as the following to run against the *v$fixed_table* to obtain the full listing.

```
SELECT NAME, TYPE
FROM V$FIXED_TABLE
WHERE NAME LIKE 'V$%';
/
SQL> SELECT NAME, TYPE
  2   FROM V$FIXED_TABLE
  3   WHERE NAME LIKE 'V$%';

NAME                              TYPE
------------------------------    -----
V$WAITSTAT                        VIEW
V$BH                              VIEW
V$GC_ELEMENT                      VIEW
```

```
V$CR_BLOCK_SERVER                VIEW
V$CURRENT_BLOCK_SERVER           VIEW
V$ENCRYPTED_TABLESPACES          VIEW
V$GC_ELEMENTS_WITH_COLLISIONS    VIEW
V$FILE_CACHE_TRANSFER            VIEW
V$TEMP_CACHE_TRANSFER            VIEW
V$CLASS_CACHE_TRANSFER           VIEW

V$INSTANCE_CACHE_TRANSFER        VIEW
V$LOCK_ELEMENT                   VIEW
V$BSP                            VIEW
V$LOCKS_WITH_COLLISIONS          VIEW
V$FILE_PING                      VIEW
V$TEMP_PING                      VIEW
V$CLASS_PING                     VIEW
V$LOCK_ACTIVITY                  VIEW
V$ROWCACHE                       VIEW
V$ROWCACHE_PARENT                VIEW

V$ROWCACHE_SUBORDINATE           VIEW
V$PROCESS                        VIEW
V$BGPROCESS                      VIEW
V$PROCESS_MEMORY                 VIEW
V$PROCESS_MEMORY_DETAIL          VIEW
V$PROCESS_MEMORY_DETAIL_PROG     VIEW
V$SESSION                        VIEW
V$RSRC_SESSION_INFO              VIEW
V$BLOCKING_QUIESCE               VIEW
V$PX_SESSION                     VIEW


NAME                             TYPE
------------------------------   -----
V$PX_SESSTAT                     VIEW
V$SESSION_CONNECT_INFO           VIEW
V$SESSION_WAIT_HISTORY           VIEW
V$WAIT_CHAINS                    VIEW
V$SESSION_WAIT                   VIEW
V$SESSION_WAIT_CLASS             VIEW
V$SYSTEM_WAIT_CLASS              VIEW
V$SESSION_EVENT                  VIEW
V$EVENT_HISTOGRAM                VIEW
V$SYSTEM_EVENT                   VIEW

V$EVENT_NAME                     VIEW
V$LICENSE                        VIEW
V$TRANSACTION                    VIEW
V$LOCKED_OBJECT                  VIEW
V$LATCH                          VIEW
V$LATCH_CHILDREN                 VIEW
V$LATCH_PARENT                   VIEW
V$LATCHNAME                      VIEW
V$LATCHHOLDER                    VIEW
V$LATCH_MISSES                   VIEW

V$RESOURCE                       VIEW
V$_LOCK1                         VIEW
V$_LOCK                          VIEW
```

```
V$LOCK                          VIEW
V$ENQUEUE_LOCK                  VIEW
V$TRANSACTION_ENQUEUE           VIEW
V$TIMER                         VIEW
V$SESSTAT                       VIEW
V$MYSTAT                        VIEW
V$SESS_IO                       VIEW

V$SYSSTAT                       VIEW
V$STATNAME                      VIEW
V$OSSTAT                        VIEW
V$RESOURCE_LIMIT                VIEW
V$ACCESS                        VIEW
V$OBJECT_DEPENDENCY             VIEW
V$DBFILE                        VIEW
V$ARCHIVE                       VIEW
V$FILESTAT                      VIEW
V$FILE_HISTOGRAM                VIEW

V$TEMPSTAT                      VIEW
V$LOGFILE                       VIEW
V$ROLLSTAT                      VIEW
V$FAST_START_SERVERS            VIEW
V$FAST_START_TRANSACTIONS       VIEW
V$SGA                           VIEW
V$SGASTAT                       VIEW
V$SGAINFO                       VIEW
V$SGA_CURRENT_RESIZE_OPS        VIEW
V$SGA_RESIZE_OPS                VIEW
NAME                            TYPE
------------------------------- -----
V$SGA_DYNAMIC_COMPONENTS        VIEW
V$SGA_DYNAMIC_FREE_MEMORY       VIEW
V$MEMORY_CURRENT_RESIZE_OPS     VIEW
V$MEMORY_RESIZE_OPS             VIEW
V$MEMORY_DYNAMIC_COMPONENTS     VIEW
V$PARAMETER                     VIEW
V$SYSTEM_PARAMETER              VIEW
V$PARAMETER2                    VIEW
V$SYSTEM_PARAMETER2             VIEW
V$SYSTEM_PARAMETER4             VIEW

V$OBSOLETE_PARAMETER            VIEW
V$SPPARAMETER                   VIEW
V$PARAMETER_VALID_VALUES        VIEW
V$CLUSTER_INTERCONNECTS         VIEW
V$CONFIGURED_INTERCONNECTS      VIEW
V$ENABLEDPRIVS                  VIEW
V$DISPATCHER                    VIEW
V$DISPATCHER_CONFIG             VIEW
V$DISPATCHER_RATE               VIEW
V$SHARED_SERVER                 VIEW

V$QUEUE                         VIEW
V$REQDIST                       VIEW
V$CIRCUIT                       VIEW
V$LOADPSTAT                     VIEW
V$LOADISTAT                     VIEW
V$LIBRARY_CACHE_MEMORY          VIEW
```

```
V$SHARED_POOL_ADVICE            VIEW
V$JAVA_LIBRARY_CACHE_MEMORY     VIEW
V$JAVA_POOL_ADVICE              VIEW
V$STREAMS_POOL_ADVICE           VIEW

V$LIBRARYCACHE                  VIEW
V$SQLAREA                       VIEW
V$SQL                           VIEW
V$SQLAREA_PLAN_HASH             VIEW
V$SQL_SHARED_MEMORY             VIEW
V$SQLTEXT                       VIEW
V$SQLTEXT_WITH_NEWLINES         VIEW
V$OPEN_CURSOR                   VIEW
V$SUBCACHE                      VIEW
V$DB_OBJECT_CACHE               VIEW

V$DB_PIPES                      VIEW
V$VERSION                       VIEW
V$CONTROLFILE                   VIEW
V$DATABASE                      VIEW
V$THREAD                        VIEW
V$INSTANCE_LOG_GROUP            VIEW
V$LOG                           VIEW
V$STANDBY_LOG                   VIEW
V$DATAFILE                      VIEW
V$TEMPFILE                      VIEW

NAME                            TYPE
------------------------------  -----
V$LOGHIST                       VIEW
V$SEGSTAT_NAME                  VIEW
V$SEGSTAT                       VIEW
V$SEGMENT_STATISTICS            VIEW
V$LOBSTAT                       VIEW
V$BUFFER_POOL                   VIEW
V$BUFFER_POOL_STATISTICS        VIEW
V$INSTANCE                      VIEW
V$TYPE_SIZE                     VIEW
V$NLS_PARAMETERS                VIEW

V$NLS_VALID_VALUES              VIEW
V$OPTION                        VIEW
V$RECOVER_FILE                  VIEW
V$BACKUP                        VIEW
V$LOG_HISTORY                   VIEW
V$ARCHIVE_GAP                   VIEW
V$RECOVERY_LOG                  VIEW
V$FIXED_TABLE                   VIEW
V$INDEXED_FIXED_COLUMN          VIEW
V$FIXED_VIEW_DEFINITION         VIEW

V$SESSION_CURSOR_CACHE          VIEW
V$SYSTEM_CURSOR_CACHE           VIEW
V$SHARED_SERVER_MONITOR         VIEW
V$PWFILE_USERS                  VIEW
V$DBLINK                        VIEW
V$PQ_SLAVE                      VIEW
V$PX_PROCESS                    VIEW
V$PQ_SESSTAT                    VIEW
```

```
V$PQ_SYSSTAT                    VIEW
V$PX_PROCESS_SYSSTAT            VIEW

V$PX_BUFFER_ADVICE             VIEW
V$EXECUTION                     VIEW
V$RECOVERY_STATUS              VIEW
V$RECOVERY_FILE_STATUS         VIEW
V$SHARED_POOL_RESERVED         VIEW
V$SORT_SEGMENT                 VIEW
V$SORT_USAGE                   VIEW
V$TEMP_EXTENT_MAP              VIEW
V$TEMP_EXTENT_POOL             VIEW
V$TEMP_SPACE_HEADER            VIEW

V$_SEQUENCES                   VIEW
V$PQ_TQSTAT                    VIEW
V$PX_INSTANCE_GROUP            VIEW
V$ACTIVE_INSTANCES             VIEW
V$SQL_CURSOR                   VIEW
V$SQL_BIND_METADATA            VIEW
V$SQL_SHARED_CURSOR            VIEW
V$SQL_BIND_DATA                VIEW
V$TABLESPACE                   VIEW
V$RMAN_CONFIGURATION           VIEW
NAME                            TYPE
------------------------------- -----
V$OFFLINE_RANGE                VIEW
V$ARCHIVED_LOG                 VIEW
V$FOREIGN_ARCHIVED_LOG         VIEW
V$ARCHIVE_PROCESSES            VIEW
V$MANAGED_STANDBY              VIEW
V$DATAGUARD_STATUS             VIEW
V$ARCHIVE_DEST                 VIEW
V$ARCHIVE_DEST_STATUS          VIEW
V$DATAGUARD_CONFIG             VIEW
V$SESSION_LONGOPS              VIEW

V$ADVISOR_PROGRESS             VIEW
V$DATAFILE_COPY                VIEW
V$COPY_CORRUPTION              VIEW
V$BACKUP_SET                   VIEW
V$BACKUP_PIECE                 VIEW
V$BACKUP_DATAFILE              VIEW
V$BACKUP_REDOLOG               VIEW
V$BACKUP_CORRUPTION            VIEW
V$DELETED_OBJECT               VIEW
V$CONTROLFILE_RECORD_SECTION   VIEW

V$DATAFILE_HEADER              VIEW
V$SESSION_OBJECT_CACHE         VIEW
V$GLOBAL_TRANSACTION           VIEW
V$BACKUP_DEVICE                VIEW
V$DYNAMIC_REMASTER_STATS       VIEW
V$DLM_MISC                     VIEW
V$DLM_LATCH                    VIEW
V$DLM_CONVERT_LOCAL            VIEW
V$DLM_CONVERT_REMOTE           VIEW
V$RECOVERY_PROGRESS            VIEW
```

```
V$GES_ENQUEUE                    VIEW
V$GES_BLOCKING_ENQUEUE           VIEW
V$DLM_ALL_LOCKS                  VIEW
V$DLM_LOCKS                      VIEW
V$DLM_RESS                       VIEW
V$GLOBAL_BLOCKED_LOCKS           VIEW
V$AQ1                            VIEW
V$CONTEXT                        VIEW
V$RSRC_CONSUMER_GROUP_CPU_MTH    VIEW
V$RSRC_PLAN_CPU_MTH              VIEW

V$MAX_ACTIVE_SESS_TARGET_MTH     VIEW
V$ACTIVE_SESS_POOL_MTH           VIEW
V$PARALLEL_DEGREE_LIMIT_MTH      VIEW
V$QUEUEING_MTH                   VIEW
V$RSRC_CONSUMER_GROUP            VIEW
V$RSRC_PLAN                      VIEW
V$RSRC_PLAN_HISTORY              VIEW
V$RSRC_CONS_GROUP_HISTORY        VIEW
V$RSRCMGRMETRIC                  VIEW
V$RSRCMGRMETRIC_HISTORY          VIEW

NAME                             TYPE
------------------------------   -----
V$HS_AGENT                       VIEW
V$HS_SESSION                     VIEW
V$INSTANCE_RECOVERY              VIEW
V$LOGMNR_CONTENTS                VIEW
V$LOGMNR_LOGS                    VIEW
V$LOGMNR_DICTIONARY              VIEW
V$LOGMNR_PARAMETERS              VIEW
V$TEMPORARY_LOBS                 VIEW
V$PROXY_DATAFILE                 VIEW
V$PROXY_ARCHIVEDLOG              VIEW

V$BACKUP_SPFILE                  VIEW
V$BACKUP_SYNC_IO                 VIEW
V$BACKUP_ASYNC_IO                VIEW
V$RESERVED_WORDS                 VIEW
V$DLM_TRAFFIC_CONTROLLER         VIEW
V$HS_PARAMETER                   VIEW
V$UNDOSTAT                       VIEW
V$MEMORY_TARGET_ADVICE           VIEW
V$SGA_TARGET_ADVICE              VIEW
V$DB_CACHE_ADVICE                VIEW

V$MTTR_TARGET_ADVICE             VIEW
V$LOGMNR_LOGFILE                 VIEW
V$LOGMNR_PROCESS                 VIEW
V$LOGMNR_TRANSACTION             VIEW
V$LOGMNR_REGION                  VIEW
V$LOGMNR_CALLBACK                VIEW
V$LOGMNR_SESSION                 VIEW
V$LOGMNR_LATCH                   VIEW
V$LOGMNR_DICTIONARY_LOAD         VIEW
V$LOGMNR_SYS_OBJECTS             VIEW

V$LOGMNR_SYS_DBA_SEGS            VIEW
V$LOGMNR_EXTENTS                 VIEW
```

```
V$LOGMNR_DBA_OBJECTS            VIEW
V$LOGMNR_OBJECT_SEGMENTS        VIEW
V$SQL_WORKAREA                  VIEW
V$SQL_WORKAREA_ACTIVE           VIEW
V$PGASTAT                       VIEW
V$SQL_WORKAREA_HISTOGRAM        VIEW
V$PGA_TARGET_ADVICE_HISTOGRAM   VIEW
V$PGA_TARGET_ADVICE             VIEW

V$SYS_OPTIMIZER_ENV             VIEW
V$SES_OPTIMIZER_ENV             VIEW
V$SQL_OPTIMIZER_ENV             VIEW
V$SQL_PLAN                      VIEW
V$SQL_PLAN_STATISTICS           VIEW
V$SQL_PLAN_STATISTICS_ALL       VIEW
V$GLOBALCONTEXT                 VIEW
V$RESUMABLE                     VIEW
V$STREAMS_APPLY_COORDINATOR     VIEW
V$STREAMS_APPLY_SERVER          VIEW
NAME                            TYPE
------------------------------- -----
V$STREAMS_APPLY_READER          VIEW
V$STREAMS_CAPTURE               VIEW
V$STREAMS_TRANSACTION           VIEW
V$STREAMS_MESSAGE_TRACKING      VIEW
V$TIMEZONE_NAMES                VIEW
V$TIMEZONE_FILE                 VIEW
V$ENQUEUE_STAT                  VIEW
V$ENQUEUE_STATISTICS            VIEW
V$LOCK_TYPE                     VIEW
V$REPLQUEUE                     VIEW

V$REPLPROP                      VIEW
V$MVREFRESH                     VIEW
V$LOGSTDBY                      VIEW
V$LOGSTDBY_STATS                VIEW
V$LOGSTDBY_TRANSACTION          VIEW
V$LOGSTDBY_PROCESS              VIEW
V$LOGSTDBY_PROGRESS             VIEW
V$LOGSTDBY_STATE                VIEW
V$VPD_POLICY                    VIEW
V$SQL_REDIRECTION               VIEW

V$HVMASTER_INFO                 VIEW
V$GCSHVMASTER_INFO              VIEW
V$GCSPFMASTER_INFO              VIEW
V$DATABASE_BLOCK_CORRUPTION     VIEW
V$LOGMNR_STATS                  VIEW
V$ASM_TEMPLATE                  VIEW
V$ASM_ALIAS                     VIEW
V$ASM_FILE                      VIEW
V$ASM_CLIENT                    VIEW
V$ASM_DISKGROUP                 VIEW

V$ASM_DISKGROUP_STAT            VIEW
V$ASM_DISK                      VIEW
V$ASM_DISK_STAT                 VIEW
V$ASM_DISK_IOSTAT               VIEW
V$ASM_OPERATION                 VIEW
```

```
V$ASM_ATTRIBUTE                   VIEW
V$STATISTICS_LEVEL                VIEW
V$DATABASE_INCARNATION            VIEW
V$AW_OLAP                         VIEW
V$AW_CALC                         VIEW

V$AW_SESSION_INFO                 VIEW
V$MAP_FILE                        VIEW
V$MAP_FILE_EXTENT                 VIEW
V$MAP_ELEMENT                     VIEW
V$MAP_EXT_ELEMENT                 VIEW
V$MAP_COMP_LIST                   VIEW
V$MAP_SUBELEMENT                  VIEW
V$MAP_FILE_IO_STACK               VIEW
V$MAP_LIBRARY                     VIEW
V$DATAPUMP_JOB                    VIEW

NAME                              TYPE
------------------------------    -----
V$DATAPUMP_SESSION                VIEW
V$RULE_SET                        VIEW
V$RULE_SET_AGGREGATE_STATS        VIEW
V$JAVAPOOL                        VIEW
V$SYSAUX_OCCUPANTS                VIEW
V$RECOVERY_FILE_DEST              VIEW
V$FLASH_RECOVERY_AREA_USAGE       VIEW
V$AW_AGGREGATE_OP                 VIEW
V$AW_ALLOCATE_OP                  VIEW
V$TRANSPORTABLE_PLATFORM          VIEW

V$BLOCK_CHANGE_TRACKING           VIEW
V$RULE                            VIEW
V$FLASHBACK_DATABASE_LOGFILE      VIEW
V$FLASHBACK_DATABASE_LOG          VIEW
V$FLASHBACK_DATABASE_STAT         VIEW
V$ACTIVE_SESSION_HISTORY          VIEW
V$WORKLOAD_REPLAY_THREAD          VIEW
V$RMAN_STATUS                     VIEW
V$RMAN_OUTPUT                     VIEW
V$ACTIVE_SERVICES                 VIEW

V$SERVICE_WAIT_CLASS              VIEW
V$SERVICE_EVENT                   VIEW
V$SERVICES                        VIEW
V$AW_LONGOPS                      VIEW
V$METRICGROUP                     VIEW
V$METRICNAME                      VIEW
V$METRIC                          VIEW
V$METRIC_HISTORY                  VIEW
V$SYSMETRIC                       VIEW
V$SYSMETRIC_HISTORY               VIEW

V$FILESPACE_USAGE                 VIEW
V$SCHEDULER_RUNNING_JOBS          VIEW
V$BUFFERED_QUEUES                 VIEW
V$BUFFERED_SUBSCRIBERS            VIEW
V$BUFFERED_PUBLISHERS             VIEW
V$TSM_SESSIONS                    VIEW
V$PROPAGATION_SENDER              VIEW
```

```
V$PROPAGATION_RECEIVER          VIEW
V$SUBSCR_REGISTRATION_STATS     VIEW
V$CLIENT_STATS                  VIEW

V$SERV_MOD_ACT_STATS            VIEW
V$SERVICE_STATS                 VIEW
V$SYS_TIME_MODEL                VIEW
V$SESS_TIME_MODEL               VIEW
V$SYSMETRIC_SUMMARY             VIEW
V$SESSMETRIC                    VIEW
V$FILEMETRIC                    VIEW
V$FILEMETRIC_HISTORY            VIEW
V$IOFUNCMETRIC                  VIEW
V$IOFUNCMETRIC_HISTORY          VIEW
NAME                            TYPE
------------------------------  -----
V$EVENTMETRIC                   VIEW
V$WAITCLASSMETRIC               VIEW
V$WAITCLASSMETRIC_HISTORY       VIEW
V$SERVICEMETRIC                 VIEW
V$SERVICEMETRIC_HISTORY         VIEW
V$XML_AUDIT_TRAIL               VIEW
V$ALERT_TYPES                   VIEW
V$THRESHOLD_TYPES               VIEW
V$RESTORE_POINT                 VIEW
V$DB_TRANSPORTABLE_PLATFORM     VIEW

V$SQL_JOIN_FILTER               VIEW
V$RMAN_BACKUP_SUBJOB_DETAILS    VIEW
V$RMAN_BACKUP_JOB_DETAILS       VIEW
V$BACKUP_SET_DETAILS            VIEW
V$BACKUP_PIECE_DETAILS          VIEW
V$BACKUP_COPY_DETAILS           VIEW
V$PROXY_COPY_DETAILS            VIEW
V$PROXY_ARCHIVELOG_DETAILS      VIEW
V$BACKUP_DATAFILE_DETAILS       VIEW
V$BACKUP_CONTROLFILE_DETAILS    VIEW

V$BACKUP_ARCHIVELOG_DETAILS     VIEW
V$BACKUP_SPFILE_DETAILS         VIEW
V$BACKUP_DATAFILE_SUMMARY       VIEW
V$BACKUP_CONTROLFILE_SUMMARY    VIEW
V$BACKUP_ARCHIVELOG_SUMMARY     VIEW
V$BACKUP_SPFILE_SUMMARY         VIEW
V$BACKUP_SET_SUMMARY            VIEW
V$BACKUP_COPY_SUMMARY           VIEW
V$PROXY_COPY_SUMMARY            VIEW
V$PROXY_ARCHIVELOG_SUMMARY      VIEW

V$UNUSABLE_BACKUPFILE_DETAILS   VIEW
V$SQLSTATS                      VIEW
V$WALLET                        VIEW
V$RFS_THREAD                    VIEW
V$DATAGUARD_STATS               VIEW
V$STANDBY_APPLY_SNAPSHOT        VIEW
V$RMAN_BACKUP_TYPE              VIEW
V$MUTEX_SLEEP_HISTORY           VIEW
V$MUTEX_SLEEP                   VIEW
V$RMAN_ENCRYPTION_ALGORITHMS    VIEW
```

```
V$OBJECT_PRIVILEGE                VIEW
V$SYSTEM_FIX_CONTROL              VIEW
V$SESSION_FIX_CONTROL            VIEW
V$FS_FAILOVER_HISTOGRAM          VIEW
V$FS_FAILOVER_STATS              VIEW
V$NFS_CLIENTS                    VIEW
V$NFS_OPEN_FILES                 VIEW
V$NFS_LOCKS                      VIEW
V$IOSTAT_NETWORK                 VIEW
V$SQL_FEATURE                    VIEW

NAME                             TYPE
-------------------------------- -----
V$SQL_FEATURE_HIERARCHY          VIEW
V$SQL_FEATURE_DEPENDENCY         VIEW
V$REDO_DEST_RESP_HISTOGRAM       VIEW
V$CORRUPT_XID_LIST               VIEW
V$FLASHBACK_TXN_MODS             VIEW
V$FLASHBACK_TXN_GRAPH            VIEW
V$SQL_HINT                       VIEW
V$RESULT_CACHE_STATISTICS        VIEW
V$RESULT_CACHE_MEMORY            VIEW
V$RESULT_CACHE_OBJECTS           VIEW

V$RESULT_CACHE_DEPENDENCY        VIEW
V$CLIENT_RESULT_CACHE_STATS      VIEW
V$IR_FAILURE                     VIEW
V$IR_REPAIR                      VIEW
V$IR_MANUAL_CHECKLIST            VIEW
V$IR_FAILURE_SET                 VIEW
V$HM_CHECK                       VIEW
V$HM_CHECK_PARAM                 VIEW
V$HM_RUN                         VIEW
V$HM_FINDING                     VIEW

V$HM_RECOMMENDATION              VIEW
V$HM_INFO                        VIEW
V$IOSTAT_CONSUMER_GROUP          VIEW
V$IOSTAT_FUNCTION                VIEW
V$IOSTAT_FILE                    VIEW
V$SQL_CS_HISTOGRAM               VIEW
V$SQL_CS_SELECTIVITY             VIEW
V$SQL_CS_STATISTICS              VIEW
V$CPOOL_CC_INFO                  VIEW
V$CPOOL_CC_STATS                 VIEW

V$PERSISTENT_QUEUES              VIEW
V$PERSISTENT_SUBSCRIBERS         VIEW
V$PERSISTENT_PUBLISHERS          VIEW
V$SSCR_SESSIONS                  VIEW
V$CALLTAG                        VIEW
V$SQL_MONITOR                    VIEW
V$SQL_PLAN_MONITOR               VIEW
V$DNFS_STATS                     VIEW
V$DNFS_SERVERS                   VIEW
V$DNFS_FILES                     VIEW

V$ENCRYPTION_WALLET              VIEW
```

```
V$CPOOL_STATS                    VIEW
V$INCMETER_CONFIG                VIEW
V$INCMETER_SUMMARY               VIEW
V$INCMETER_INFO                  VIEW
V$SQLFN_METADATA                 VIEW
V$SQLFN_ARG_METADATA             VIEW
V$RMA_COMPRESSION_ALGORITHM    VIEW
V$DIAG_INFO                      VIEW
V$IO_CALIBRATION_STATUS          VIEW

V$PROCESS_GROUP                  VIEW
V$DETACHED_SESSION               VIEW
V$SECUREFILE_TIMER               VIEW
V$DNFS_CHANNELS                  VIEW

484 rows selected.
```

Due to the large number of *v$* views for 11g, it would take a massive set of encyclopedias to describe each and every *v$* dynamic performance view in great detail! Therefore, the most important new *v$* dynamic performance views for Oracle 11g will be described here as well as how to understand database internal operations by using these *v$* views.

Investigating Oracle 11g Internals with V$ Views

As has been observed in the previous section of the *v$* views, there are hundreds of different *v$* views in each release of Oracle. Next take a look into how to best tap into the new features of Oracle 11g internals with some key techniques. One way to better understand Oracle 11g database internals is to query the new Oracle 11g memory buffers via the *v$* views for 11g memory enhancements. The following example shows how to examine the various memory buffers for 11g.

```
SQL> describe V$MEMORY_DYNAMIC_COMPONENTS

 Name                                      Null?    Type
 ----------------------------------------- -------- -----------
 COMPONENT                                          VARCHAR2(64)
 CURRENT_SIZE                                       NUMBER
 MIN_SIZE                                           NUMBER
 MAX_SIZE                                           NUMBER
 USER_SPECIFIED_SIZE                                NUMBER
 OPER_COUNT                                         NUMBER
 LAST_OPER_TYPE                                     VARCHAR2(13)
 LAST_OPER_MODE                                     VARCHAR2(9)
 LAST_OPER_TIME                                     DATE
 GRANULE_SIZE                                       NUMBER
```

If *v$memory_dynamic_components* is queried, one can obtain details on 11g memory operations with the following script.

```
SQL> select component, current_size, max_size, granule_size, last_oper_type
  2  from v$memory_dynamic_components;
```

COMPONENT	CURRENT_SIZE	MAX_SIZE	GRANULE_SIZE	LAST_OPER_TYPE
shared pool	184549376	184549376	4194304	GROW
large pool	4194304	4194304	4194304	STATIC
java pool	12582912	12582912	4194304	GROW
streams pool	0	4194304		STATIC
SGA Target	536870912	536870912	4194304	STATIC
DEFAULT buffer cache	327155712	360710144	4194304	SHRINK
KEEP buffer cache	0	0	4194304	STATIC
RECYCLE buffer cache	0	0	4194304	STATIC
DEFAULT 2K buffer cache	0	0	4194304	STATIC
DEFAULT 4K buffer cache	0	0	4194304	STATIC
DEFAULT 8K buffer cache	0	0	4194304	STATIC
DEFAULT 16K buffer cache	0	0	4194304	STATIC
DEFAULT 32K buffer cache	0	0	4194304	STATIC
Shared IO Pool	0	0	4194304	STATIC
PGA Target	318767104	318767104	4194304	STATIC
ASM Buffer Cache	0	0	4194304	STATIC

```
16 rows selected.
```

By issuing a describe from SQL*Plus for each Oracle 11g *v$* dynamic performance view, the contents can be displayed, thereby providing insight into how to best tap the power of these useful views.

This chapter will conclude with a visit to the *v$* views and some further example scripts to best harness the power of these dynamic performance views available with Oracle 11g to tap into the data dictionary.

Scripts and Tips for *v$* and Data Dictionary - Oracle 11g

Now take a look into how to explore some of the key new features for Oracle 11g by using the new *v$* dynamic performance views. While a comprehensive look at all new features for the *v$* views would require an entire book, an example for 11g ADR to illustrate the power of scripts and *v$* views within Oracle 11g will be used as a sample.

For this study, examine the new 11g feature for the Automatic Diagnostic Repository (ADR) to investigate how incident packaging functions. The Oracle 11g ADR uses a set of *v$* views stored within the Oracle data dictionary to perform its operations based on the following key *v$* views listed below:

```
SQL> select name from v$fixed_table where name like 'V$IR%';

NAME
-------------------------------
V$IR_FAILURE
V$IR_REPAIR
V$IR_MANUAL_CHECKLIST
V$IR_FAILURE_SET
```

For instance, check out the current *v$* view for incident repair operations by first understanding the *v$ir_repair* view.

```
SQL> desc V$IR_REPAIR

Name                                     Null?    Type
---------------------------------------- -------- ---------------
REPAIR_ID                                         NUMBER
ADVISE_ID                                         NUMBER
SUMMARY                                           VARCHAR2(32)
RANK                                              NUMBER
TIME_DETECTED                                     DATE
EXECUTED                                          DATE
ESTIMATED_DATA_LOSS                               VARCHAR2(20)
DETAILED_DESCRIPTION                              VARCHAR2(1024)
REPAIR_SCRIPT                                     VARCHAR2(512)
ESTIMATED_REPAIR_TIME                             NUMBER
ACTUAL_REPAIR_TIME                                NUMBER
STATUS                                            VARCHAR2(7)
```

From the *v$ir_repair* dyamic performance view, query results after new and current incidents are created via the ADR facility from Oracle 11g.

Summary

In this chapter, insight was provided into the following topics regarding *v$* dynamic performance views for the Oracle 11g database:

- Purpose of *v$* dynamic performance views for 11g

- Tips for using *v$* views

- New features for 11g dynamic *v$* performance views

The next chapter will offer coverage on the mystery surrounding the *v$* tables that underlie all *v$* views for Oracle 11g.

Inside the *x$* Tables of Oracle 11g

In the last chapter, the power inherent in the dynamic performance *v$* views available with Oracle 11g for the serious Oracle database professional was explored. This chapter will provide further coverage of the inner sanctum of Oracle 11g which is contained in the *x$* tables and which form the basis for the dynamic performance *v$* views. This chapter will examine:

- Exploring Oracle 11g new features and internals with the *x$* tables

- Using the *x$* tables for Oracle 11g database analysis

- Scripts using *x$* tables with Oracle 11g

Classification of x$ Tables

As one can expect, the structure of the *x$* tables is quite cryptic and poorly documented, if at all, within the Oracle literature. What is key is to establish a naming convention for the categories of *x$* tables so that the Oracle expert can better understand their meaning and usage. Due to the nature of Oracle database internals, the *x$* tables are not documented and their secrets remain internal to Oracle development.

However, there is a useful method to categorize the *x$* tables into various functions based on how they operate. Fortunately, in most cases it is quite safe to query the *x$* tables without causing any harm. They provide insight into the Oracle database internals for the advanced DBA.

This chapter will provide a useful classification system that can allow the DBA to better understand the nature of *x$* tables. At first glance they appear cryptic but are quite easy to decipher once a system has been provided. Yet one needs to review the layers that make up the Oracle 11g database kernel first. Following are the Oracle 11g kernel database layers:

Oracle 11g Kernel Database Layers

KS: Kernel Services
KX: Kernel Execution
K2: Kernel Distributed Transactions
KK: Kernel Compilation
KZ: Kernel Security
KQ: Kernel Query
KA: Kernel Access
KD: Kernel Data
KT: Kernel Transactions
KC: Kernel Cache
KJ: Kernel Locking
KG: Kernel Generic

A short explanation of these kernel layers follows so that one can better understand the relationship between $x\$$ tables and the database kernel for Oracle 11g. The Kernel Services (KS) layer gives one the required database services for all other layers in the database kernel stack. For instance, it regulates the initialization parameters in the database for the session and instance levels as well as manages database concurrency operations for locking, latching operations and wait event management for database and instance level statistics. Next to be covered is the Kernel Execution layer.

The Kernel Execution (KX) layer performs code executions from the Kernel Compilation layer (KK) and handles bind operations for PL/SQL code as well as recursive calls within the shared pool area for the Oracle 11g SGA.

The Kernel Distributed Transaction (K2) layer manages operations involved within distributed transactions including two-phase commit tasks within the Oracle 11g database.

The Kernel Compilation (KK) layer is responsible for managing the compilation of PL/SQL objects along with tasks performed by the Oracle optimizer.

Next is the Kernel Security layer (KZ) which manages role and system privileges within the Oracle 11g database for security operations.

The Kernel Query (KQ) layer handles row caching operations from the data dictionary. It provides critical tasks so that the Kernel Security (KZ) and Kernel Compilation (KK) layers are able to receive data from the query results performed at this Kernel Query layer.

Kernel Access (KA) provides operations that permit access to database segments as well as routing information to other kernel layers within the Oracle 11g database kernel stack.

Kernel Data (KD) manages the storage layer for segments and data retrieval as well as formatting operations of database segments for storage of table data and index data.

Kernel Transactions (KT) manages freelist operations along with rollback segments including interested transaction list (ITL) allocation for operations that occur within data blocks, undo tasks, and transaction consistency based on the ACID model for relational databases.

Kernel Cache (KC) handles operations around the database buffer cache for Oracle 11g. It works hand-in-hand with system functions to manage shared memory resources including the buffer cache and redo log memory operations.

Kernel Locking (KJ) provides for lock management for RAC environments. It does not manage single instance non-RAC lock operations.

The Kernel Generic layer performs basic database kernel operations.

Following is a brief summary of the different kernel services available for review via the *x$* tables. First to be examined are the *x$* tables around the Kernel Services (KS) layer for Oracle 11g.

Exploring Oracle 11g Database Internals with x$ Tables

In order to query the *x$* tables, one must have SYS level privileges within the Oracle 11g database environment. Due to the hundreds of *x$* tables in each major release of Oracle, it would take a huge amount of material to cover each and every one in great detail. Therefore, this chapter will provide a listing of the key *x$* tables centered around the kernel layers with some example scripts to explain how to access the Oracle 11g database kernel internal information. The following family listing of *x$* tables allows one to view the status for kernel services (KS) within Oracle 11g.

X$KS – Kernel Services

x$ksmfs	Memory fixed SGA
x$ksmfsv	Memory fixed SGA vectors
x$ksmjs	Java Pool memory
x$ksmlru	Memory LRU (least recently used)
x$ksmls	Large pool memory
x$ksmmem	Memory
x$ksmpp	Memory Process Pool
x$ksmsd	Memory SGA definitions
x$ksmsp	Shared pool memory
x$ksmspr	Shared pool reserved memory
x$ksmss	Shared pool summary
x$ksmup	User pool memory
x$ksqst	Enqueue status
x$ksulop	User long operation

x$ksulv   User locale value

x$ksupr   User process

It is demonstrated here how to understand shared pool memory by performing a describe on the *x$ksmsp* table:

```
SQL> describe x$ksmsp

Name                                    Null?    Type
---------------------------------------- -------- ----------------
ADDR                                             RAW(4)
INDX                                             NUMBER
INST_ID                                          NUMBER
KSMCHIDX                                         NUMBER
KSMCHDUR                                         NUMBER
KSMCHCOM                                         VARCHAR2(16)
KSMCHPTR                                         RAW(4)
KSMCHSIZ                                         NUMBER
KSMCHCLS                                         VARCHAR2(8)
KSMCHTYP                                         NUMBER
KSMCHPAR                                         RAW(4)
```

The following example query against the *x$ksmsp* table allows one to understand how shared pool memory is currently being used by the Oracle 11g database.

```
SQL> select ksmchcom AComment,
  2    ksmchcls Status,
  3    sum(ksmchsiz) Bytes
  4    from x$ksmsp
  5    group by ksmchcom, ksmchcls;

ACOMMENT          STATUS      BYTES
----------------  --------  ----------
sql area          recr       3354624
PL/SQL DIANA      freeabl    8753152
trigger defini    recr         94404
joxlod exec hp    recr        269792
partitioning d    recr         18052
sql area:KOKA     recr         40960
policy hash tab   freeabl        164
Label Cache Hea   freeabl        104
qtree_kwqspqctx   freeabl         40
dbgefgHtAddSK-1   freeabl     450996
Session Page      freeabl       6776
```

Now review an example of how to understand *x$* tables by querying against one of the key *x$kc* tables for the Kernel Cache (KC) layer with Oracle 11g.

X$KC – Kernel Cache

x$kcbfwai	Block file wait
x$kcbwait	Block wait
x$kcccp	Checkpoint progress controlfile
x$kcfio	File I/O
x$kclfh	Lock file header
x$kclfi	Lock file index
x$kcluh	Lock undo header
x$kclui	Lock undo index

For this case study of the Kernel Cache (KC) family of *x$* tables, give a code example with the *x$kcbfwait* table to examine buffer busy wait issues.

One can use the following example to find the data files that have poor performance in terms of wait time:.

```
SQL> select count, file#, name
  2  from x$kcbfwait, v$datafile
  3  where indx+1=file#
  4  order by count;

   COUNT    FILE#   NAME
----------------------------------------------------
       0        3   C:\WIN11G1\ORADATA\WIN11G\UNDOTBS01.DBF

       0        2   C:\WIN11G1\ORADATA\WIN11G\SYSAUX01.DBF

       0        5   C:\WIN11G1\ORADATA\WIN11G\EXAMPLE01.DBF


   COUNT    FILE#   NAME
----------------------------------------------------
       0        4   C:\WIN11G1\ORADATA\WIN11G\USERS01.DBF

      33        1   C:\WIN11G1\ORADATA\WIN11G\SYSTEM01.DBF

SQL>
```

Next to be used is an example to understand the kernel query layer of the 11g database kernel from the *x$kq* family.

X$KQ – Kernel Query

x$kqfco	Fixed table columns
x$kqfdt	Fixed table
x$kqfp	Fixed procedure
x$kqfsz	Fixed size
x$kqfta	Fixed table
x$kqfvi	Fixed view
x$kqfvt	Fixed view table

Now one can examine the 11g database internal structures for fixed tables and views by usage of the *x$kq* kernel query tables. For instance, issue a query against the *x$kqfvi* table which will provide the complete listing for all *v$* and *gv$* views based on the *x$* tables for Oracle 11g.

```
SQL> select kqfvinam from x$kqfvi;

KQFVINAM
------------------------------
GV$WAITSTAT
V$WAITSTAT
GV$BH
V$BH
GV$GC_ELEMENT
V$GC_ELEMENT
GV$CR_BLOCK_SERVER
V$CR_BLOCK_SERVER
GV$CURRENT_BLOCK_SERVER
V$CURRENT_BLOCK_SERVER
GV$ENCRYPTED_TABLESPACES
V$ENCRYPTED_TABLESPACES
GV$GC_ELEMENTS_WITH_COLLISIONS
V$GC_ELEMENTS_WITH_COLLISIONS
GV$FILE_CACHE_TRANSFER
V$FILE_CACHE_TRANSFER
GV$TEMP_CACHE_TRANSFER
V$TEMP_CACHE_TRANSFER
GV$CLASS_CACHE_TRANSFER
V$CLASS_CACHE_TRANSFER
GV$INSTANCE_CACHE_TRANSFER
V$INSTANCE_CACHE_TRANSFER
GV$LOCK_ELEMENT
V$LOCK_ELEMENT
GV$BSP
V$BSP
GV$LOCKS_WITH_COLLISIONS
V$LOCKS_WITH_COLLISIONS
GV$FILE_PING
V$FILE_PING
GV$TEMP_PING
```

```
V$TEMP_PING
GV$CLASS_PING
```

The listing from *x$kqfvi* is now available, so proceed to examine other Oracle 11g database structures within the database kernel by accessing the *x$kq* layer of the generic kernel database structures. The following table lists the most frequently used *x$kq* kernel generic *x$* tables.

X$KG – Kernel Generic

x$kghlu	Heap LRU (Least Recently Used)
x$kgllk	Library cache lock
x$kglob	Library cache object
x$kglpn	Library cache pin
x$kglst	Library cache status

If a DBA is experiencing performance degradation issues due to library cache issues, then query the *x$kgllk* table to investigate further.

```
C:\>sqlplus "/as sysdba"
SQL*Plus: Release 11.1.0.6.0 - Production on Thu May 14 16:43:01 2009

Copyright (c) 1982, 2007, Oracle.  All rights reserved.

Connected to:
Oracle Database 11g Enterprise Edition Release 11.1.0.6.0 - Production
With the Partitioning, OLAP, Data Mining and Real Application Testing
options

SQL> select
  2    kglnaobj, kgllkreq
  3  from
  4    x$kgllk x join v$session s on
  5      s.saddr = x.kgllkses;

KGLNAOBJ                                                       KGLLKREQ
------------------------------------------------------------- ----------
table_4_9_1322_0_0_0                                                  0
table_4_9_1322_0_0_0                                                  0
STANDARD                                                              0
DBMS_PRVT_TRACE                                                       0
table_1_ff_20b_0_0_0                                                  0
table_1_ff_20b_0_0_0                                                  0
select 1 from sys.aq$_subscriber_table where rownum < 2 and           0
select 1 from sys.aq$_subscriber_table where rownum < 2 and           0
select decode(bitand(a.flags, 16384), 0, a.next_run_date,             0
select decode(bitand(a.flags, 16384), 0, a.next_run_date,             0
select con#,obj#,rcon#,enabled,nvl(defer,0) from cdef$ where          0

select con#,obj#,rcon#,enabled,nvl(defer,0) from cdef$ where          0
insert into smon_scn_time (thread, time_mp, time_dp, scn, sc          0
select obj#,type#,ctime,mtime,stime,status,dataobj#,flags,oi          0
select obj#,type#,ctime,mtime,stime,status,dataobj#,flags,oi          0
select obj#,type#,ctime,mtime,stime,status,dataobj#,flags,oi          0
select obj#,type#,ctime,mtime,stime,status,dataobj#,flags,oi          0
```

```
table_1_ff_207_0_0_0                                                   0
table_1_ff_207_0_0_0                                                   0
select con#,type#,condlength,intcols,robj#,rcon#,match#,refa           0
select con#,type#,condlength,intcols,robj#,rcon#,match#,refa           0
AQ$_ALERT_QT_E                                                         0

select name,intcol#,segcol#,type#,length,nvl(precision#,0),d           0
select name,intcol#,segcol#,type#,length,nvl(precision#,0),d           0
select name,intcol#,segcol#,type#,length,nvl(precision#,0),d           0
select name,intcol#,segcol#,type#,length,nvl(precision#,0),d           0
DELETE FROM RECENT_RESOURCE_INCARNATIONS$ WHERE RESOURCE_TYP           0
DELETE FROM RECENT_RESOURCE_INCARNATIONS$ WHERE RESOURCE_TYP           0
select decode(bitand(a.flags, 16384), 0, a.next_run_date,             0
select decode(bitand(a.flags, 16384), 0, a.next_run_date,             0
DBMS_HA_ALERTS_PRVT                                                    0
BEGIN   dbms_ha_alerts_prvt.clear_instance_resources(   :dbdo          0
BEGIN   dbms_ha_alerts_prvt.clear_instance_resources(   :dbdo          0

select   kglnaobj, kgllkreq from   x$kgllk x join v$session            0
select   kglnaobj, kgllkreq from   x$kgllk x join v$session            0
select   tab.rowid, tab.msgid, tab.corrid, tab.priority, tab.          0
select   tab.rowid, tab.msgid, tab.corrid, tab.priority, tab.          0
select subscriber_id, name, address, protocol, subscriber_ty          0
select subscriber_id, name, address, protocol, subscriber_ty          0
STANDARD                                                               0
table_1_ff_213_0_0_0                                                   0
table_1_ff_213_0_0_0                                                   0
ALERT_QUE_R                                                            0
table_1_ff_20f_0_0_0                                                   0

table_1_ff_20f_0_0_0                                                   0
select a.next_start_date, a.objid, a.w_open from  (select b.          0
select a.next_start_date, a.objid, a.w_open from  (select b.          0
KGLNAOBJ                                                        KGLLKREQ
------------------------------------------------------------- ----------
PLITBLM                                                                0
ALERT_QUE                                                              0
select /*+ FIRST_ROWS(1) */ x.C1, x.C2, x.C3 from  (select a          0
select /*+ FIRST_ROWS(1) */ x.C1, x.C2, x.C3 from  (select a          0
select OBJOID,   CLSOID, RUNTIME, PRI, JOBTYPE,   SCHLIM,   WT,        0
select OBJOID,   CLSOID, RUNTIME, PRI, JOBTYPE,   SCHLIM,   WT,        0
insert into "SYS"."ALERT_QT"  (q_name, msgid, corrid, priori          0
insert into "SYS"."ALERT_QT"  (q_name, msgid, corrid, priori          0

DBMS_HA_ALERTS_PRVT                                                    0
SELECT INSTANCE_NAME, HOST_NAME, NVL(GVI_STARTUP_TIME, SYSTI          0
SELECT INSTANCE_NAME, HOST_NAME, NVL(GVI_STARTUP_TIME, SYSTI          0
table_1_ff_203_0_0_0                                                   0
table_1_ff_203_0_0_0                                                   0
table_1_ff_203_0_0_0                                                   0
table_1_ff_203_0_0_0                                                   0
select intcol#,nvl(pos#,0),col#,nvl(spare1,0) from ccol$ whe          0
select intcol#,nvl(pos#,0),col#,nvl(spare1,0) from ccol$ whe          0
select CONNECTION_POOL_NAME, STATUS, MINSIZE, MAXSIZE,                0
select CONNECTION_POOL_NAME, STATUS, MINSIZE, MAXSIZE,                0

select i.obj#,i.ts#,i.file#,i.block#,i.intcols,i.type#,i.fla          0
select i.obj#,i.ts#,i.file#,i.block#,i.intcols,i.type#,i.fla          0
select i.obj#,i.ts#,i.file#,i.block#,i.intcols,i.type#,i.fla          0
select i.obj#,i.ts#,i.file#,i.block#,i.intcols,i.type#,i.fla          0
select max(RETENTION) from SYS_FBA_FA                                 0
select max(RETENTION) from SYS_FBA_FA                                 0
DATABASE                                                              0
select t.ts#,t.file#,t.block#,nvl(t.bobj#,0),nvl(t.tab#,0),t          0
select t.ts#,t.file#,t.block#,nvl(t.bobj#,0),nvl(t.tab#,0),t          0
select t.ts#,t.file#,t.block#,nvl(t.bobj#,0),nvl(t.tab#,0),t          0
select t.ts#,t.file#,t.block#,nvl(t.bobj#,0),nvl(t.tab#,0),t          0

update sys.mon_mods$ set inserts = inserts + :ins, updates =          0
ALTER SESSION SET NLS_LANGUAGE= 'AMERICAN' NLS_TERRITORY= 'A          0
select value, flags, modified_inst, additional_info,                 0
select value, flags, modified_inst, additional_info,                 0
SELECT OBJOID, CLSOID,    DECODE(BITAND(FLAGS, 16384), 0, RU          0
SELECT OBJOID, CLSOID,    DECODE(BITAND(FLAGS, 16384), 0, RU          0
select f.file#, f.block#, f.ts#, f.length from fet$ f, ts$ t          0
DBMS_PRVT_TRACE                                                       0
COMMIT                                                                0
select 1 from obj$ where name='DBA_QUEUE_SCHEDULES'                   0
```

Classification of x$ Tables   **175**

```
select 1 from obj$ where name='DBA_QUEUE_SCHEDULES'                    0

88 rows selected.

SQL>
```

The advantage of using the above *x$* table query against the *x$kgllk* table is that more information is provided by using this *x$* table than the *v$lock* query. Recalling from earlier on, it was mentioned that all of the *v$* dynamic performance views are based upon *x$* tables. In the above query code listing, the *x$kgllk* table lists all held and requested library object locks for all sessions within Oracle 11g.

Now decipher some of the columns in the *x$kgllk* table from the query that was just ran against the Oracle 11g database. In the *x$kgllk* table, the column kglnaobj displays the name of the object in terms of the first 80 characters of the object name. If one examines the kgllkreq column, it can be determined that a value of zero indicates that a lock is being held, whereas a value greater than zero for the kgllkreq column indicates that a lock has been requested within the Oracle database. As can be seen, using *x$* tables will expand the realm of performance and database analysis for complex Oracle issues. Now examine the *x$* tables for the kernel security (KZ) layer within Oracle 11g.

X$KZ – Kernel Security (KZ) Layer

x$kzspr	Enabled privileges
x$kzsro	Enabled roles
x$kzsrt	Remote password file table entries

As these *x$* tables are undocumented, next to be reviewed is an example of the security kernel layer for Oracle 11g roles and privileges by querying against the *x$kzspr* and *x$kzsrt* tables. First, obtain the column definitions for the three security *x$* tables.

```
SQL> desc x$kzspr

Name                                      Null?    Type
----------------------------------------- -------- ----------------
ADDR                                               RAW(4)
INDX                                               NUMBER
INST_ID                                            NUMBER
KZSPRPRV                                           NUMBER
```

```
SQL> desc x$kzsro

Name                                      Null?    Type
----------------------------------------- -------- ----------------
  ADDR                                              RAW(4)
  INDX                                              NUMBER
  INST_ID                                           NUMBER
  KZSROROL                                          NUMBER

SQL> desc x$kzsrt

Name                                      Null?    Type
----------------------------------------- -------- ----------------
  ADDR                                              RAW(4)
  INDX                                              NUMBER
  INST_ID                                           NUMBER
  USERNAME                                          VARCHAR2(30)
  SYSDBA                                            NUMBER
  SYSOPER                                           NUMBER
  SYSASM                                            NUMBER
  VALID                                             NUMBER
```

Now that the table definitions for the above three *x$* tables for the kernel security (KZ) layer are defined, drill down with the following code example to obtain details for Oracle 11g security roles and privileges.

```
SQL> select username, sysdba, sysoper, sysasm, valid
  2  from x$kzsrt;

USERNAME                      SYSDBA     SYSOPER    SYSASM     VALID
----------------------------- ---------- ---------- ---------- ----
INTERNAL                          1          1          0        1
SYS                               1          1          0        1
```

The above query against the *x$kzsrt* table yields details for the Oracle 11g remote password entries for 11g roles including that for SYSDBA, SYSOPER and SYSASM along with a status value for whether the elevated privilege has been enabled or not within the Oracle 11g database. A value of 1 indicates that an account has been enabled for these privileges while a value of 0 would indicate that no user has these privileges enabled in the Oracle database.

A cursory walkthrough of the *x$* tables for Oracle 11g has now been provided, so the survey will conclude with how *x$* tables can be used by the experienced Oracle professional to investigate and understand Oracle 11g new features.

Oracle 11g New Features – Useful x$ Tables

As already stated, the *x$* views are not documented and Oracle does not provide support on the meaning and usage of these *x$* tables. With that said, some useful queries can be derived to better understand internal operations within Oracle 11g. Dozens of Metalink support notes reference many of these key *x$* tables for tapping into the power of the Oracle database engine.

For the case study, examine the 11g new feature for incident packaging and reporting which is part of the Oracle 11g Automatic Diagnostic Repository (ADR). Since the *v$* dynamic performance views are built upon the *x$* structures, one can see the core ADR functions for 11g based on the following set of *x$* tables for 11g:

```
SQL> select * from v$fixed_table
  2  where name like 'X$IR%';

NAME                          OBJECT_ID TYPE   TABLE_NUM
----------------------------- --------- -----  ----------
X$IR_WORKING_FAILURE_SET     4294952913 TABLE        750
X$IR_WORKING_REPAIR_SET      4294952914 TABLE        751
X$IR_REPAIR_OPTION           4294952915 TABLE        752
X$IR_MANUAL_OPTION           4294952917 TABLE        753
X$IR_REPAIR_STEP             4294952916 TABLE        754
X$IR_WF_PARAM                4294952918 TABLE        755
X$IR_WR_PARAM                4294952919 TABLE        756
X$IR_RS_PARAM                4294952920 TABLE        757

8 rows selected.
```

By issuing queries against the *x$ir_repair_option*, it is better understood how the 11g ADR incident packaging and repair feature behaves. There is also the *x$diag_info* table that uncovers more 11g new features for the 11g Health Monitor (HM) diagnostic tools new to this release of the Oracle database.

For instance, if the following query is issued against *x$diag_info* for the Oracle 11g database, obtain the following useful details for diagnostics with 11g.

```
SQL> desc x$diag_info
```

```
Name                                        Null?    Type
----------------------------------------    -------- ----------------
ADDR                                                 RAW(4)
INDX                                                 NUMBER
INST_ID                                              NUMBER
NAME                                                 VARCHAR2(64)
VALUE                                                VARCHAR2(512)

SQL> col name format a25
SQL> col value format a50
SQL> select name, value from x$diag_info;

NAME                    VALUE
--------------------    ----------------------------------------
Diag Enabled            TRUE
ADR Base                c:\win11g1
ADR Home                c:\win11g1\diag\rdbms\win11g\win11g
Diag Trace              c:\win11g1\diag\rdbms\win11g\win11g\trace
Diag Alert              c:\win11g1\diag\rdbms\win11g\win11g\alert
Diag Incident           c:\win11g1\diag\rdbms\win11g\win11g\incident
Diag Cdump              c:\win11g1\diag\rdbms\win11g\win11g\cdump
Health Monitor          c:\win11g1\diag\rdbms\win11g\win11g\hm
Default Trace File      c:\win11g1\diag\rdbms\win11g\win11g\trace\win11g_ora_3020.trc

Active Problem Count    0
Active Incident Count   0

11 rows selected.
```

The above query against *x$diag_info* displays more information than if a
query had been issued against the dynamic performance view for
v$diag_info. For comparison, obtain address and system values with
x$diag_info that are not available with *v$diag_info* as shown in the
difference listed below.

```
SQL> desc v$diag_info

Name                                        Null?    Type
----------------------------------------    -------- ----------
INST_ID                                              NUMBER
NAME                                                 VARCHAR2(6
VALUE                                                VARCHAR2(5

SQL> desc x$diag_info

Name                                        Null?    Type
----------------------------------------    -------- ----------
ADDR                                                 RAW(4)
INDX                                                 NUMBER
INST_ID                                              NUMBER
NAME                                                 VARCHAR2(6
VALUE                                                VARCHAR2(5
```

For the serious Oracle database professional, understanding *x$* tables
provides an even more fine grain level of detailed information than is
available with the *v$* dynamic performance views. In most cases, the *v$*
dynamic performance views are sufficient for analysis, yet in rare times

---

of difficult situations, the *x$* tables offer even deeper root cause analysis tools to separate the wheat from the chaff and to distinguish from the average DBA versus the true Oracle expert!

Using the X$ Tables for Oracle 11g Analysis

Earlier an introduction was given to the structure of *x$* tables within Oracle 11g. To use these *x$* tables for database analysis for Oracle 11g, one simply needs to login to the Oracle 11g database via the SQL*Plus utility as a privileged user database account that has been granted SYSDBA level privileges.

Scripts Using X$ Tables with Oracle 11g

No coverage of database internals with *x$* tables would be complete without a few useful scripts that harness the power of the *x$* tables within Oracle 11g. However, since the *x$* tables are completely undocumented for each major release of Oracle, one needs a script to obtain these hidden tables for Oracle 11g. By querying against the *v$fixed_table*, obtain a comprehensive listing.

```
SQL> select * from v$fixed_table where name like 'X$%';

NAME                         OBJECT_ID TYPE   TABLE_NUM
---------------------------- ---------- ------ ----------
X$KQFTA                      4294950912 TABLE          0
X$KQFVI                      4294950913 TABLE          1
NAME                         OBJECT_ID TYPE   TABLE_NUM
---------------------------- ---------- ------ ----------
X$KQFVT                      4294951149 TABLE          2
X$KQFDT                      4294950914 TABLE          3
X$KQFCO                      4294951036 TABLE          4
X$KQFOPT                     4294952712 TABLE          5
X$KYWMPCTAB                  4294952922 TABLE          6
X$KYWMWRCTAB                 4294953009 TABLE          7
X$KYWMCLTAB                  4294952923 TABLE          8
X$KYWMNF                     4294952924 TABLE          9
X$KSDAF                      4294952775 TABLE         10
X$KSDAFT                     4294952776 TABLE         11

X$KSLLTR                     4294950993 TABLE         12
X$KSLHOT                     4294952169 TABLE         13
X$KSLLCLASS                  4294951813 TABLE         14
X$KSLECLASS                  4294951830 TABLE         15
X$KSLEMAP                    4294951831 TABLE         16
X$KSLLD                      4294950994 TABLE         17
```

```
X$KSLED                          4294951094 TABLE            18
X$KSLCS                          4294952078 TABLE            19
X$KSLSCS                         4294952079 TABLE            20
X$KSLES                          4294951095 TABLE            21

X$KSLSESHIST                     4294951973 TABLE            22
X$KSLEI                          4294951102 TABLE            23
X$KSLLW                          4294951183 TABLE            24
X$KSLPO                          4294951184 TABLE            25
X$KSLWSC                         4294951185 TABLE            26
X$KSLWH                          4294952866 TABLE            27
X$KSLWT                          4294952867 TABLE            28
X$KSQEQTYP                       4294951983 TABLE            29
X$KSQRS                          4294950999 TABLE            30
X$KSQDN                          4294951001 TABLE            31

X$KSQST                          4294951085 TABLE            32
X$KSUINSTSTAT                    4294953015 TABLE            33
X$KSUSE                          4294951004 TABLE            34
X$KSUSEX                         4294951428 TABLE            35
X$KSUPR                          4294951005 TABLE            36
X$KSUPRLAT                       4294951006 TABLE            37
X$KSURLMT                        4294951396 TABLE            38
X$KSUSD                          4294951007 TABLE            39
X$KSUSGSTA                       4294951008 TABLE            40
X$KSUTM                          4294951067 TABLE            41

X$KSUSGIF                        4294951930 TABLE            42
X$KSUSESTA                       4294951009 TABLE            43
X$KSUMYSTA                       4294951106 TABLE            44
X$KSUSIO                         4294951079 TABLE            45
X$KSUSECST                       4294951096 TABLE            46
X$KSULOP                         4294951244 TABLE            47
X$KSUPGP                         4294951577 TABLE            48
X$KSUPGS                         4294951578 TABLE            49
X$KSURU                          4294951010 TABLE            50
X$KSUPL                          4294951011 TABLE            51

X$KSUCF                          4294951012 TABLE            52
X$KSULL                          4294951082 TABLE            53
X$KSUCPUSTAT                     4294952112 TABLE            54
X$KSUVMSTAT                      4294952113 TABLE            55
X$KSUNETSTAT                     4294953033 TABLE            56
X$KSUSM                          4294952182 TABLE            57
X$KSIRESTYP                      4294951982 TABLE            58
X$KSIMSI                         4294951178 TABLE            59
X$KSIMAV                         4294951179 TABLE            60
X$KSIMAT                         4294951180 TABLE            61

X$KSMSD                          4294950995 TABLE            62
X$KSMSS                          4294950997 TABLE            63
X$KSMNS                          4294951493 TABLE            64
X$KSMNIM                         4294951494 TABLE            65
NAME                             OBJECT_ID TYPE   TABLE_NUM
-------------------------------- ---------- ----- ----------
X$KSMLS                          4294951383 TABLE            66
X$KSMFS                          4294951384 TABLE            67
X$KSMJS                          4294951595 TABLE            68
X$KSMSTRS                        4294952000 TABLE            69
```

```
X$KSMMEM                4294951147 TABLE              70
X$KSMFSV                4294951146 TABLE              71

X$KSMLRU                4294951099 TABLE              72
X$KGHLU                 4294951105 TABLE              73
X$KSMSP                 4294951100 TABLE              74
X$KSMSPR                4294951170 TABLE              75
X$KSMPP                 4294951191 TABLE              76
X$KSMUP                 4294951192 TABLE              77
X$KSMHP                 4294951193 TABLE              78
X$KSMJCH                4294951609 TABLE              79
X$KSMSST                4294952688 TABLE              80
X$KSMSP_DSNEW           4294951768 TABLE              81

X$KSMSP_NWEX            4294951769 TABLE              82
X$KGLSIM                4294951882 TABLE              83
X$KGLJSIM               4294951994 TABLE              84
X$KGLMEM                4294951885 TABLE              85
X$KGLJMEM               4294951997 TABLE              86
X$KSMSGMEM              4294952475 TABLE              87
X$KSMPGST               4294952646 TABLE              88
X$KSMPGDST              4294952673 TABLE              89
X$KSMPGDP               4294952674 TABLE              90
X$KSPPI                 4294950998 TABLE              91

X$KSPPCV                4294951198 TABLE              92
X$KSPPSV                4294951199 TABLE              93
X$KSPPCV2               4294951587 TABLE              94
X$KSPPSV2               4294951588 TABLE              95
X$KSPSPFILE             4294951746 TABLE              96
X$KSPSPFH               4294951933 TABLE              97
X$KSPVLD_VALUES         4294952694 TABLE              98
X$KSPPO                 4294951486 TABLE              99
X$KSBDP                 4294950990 TABLE             100
X$KSBDD                 4294950991 TABLE             101

X$MESSAGES              4294950992 TABLE             102
X$KSBFT                 4294952690 TABLE             103
X$KSBTABACT             4294952582 TABLE             104
X$KSQEQ                 4294951000 TABLE             105
X$TRACE                 4294951002 TABLE             106
X$TRACE_EVENTS          4294951003 TABLE             107
X$KSTEX                 4294951145 TABLE             108
X$NLS_PARAMETERS        4294951043 TABLE             109
X$KSULV                 4294951130 TABLE             110
X$TIMEZONE_NAMES        4294951704 TABLE             111

X$TIMEZONE_FILE         4294952589 TABLE             112
X$KSUXSINST             4294951046 TABLE             113
X$KSUSECON              4294951158 TABLE             114
X$KSRPCIOS              4294952737 TABLE             115

NAME                    OBJECT_ID TYPE   TABLE_NUM
------------------------------- ---------- ----- ----------
X$KSFDSTCG              4294952842 TABLE             116
X$KSFDSTCMP             4294952843 TABLE             117
X$KSFDSTFILE            4294952844 TABLE             118
X$KSFDSTHIST            4294952845 TABLE             119
X$KSFDSTTHIST           4294952846 TABLE             120
```

```
X$DNFS_STATS                      4294952964 TABLE          121

X$DNFS_HIST                       4294952952 TABLE          122
X$DNFS_SERVERS                    4294952955 TABLE          123
X$DNFS_META                       4294952961 TABLE          124
X$DNFS_FILES                      4294952958 TABLE          125
X$DNFS_CHANNELS                   4294953014 TABLE          126
X$KSFQP                           4294951563 TABLE          127
X$KSFQDVNT                        4294951380 TABLE          128
X$KSFVQST                         4294951441 TABLE          129
X$KSFVSTA                         4294951427 TABLE          130
X$KSFVSL                          4294951426 TABLE          131

X$KGSKTE                          4294951465 TABLE          132
X$KGSKTO                          4294951466 TABLE          133
X$KGSKCP                          4294951467 TABLE          134
X$KGSKPP                          4294951468 TABLE          135
X$KGSKASP                         4294951571 TABLE          136
X$KGSKDOPP                        4294951572 TABLE          137
X$KGSKQUEP                        4294951701 TABLE          138
X$KGSKVFT                         4294952667 TABLE          139
X$KGSKCFT                         4294951469 TABLE          140
X$KGSKNCFT                        4294952945 TABLE          141

X$KGSKPFT                         4294951470 TABLE          142
X$KSKPLW                          4294952188 TABLE          143
X$KGSKSCS                         4294952189 TABLE          144
X$KSRCDES                         4294951579 TABLE          145
X$KSRCCTX                         4294951580 TABLE          146
X$KSRMSGDES                       4294951581 TABLE          147
X$KSRMPCTX                        4294951582 TABLE          148
X$KSRCHDL                         4294951583 TABLE          149
X$KSRMSGO                         4294951584 TABLE          150
X$KSXPPING                        4294952378 TABLE          151

X$KSXPCLIENT                      4294952380 TABLE          152
X$KSXPIF                          4294952379 TABLE          153
X$KSXPIA                          4294952165 TABLE          154
X$SKGXPIA                         4294952166 TABLE          155
X$KSMDD                           4294951622 TABLE          156
X$KSMDUT1                         4294952607 TABLE          157
X$KSMGE                           4294951733 TABLE          158
X$KSXRMSG                         4294951728 TABLE          159
X$KSXRREPQ                        4294951729 TABLE          160
X$KSXRCONQ                        4294951730 TABLE          161

X$KSXRCH                          4294951731 TABLE          162
X$KSXRSG                          4294951732 TABLE          163
X$KSFMLIB                         4294951910 TABLE          164
NAME                              OBJECT_ID TYPE   TABLE_NUM
-------------------------------   ---------- -----  ----------
X$KSFMIOST                        4294951817 TABLE          165
X$KSFMFILE                        4294951818 TABLE          166
X$KSFMFILEEXT                     4294951819 TABLE          167
X$KSFMSUBELEM                     4294951820 TABLE          168
X$KSFMELEM                        4294951821 TABLE          169
X$KSFMEXTELEM                     4294951822 TABLE          170
X$KSFMCOMPL                       4294951823 TABLE          171
```

```
X$KSOLSSTAT                     4294951842 TABLE          172
X$KSOLSFTS                      4294951841 TABLE          173
X$KSWSCLSTAB                    4294952155 TABLE          174
X$KSWSEVTAB                     4294952154 TABLE          175
X$KSWSASTAB                     4294952091 TABLE          176
X$GIMSA                         4294952863 TABLE          177
X$KSIRGD                        4294952708 TABLE          178
X$KSDHNG_CHAINS                 4294952927 TABLE          179
X$KJREQFP                       4294952613 TABLE          180
X$KJLEQFP                       4294952612 TABLE          181

X$KJISFT                        4294951415 TABLE          182
X$KJILFT                        4294951416 TABLE          183
X$KJICVT                        4294951421 TABLE          184
X$KJILKFT                       4294951430 TABLE          185
X$KJIRFT                        4294951433 TABLE          186
X$KJITRFT                       4294951603 TABLE          187
X$KJXM                          4294951770 TABLE          188
X$KJCTFS                        4294951927 TABLE          189
X$KJCTFR                        4294951928 TABLE          190
X$KJCTFRI                       4294951929 TABLE          191

X$KJBR                          4294951616 TABLE          192
X$KJBRFX                        4294951617 TABLE          193
X$KJBL                          4294951614 TABLE          194
X$KJBLFX                        4294951615 TABLE          195
X$KJMSDP                        4294951693 TABLE          196
X$KJMDDP                        4294951694 TABLE          197
X$KJDRHV                        4294951781 TABLE          198
X$KJDRPCMHV                     4294951784 TABLE          199
X$KJDRPCMPF                     4294951787 TABLE          200
X$KJDRMAFNSTATS                 4294952142 TABLE          201

X$KJDRMHVSTATS                  4294952143 TABLE          202
X$KJDRMREQ                      4294952144 TABLE          203
X$KJPNPX                        4294952120 TABLE          204
X$KMGSCT                        4294951662 TABLE          205
X$KMGSTFR                       4294952192 TABLE          206
X$KMGSOP                        4294951663 TABLE          207
X$KMGSBSADV                     4294952614 TABLE          208
X$KMGSBSMEMADV                  4294952877 TABLE          209
X$KCCCF                         4294951110 TABLE          210
X$KCCRS                         4294951217 TABLE          211

X$KCCDI                         4294951038 TABLE          212
X$KCCDI2                        4294951840 TABLE          213
X$KCCRT                         4294951041 TABLE          214
NAME                            OBJECT_ID TYPE   TABLE_NUM
------------------------------- ---------- ----- ----------
X$KCCTIR                        4294952471 TABLE          215
X$KCCLE                         4294951040 TABLE          216
X$KCCSL                         4294951665 TABLE          217
X$KCCFE                         4294951039 TABLE          218
X$KCCTF                         4294951460 TABLE          219
X$KCCFN                         4294951037 TABLE          220
X$KCCTS                         4294951206 TABLE          221

X$KCCRM                         4294951669 TABLE          222
X$KCCLH                         4294951042 TABLE          223
```

```
X$KCCOR              4294951207 TABLE           224
X$KCCAL              4294951208 TABLE           225
X$KCCRL              4294952933 TABLE           226
X$KCCBS              4294951209 TABLE           227
X$KCCBP              4294951210 TABLE           228
X$KCCBF              4294951211 TABLE           229
X$KCCBL              4294951212 TABLE           230
X$KCCDC              4294951213 TABLE           231

X$KCCFC              4294951214 TABLE           232
X$KCCCC              4294951215 TABLE           233
X$KCCDL              4294951216 TABLE           234
X$KCCPD              4294951557 TABLE           235
X$KCCPA              4294951560 TABLE           236
X$KCCBI              4294951810 TABLE           237
X$KCCIC              4294951906 TABLE           238
X$KCCRDI             4294952047 TABLE           239
X$KCCIRT             4294952048 TABLE           240
X$KCCAGF             4294952049 TABLE           241

X$KCCFLE             4294952037 TABLE           242
X$KCCRSP             4294952655 TABLE           243
X$KCCNRS             4294952659 TABLE           244
X$KCCRSR             4294952064 TABLE           245
X$KCCDFHIST          4294952133 TABLE           246
X$KCCBLKCOR          4294952377 TABLE           247
X$KCCACM             4294952921 TABLE           248
X$KCBWDS             4294951172 TABLE           249
X$KCBWBPD            4294951394 TABLE           250
X$KCBBHS             4294951429 TABLE           251

X$KCBBES             4294951503 TABLE           252
X$ACTIVECKPT         4294951387 TABLE           253
X$CKPTBUF            4294951388 TABLE           254
X$KCBKWRL            4294951613 TABLE           255
X$KCBKPFS            4294951775 TABLE           256
X$BH                 4294950954 TABLE           257
X$KCBBF              4294951246 TABLE           258
X$KCBWH              4294951247 TABLE           259
X$KCBSW              4294951248 TABLE           260
X$KCBUWHY            4294952724 TABLE           261

X$KCBWAIT            4294950955 TABLE           262
X$KCBFWAIT           4294951081 TABLE           263
X$KCBTEK             4294952993 TABLE           264
NAME                 OBJECT_ID TYPE  TABLE_NUM
-------------------- ---------- ----- ----------
X$KCBDBK             4294952994 TABLE           265
X$KCBSC              4294951626 TABLE           266
X$KCBSH              4294951629 TABLE           267
X$KCBSDS             4294951630 TABLE           268
X$KCBMMAV            4294951824 TABLE           269
X$KCBOBH             4294952086 TABLE           270
X$KCBOQH             4294952087 TABLE           271

X$KCRMF              4294951160 TABLE           272
X$KCRMT              4294951161 TABLE           273
X$KCRMX              4294951163 TABLE           274
X$KCRRDSTAT          4294951650 TABLE           275
```

```
X$KCRRARCH                       4294951556 TABLE           276
X$KCRRLNS                        4294951903 TABLE           277
X$KCRRNHG                        4294952209 TABLE          .278
X$KCRRASTATS                     4294952210 TABLE           279
X$KRFSTHRD                       4294952193 TABLE           280
X$KCRRPTDGSTATS                  4294952206 TABLE           281

X$KRSSMS                         4294951618 TABLE           282
X$KRSTDGC                        4294951963 TABLE           283
X$KRSTDEST                       4294951242 TABLE           284
X$KRSTPVRS                       4294952201 TABLE           285
X$KRSTALG                        4294951814 TABLE           286
X$KCRFWS                         4294951809 TABLE           287
X$LOGBUF_READHIST                4294953010 TABLE           288
X$KCRFSTRAND                     4294952164 TABLE           289
X$KCRFDEBUG                      4294952088 TABLE           290
X$KCRFX                          4294951162 TABLE           291

X$KCFIOHIST                      4294951974 TABLE           292
X$KCFIO                          4294950957 TABLE           293
X$KCFTIO                         4294951521 TABLE           294
X$KCLFX                          4294951174 TABLE           295
X$KCLQN                          4294951175 TABLE           296
X$KCLFH                          4294951141 TABLE           297
X$KCLFI                          4294951142 TABLE           298
X$LE                             4294950958 TABLE           299
X$KCLLS                          4294951173 TABLE           300
X$KCLCRST                        4294951504 TABLE           301

X$INSTANCE_CACHE_TRANSFER        4294952150 TABLE           302
X$KCLCURST                       4294951774 TABLE           303
X$KCLRCVST                       4294952020 TABLE           304
X$OBJECT_POLICY_STATISTICS       4294952185 TABLE           305
X$POLICY_HISTORY                 4294952231 TABLE           306
X$KCBLDRHIST                     4294951707 TABLE           307
X$KCBLSC                         4294951612 TABLE           308
X$KCCCP                          4294951392 TABLE           309
X$ESTIMATED_MTTR                 4294951668 TABLE           310
X$KCTLAX                         4294952474 TABLE           311

X$KCTICW                         4294952476 TABLE           312
X$TARGETRBA                      4294951551 TABLE           313
X$KCVFH                          4294951072 TABLE           314
NAME                             OBJECT_ID  TYPE   TABLE_NUM
-------------------------------- ---------- ----- ----------
X$KCVFHTMP                       4294951522 TABLE           315
X$KRBAFF                         4294951455 TABLE           316
X$KRBMSFT                        4294952008 TABLE           317
X$KRBMRST                        4294952063 TABLE           318
X$KRBMROT                        4294952067 TABLE           319
X$KRBMCA                         4294953006 TABLE           320
X$LOGMNR_LOGS                    4294951536 TABLE           321

X$LOGMNR_PARAMETERS              4294951538 TABLE           322
X$LOGMNR_DICTIONARY              4294951537 TABLE           323
X$LOGMNR_CONTENTS                4294951535 TABLE           324
X$LOGMNR_ROOT$                   4294951751 TABLE           325
X$LOGMNR_COL$                    4294951752 TABLE           326
X$LOGMNR_TAB$                    4294951753 TABLE           327
```

```
X$LOGMNR_OBJ$                      4294951754 TABLE          328
X$LOGMNR_TS$                       4294951756 TABLE          329
X$LOGMNR_IND$                      4294951757 TABLE          330
X$LOGMNR_USER$                     4294951758 TABLE          331

X$LOGMNR_TABPART$                  4294951759 TABLE          332
X$LOGMNR_TABSUBPART$               4294951760 TABLE          333
X$LOGMNR_TABCOMPART$               4294951761 TABLE          334
X$LOGMNR_INDPART$                  4294951762 TABLE          335
X$LOGMNR_TYPE$                     4294951763 TABLE          336
X$LOGMNR_COLTYPE$                  4294951764 TABLE          337
X$LOGMNR_ATTRIBUTE$                4294951765 TABLE          338
X$LOGMNR_ENCRYPTION_PROFILE$       4294951766 TABLE          339
X$LOGMNR_ENCRYPTED_OBJ$            4294951767 TABLE          340
X$KRVXDKA                          4294952132 TABLE          341

X$KRVXDTA                          4294953031 TABLE          342
X$LOGMNR_ENC$                      4294952869 TABLE          343
X$LOGMNR_CLU$                      4294952752 TABLE          344
X$LOGMNR_FILE$                     4294952753 TABLE          345
X$LOGMNR_INDSUBPART$               4294952754 TABLE          346
X$LOGMNR_LOB$                      4294952755 TABLE          347
X$LOGMNR_LOBFRAG$                  4294952756 TABLE          348
X$LOGMNR_SEG$                      4294952757 TABLE          349
X$LOGMNR_UET$                      4294952758 TABLE          350
X$LOGMNR_KTFBUE                    4294952759 TABLE          351

X$LOGMNR_UNDO$                     4294952760 TABLE          352
X$LOGMNR_ATTRCOL$                  4294952983 TABLE          353
X$LOGMNR_INDCOMPART$               4294952984 TABLE          354
X$LOGMNR_KOPM$                     4294952985 TABLE          355
X$LOGMNR_NTAB$                     4294952986 TABLE          356
X$LOGMNR_OPQTYPE$                  4294952987 TABLE          357
X$LOGMNR_PARTOBJ$                  4294952988 TABLE          358
X$LOGMNR_PROPS$                    4294952989 TABLE          359
X$LOGMNR_REFCON$                   4294952990 TABLE          360
X$LOGMNR_SUBCOLTYPE$               4294952991 TABLE          361

X$LOGMNR_CDEF$                     4294952992 TABLE          362
X$LOGMNR_SESSION                   4294951638 TABLE          363
X$LOGMNR_LATCH                     4294952583 TABLE          364
NAME                               OBJECT_ID TYPE   TABLE_NUM
--------------------------------   ---------- ----- ----------
X$LOGMNR_DICTIONARY_LOAD           4294952586 TABLE          365
X$LOGMNR_LOGFILE                   4294951641 TABLE          366
X$LOGMNR_PROCESS                   4294951644 TABLE          367
X$KRVXTX                           4294951647 TABLE          368
X$LOGMNR_REGION                    4294951631 TABLE          369
X$LOGMNR_CALLBACK                  4294951634 TABLE          370
X$KRVXSV                           4294951832 TABLE          371

X$KRVXOP                           4294952234 TABLE          372
X$KRVXTHRD                         4294952195 TABLE          373
X$LOGMNR_LOG                       4294952199 TABLE          374
X$KRVXWARNV                        4294952203 TABLE          375
X$KCPXPL                           4294951988 TABLE          376
X$KRVSLV                           4294951709 TABLE          377
X$KRVSLVS                          4294951712 TABLE          378
X$KRVSLVPG                         4294952172 TABLE          379
```

```
X$KRVSLVST              4294952175 TABLE         380
X$KRVSLVAS              4294952200 TABLE         381

X$KRVSLVTHRD            4294952205 TABLE         382
X$DGLPARAM              4294951695 TABLE         383
X$QUIESCE               4294951708 TABLE         384
X$KCBVBL                4294951931 TABLE         385
X$KRCFH                 4294952009 TABLE         386
X$KRCEXT                4294952010 TABLE         387
X$KRCCDE                4294952011 TABLE         388
X$KRCCDS                4294952012 TABLE         389
X$KRCCDR                4294952131 TABLE         390
X$KRCGFE                4294952013 TABLE         391

X$KRCFDE                4294952014 TABLE         392
X$KRCFBH                4294952015 TABLE         393
X$KRCBIT                4294952016 TABLE         394
X$KRCSTAT               4294952109 TABLE         395
X$KRASGA                4294952214 TABLE         396
X$KRFBLOG               4294952040 TABLE         397
X$KRFGSTAT              4294952106 TABLE         398
X$KRBZA                 4294952709 TABLE         399
X$KCFISTSA              4294952982 TABLE         400
X$KTADM                 4294951013 TABLE         401

X$KTATRFIL              4294952592 TABLE         402
X$KTATRFSL              4294952593 TABLE         403
X$KTATL                 4294952594 TABLE         404
X$KTCXB                 4294951014 TABLE         405
X$KTCSP                 4294951984 TABLE         406
X$KTUGD                 4294951683 TABLE         407
X$KTURD                 4294951022 TABLE         408
X$KTUXE                 4294951205 TABLE         409
X$KTUSMST               4294951684 TABLE         410
X$KTUSMST2              4294952111 TABLE         411

X$KTUSUS                4294952619 TABLE         412
X$KTUCUS                4294952899 TABLE         413
X$KTURHIST              4294951986 TABLE         414
NAME                    OBJECT_ID TYPE   TABLE_NUM
------------------------------ ---------- ----- ----------
X$KTPRXRS               4294951457 TABLE         415
X$KTPRXRT               4294951459 TABLE         416
X$KTPRHIST              4294951987 TABLE         417
X$KTRSO                 4294951688 TABLE         418
X$KTIFP                 4294952160 TABLE         419
X$KTIFF                 4294952161 TABLE         420
X$KTIFB                 4294952162 TABLE         421

X$KTIFV                 4294952163 TABLE         422
X$KTUQQRY               4294952094 TABLE         423
X$KTCNREG               4294952202 TABLE         424
X$KTFTBTXNMODS          4294952997 TABLE         425
X$KTFTBTXNGRAPH         4294952999 TABLE         426
X$KTCNQUERY             4294952228 TABLE         427
X$KTCNREGQUERY          4294952229 TABLE         428
X$KTCNCLAUSES           4294952230 TABLE         429
X$KTCNINBAND            4294952232 TABLE         430
X$KTSTSSD               4294951176 TABLE         431
```

```
X$KTSSO                          4294951251 TABLE        432
X$KTSTFC                         4294951520 TABLE        433
X$KTSTUSC                        4294952595 TABLE        434
X$KTSTUSS                        4294952596 TABLE        435
X$KTSTUSG                        4294952597 TABLE        436
X$KTSPSTAT                       4294951779 TABLE        437
X$KTSKSTAT                       4294951985 TABLE        438
X$KTTEFINFO                      4294952465 TABLE        439
X$LOBSTATHIST                    4294952785 TABLE        440
X$LOBSTAT                        4294952781 TABLE        441

X$LOBSEGSTAT                     4294952784 TABLE        442
X$KTTVS                          4294951062 TABLE        443
X$KTTETS                         4294952780 TABLE        444
X$KTFBFE                         4294951515 TABLE        445
X$KTFBHC                         4294951516 TABLE        446
X$KTFBUE                         4294951517 TABLE        447
X$KTSLCHUNK                      4294952972 TABLE        448
X$KTFTHC                         4294951518 TABLE        449
X$KTFTME                         4294951519 TABLE        450
X$KDNSSF                         4294950965 TABLE        451

X$KDXST                          4294950966 TABLE        452
X$KDXHS                          4294950967 TABLE        453
X$KDLT                           4294951512 TABLE        454
X$KDLU_STAT                      4294953026 TABLE        455
X$KQRST                          4294950989 TABLE        456
X$KQRPD                          4294951155 TABLE        457
X$KQRSD                          4294951156 TABLE        458
X$KQRFP                          4294951449 TABLE        459
X$KQRFS                          4294951450 TABLE        460
X$KQDPG                          4294951098 TABLE        461

X$KGLOB                          4294950985 TABLE        462
X$KGLLK                          4294950986 TABLE        463
X$KGLPN                          4294950987 TABLE        464
NAME                             OBJECT_ID TYPE  TABLE_NUM
-------------------------------- ---------- ----- ----------
X$KGLST                          4294950988 TABLE        465
X$KGLAU                          4294951112 TABLE        466
X$KGLSN                          4294951379 TABLE        467
X$KGLTR                          4294951033 TABLE        468
X$KGLXS                          4294951034 TABLE        469
X$KGLRD                          4294951187 TABLE        470
X$KGLDP                          4294951035 TABLE        471

X$KGLNA                          4294951064 TABLE        472
X$KGLNA1                         4294951150 TABLE        473
X$KKSBV                          4294951063 TABLE        474
X$KKSSRD                         4294951776 TABLE        475
X$KGSCC                          4294951086 TABLE        476
X$KQLSET                         4294951230 TABLE        477
X$KGICS                          4294951087 TABLE        478
X$KGLLC                          4294951108 TABLE        479
X$KQLFXPL                        4294951672 TABLE        480
X$KQLFSQCE                       4294952031 TABLE        481

X$KQLFBC                         4294952034 TABLE        482
```

```
X$MUTEX_SLEEP_HISTORY            4294952691 TABLE        483
X$MUTEX_SLEEP                    4294952692 TABLE        484
X$VERSION                        4294951029 TABLE        485
X$KQFSZ                          4294951069 TABLE        486
X$KQFP                           4294951240 TABLE        487
X$DUAL                           4294951241 TABLE        488
X$KKKICR                         4294953019 TABLE        489
X$KKSSQLSTAT                     4294952660 TABLE        490
X$KKCNRSTAT                      4294952894 TABLE        491

X$KZDOS                          4294951023 TABLE        492
X$KZSRO                          4294951024 TABLE        493
X$KZSPR                          4294951025 TABLE        494
X$KZSRT                          4294951115 TABLE        495
X$KZRTPD                         4294951771 TABLE        496
X$CONTEXT                        4294951495 TABLE        497
X$KZEKMFVW                       4294952685 TABLE        498
X$KZEKMENCWAL                    4294952966 TABLE        499
X$GLOBALCONTEXT                  4294951685 TABLE        500
X$XML_AUDIT_TRAIL                4294952598 TABLE        501

X$KZPOPR                         4294952713 TABLE        502
X$XS_SESSION_ROLES               4294952801 TABLE        503
X$K2GTE2                         4294951052 TABLE        504
X$K2GTE                          4294951032 TABLE        505
X$KMMSI                          4294950972 TABLE        506
X$KMMDI                          4294950973 TABLE        507
X$KMMSG                          4294950974 TABLE        508
X$KMMDP                          4294950975 TABLE        509
X$KMMRD                          4294950976 TABLE        510
X$KMCQS                          4294950970 TABLE        511

X$KMCVC                          4294950971 TABLE        512
X$KMPCP                          4294953042 TABLE        513
X$KMPCSO                         4294953039 TABLE        514
NAME                             OBJECT_ID  TYPE   TABLE_NUM
-------------------------------- ---------- ----- ----------
X$KMPCMON                        4294953040 TABLE        515
X$KMPSRV                         4294953041 TABLE        516
X$KKSAI                          4294951197 TABLE        517
X$KKSCS                          4294951623 TABLE        518
X$JOXFT                          4294951596 TABLE        519
X$JOXFM                          4294951780 TABLE        520
X$KXSCC                          4294951188 TABLE        521

X$KXSBD                          4294951196 TABLE        522
X$KXFPCST                        4294951113 TABLE        523
X$KXFPCMS                        4294951117 TABLE        524
X$KXFPSMS                        4294951118 TABLE        525
X$KXFPCDS                        4294951119 TABLE        526
X$KXFPSDS                        4294951120 TABLE        527
X$KXFPDP                         4294951134 TABLE        528
X$KXFPSST                        4294951114 TABLE        529
X$KXFPYS                         4294951135 TABLE        530
X$KXFPNS                         4294951497 TABLE        531

X$KXFPPIG                        4294952838 TABLE        532
X$KXFPIG                         4294952839 TABLE        533
X$KXFPPFT                        4294951661 TABLE        534
```

```
X$KXFPBS                      4294952167 TABLE          535
X$KXFQSROW                    4294951189 TABLE          536
X$KSXAFA                      4294951204 TABLE          537
X$QESMMSGA                    4294951737 TABLE          538
X$QESMMIWT                    4294951738 TABLE          539
X$QESMMIWH                    4294951829 TABLE          540
X$QKSMMWDS                    4294951739 TABLE          541

X$QESMMAHIST                  4294951847 TABLE          542
X$QESMMAPADV                  4294951850 TABLE          543
X$QESRSTAT                    4294951853 TABLE          544
X$QESRSTATALL                 4294951856 TABLE          545
X$QKSCESYS                    4294952029 TABLE          546
X$QKSCESES                    4294952030 TABLE          547
X$KAUVRSTAT                   4294952130 TABLE          548
X$QESBLSTAT                   4294952620 TABLE          549
X$QKSBGSYS                    4294952715 TABLE          550
X$QKSBGSES                    4294952716 TABLE          551

X$QKSFM                       4294952746 TABLE          552
X$QKSFMPRT                    4294952747 TABLE          553
X$QKSFMDEP                    4294952748 TABLE          554
X$QKSHT                       4294952777 TABLE          555
X$QESRCSTA                    4294952786 TABLE          556
X$QESRCOBJ                    4294952787 TABLE          557
X$QESRCMEM                    4294952788 TABLE          558
X$QESRCDEP                    4294952789 TABLE          559
X$QESRCSO                     4294952790 TABLE          560
X$KKOCS_HISTOGRAM             4294952853 TABLE          561

X$KKOCS_SELECTIVITY           4294952856 TABLE          562
X$KKOCS_STATISTICS            4294952859 TABLE          563
X$XPLTON                      4294952524 TABLE          564
NAME                          OBJECT_ID  TYPE  TABLE_NUM
----------------------------- ---------- ----- ----------
X$XPLTOO                      4294952525 TABLE          565
X$KLPT                        4294951232 TABLE          566
X$KLCIE                       4294951600 TABLE          567
X$KVII                        4294951127 TABLE          568
X$KVIS                        4294951128 TABLE          569
X$KVIT                        4294951129 TABLE          570
X$KUPVJ                       4294951945 TABLE          571

X$KUPVA                       4294951946 TABLE          572
X$KNSTACR                     4294951653 TABLE          573
X$KNSTASL                     4294951656 TABLE          574
X$KNSTRPP                     4294951721 TABLE          575
X$KNSTMVR                     4294951715 TABLE          576
X$KNSTCAP                     4294951837 TABLE          577
X$KNSTRQU                     4294951718 TABLE          578
X$KNGFL                       4294952119 TABLE          579
X$KNGFLE                      4294952668 TABLE          580
X$KNSTTXN                     4294952698 TABLE          581

X$KNSTMT                      4294952749 TABLE          582
X$KNLAROW                     4294951991 TABLE          583
X$KNLASG                      4294952701 TABLE          584
X$TEMPORARY_LOB_REFCNT        4294951961 TABLE          585
X$ABSTRACT_LOB                4294952581 TABLE          586
```

```
X$KOCST                     4294951374 TABLE        587
X$UGANCO                    4294951109 TABLE        588
X$PRMSLTYX                  4294951900 TABLE        589
X$OPTION                    4294951132 TABLE        590
X$KPOQSTA                   4294952936 TABLE        591

X$KPONEXSTAT                4294953032 TABLE        592
X$KWDDEF                    4294951568 TABLE        593
X$OPERATORS                 4294952697 TABLE        594
X$OPVERSION                 4294952949 TABLE        595
X$OPDESC                    4294952950 TABLE        596
X$OPARG                     4294953003 TABLE        597
X$KPPLCC_INFO               4294952879 TABLE        598
X$KPPLCC_STATS              4294952880 TABLE        599
X$KPPLCP_STATS              4294952969 TABLE        600
X$KWQPS                     4294951907 TABLE        601

X$KWQPD                     4294951908 TABLE        602
X$KWQSI                     4294951434 TABLE        603
X$PERSISTENT_QUEUES         4294952891 TABLE        604
X$PERSISTENT_SUBSCRIBERS    4294952892 TABLE        605
X$PERSISTENT_PUBLISHERS     4294952893 TABLE        606
X$KWRSNV                    4294951953 TABLE        607
X$RULE_SET                  4294952207 TABLE        608
X$RULE                      4294952208 TABLE        609
X$BUFFERED_QUEUES           4294952070 TABLE        610
X$BUFFERED_SUBSCRIBERS      4294952071 TABLE        611

X$BUFFERED_PUBLISHERS       4294952072 TABLE        612
X$BUFFER2                   4294952679 TABLE        613
X$BUFFER                    4294952073 TABLE        614
NAME                        OBJECT_ID TYPE   TABLE_NUM
--------------------------- ---------- -----  ----------
X$KWQBPMT                   4294952159 TABLE        615
X$KWQMNC                    4294953034 TABLE        616
X$KWQMNSCTX                 4294953035 TABLE        617
X$KWQMNTASK                 4294953036 TABLE        618
X$KWQMNTASKSTAT             4294953037 TABLE        619
X$KWQMNJIT                  4294953038 TABLE        620
X$HS_SESSION                4294951479 TABLE        621

X$HOFP                      4294951606 TABLE        622
X$NFSCLIENTS                4294952726 TABLE        623
X$NFSOPENS                  4294952727 TABLE        624
X$NFSLOCKS                  4294952728 TABLE        625
X$RFMP                      4294951679 TABLE        626
X$RFMTE                     4294951680 TABLE        627
X$VINST                     4294951698 TABLE        628
X$NSV                       4294951808 TABLE        629
X$RFAHIST                   4294952721 TABLE        630
X$RFAFO                     4294952862 TABLE        631

X$XSAGGR                    4294951891 TABLE        632
X$XSSINFO                   4294951894 TABLE        633
X$XSAGOP                    4294951888 TABLE        634
X$XSOBJECT                  4294951889 TABLE        635
X$XSLONGOPS                 4294952060 TABLE        636
X$XSOQSEHI                  4294952051 TABLE        637
X$XSOQOJHI                  4294952054 TABLE        638
```

```
X$XSOQOPHI                      4294952055 TABLE          639
X$XSOQMEHI                      4294952056 TABLE          640
X$XSOQOPLU                      4294952057 TABLE          641

X$XSAWSO                        4294951897 TABLE          642
X$KFALS                         4294951863 TABLE          643
X$KFCBH                         4294952608 TABLE          644
X$KFCCE                         4294952610 TABLE          645
X$KFBH                          4294952611 TABLE          646
X$KFDSK                         4294951879 TABLE          647
X$KFDSK_STAT                    4294952649 TABLE          648
X$KFDAT                         4294951859 TABLE          649
X$KFDFS                         4294952223 TABLE          650
X$KFDDD                         4294952725 TABLE          651

X$KFGRP                         4294951876 TABLE          652
X$KFGRP_STAT                    4294952650 TABLE          653
X$KFGMG                         4294951966 TABLE          654
X$KFGBRB                        4294952233 TABLE          655
X$KFKID                         4294951870 TABLE          656
X$KFKLIB                        4294952168 TABLE          657
X$KFMDGRP                       4294952211 TABLE          658
X$KFNCL                         4294951871 TABLE          659
X$KFNSDSKIOST                   4294952224 TABLE          660
X$KFTMTA                        4294951860 TABLE          661

X$KFFIL                         4294951866 TABLE          662
X$KFFXP                         4294951869 TABLE          663
X$KFDPARTNER                    4294951979 TABLE          664
NAME                            OBJECT_ID TYPE   TABLE_NUM
------------------------------- ---------- ----- ----------
X$KFCLLE                        4294952609 TABLE          665
X$KFENV                         4294952220 TABLE          666
X$KFVOL                         4294952804 TABLE          667
X$KFVOLSTAT                     4294952907 TABLE          668
X$KFVOFS                        4294952910 TABLE          669
X$KFVOFSV                       4294952904 TABLE          670
X$KELTOSD                       4294952097 TABLE          671

X$KELTSD                        4294952098 TABLE          672
X$KELTGSD                       4294952099 TABLE          673
X$KEWEFXT                       4294952100 TABLE          674
X$KEWECLS                       4294952568 TABLE          675
X$KEWESMS                       4294952569 TABLE          676
X$KEWESMAS                      4294952572 TABLE          677
X$KEWRTB                        4294951956 TABLE          678
X$KEWXOCF                       4294951957 TABLE          679
X$KEWX_SEGMENTS                 4294952146 TABLE          680
X$KEWX_LOBS                     4294952147 TABLE          681

X$KEWRSQLIDTAB                  4294951981 TABLE          682
X$KEWRTSQLPLAN                  4294952429 TABLE          683
X$KEWRTOPTENV                   4294952430 TABLE          684
X$KEWRSQLCRIT                   4294952431 TABLE          685
X$KEWRATTRNEW                   4294952426 TABLE          686
X$KEWRATTRSTALE                 4294952427 TABLE          687
X$KEWRTSQLTEXT                  4294952428 TABLE          688
X$KEWRTSEGSTAT                  4294952424 TABLE          689
X$ASH                           4294952043 TABLE          690
```

```
X$KEWASH               4294952044 TABLE         691

X$KEWAM                4294952045 TABLE         692
X$KEAOBJT              4294952021 TABLE         693
X$KEACMDN              4294952022 TABLE         694
X$KEAFDGN              4294952771 TABLE         695
X$KEWSSMAP             4294952564 TABLE         696
X$KEWSSYSV             4294952565 TABLE         697
X$KEWSSESV             4294952566 TABLE         698
X$KEWSSVCV             4294952567 TABLE         699
X$KEWMRWMV             4294952412 TABLE         700
X$KEWMDRMV             4294952413 TABLE         701

X$KEWMSEMV             4294952419 TABLE         702
X$KEWMSVCMV            4294952425 TABLE         703
X$KEWMFLMV             4294952420 TABLE         704
X$KEWMIOFMV            4294952481 TABLE         705
X$KEWMRMGMV            4294952486 TABLE         706
X$KEWMEVMV             4294952421 TABLE         707
X$KEWMRSM              4294952416 TABLE         708
X$KEWMDSM              4294952417 TABLE         709
X$KEWMGSM              4294952418 TABLE         710
X$KEWMAFMV             4294952422 TABLE         711

X$KEWMSMDV             4294952423 TABLE         712
X$KELRTD               4294952602 TABLE         713
X$KELRXMR              4294952702 TABLE         714
NAME                   OBJECT_ID  TYPE  TABLE_NUM
---------------------- ---------- ----- ----------
X$KELRSGA              4294952703 TABLE         715
X$KEHR                 4294952512 TABLE         716
X$KEHR_CHILD           4294952513 TABLE         717
X$KEHRP                4294952514 TABLE         718
X$KEHF                 4294952515 TABLE         719
X$KEHSQT               4294952521 TABLE         720
X$KEHEVTMAP            4294952516 TABLE         721

X$KEHECLMAP            4294952517 TABLE         722
X$KEHSYSMAP            4294952518 TABLE         723
X$KEHOSMAP             4294952522 TABLE         724
X$KEHTIMMAP            4294952519 TABLE         725
X$KEHPRMMAP            4294952520 TABLE         726
X$KETTG                4294952502 TABLE         727
X$KETOP                4294952503 TABLE         728
X$KETCL                4294952504 TABLE         729
X$KECPDENTRY           4294952523 TABLE         730
X$KECPRT               4294952526 TABLE         731

X$KESWXMON             4294952939 TABLE         732
X$KESWXMON_PLAN        4294952942 TABLE         733
X$JSKJOBQ              4294952128 TABLE         734
X$JSKSLV               4294952116 TABLE         735
X$DBGRICX              4294952772 TABLE         736
X$DBGRIPX              4294952773 TABLE         737
X$DBGRIKX              4294952774 TABLE         738
X$DBGRIFX              4294952946 TABLE         739
X$DBGDIREXT            4294952491 TABLE         740
X$DBGALERTEXT          4294952492 TABLE         741
```

```
X$DBKFDG                         4294952812 TABLE        742
X$DBKRECO                        4294952813 TABLE        743
X$DBKFSET                        4294952814 TABLE        744
X$DBKRUN                         4294952811 TABLE        745
X$DBKINFO                        4294952815 TABLE        746
X$DBKH_CHECK                     4294952830 TABLE        747
X$DBKH_CHECK_PARAM               4294952831 TABLE        748
X$DIAG_INFO                      4294953011 TABLE        749
X$IR_WORKING_FAILURE_SET         4294952913 TABLE        750
X$IR_WORKING_REPAIR_SET          4294952914 TABLE        751

X$IR_REPAIR_OPTION               4294952915 TABLE        752
X$IR_MANUAL_OPTION               4294952917 TABLE        753
X$IR_REPAIR_STEP                 4294952916 TABLE        754
X$IR_WF_PARAM                    4294952918 TABLE        755
X$IR_WR_PARAM                    4294952919 TABLE        756
X$IR_RS_PARAM                    4294952920 TABLE        757
X$DBKINCMETCFG                   4294952973 TABLE        758
X$DBKINCMETSUMMARY               4294952974 TABLE        759
X$DBKINCMETINFO                  4294952975 TABLE        760
X$DBKEFEFC                       4294952805 TABLE        761

X$DBKEFAFC                       4294952806 TABLE        762
X$DBKEFIEFC                      4294952807 TABLE        763
X$DBKEFDEAFC                     4294952808 TABLE        764
NAME                             OBJECT_ID  TYPE  TABLE_NUM
------------------------------   ---------- ----- ----------
X$KSXPTESTTBL                    4294952215 TABLE        765
X$KTCNQROW                       4294952227 TABLE        766
X$KSLLTR_CHILDREN                4294952735 TABLE      65537
X$KSLLTR_PARENT                  4294952736 TABLE      65537
X$KCVFHONL                       4294951073 TABLE      65537
X$KCVFHMRR                       4294951074 TABLE      65537
X$KCVFHALL                       4294951440 TABLE      65537

X$KGLTABLE                       4294951056 TABLE      65537
X$KGLBODY                        4294951057 TABLE      65537
X$KGLTRIGGER                     4294951058 TABLE      65537
X$KGLINDEX                       4294951059 TABLE      65537
X$KGLCLUSTER                     4294951060 TABLE      65537
X$KGLCURSOR                      4294951061 TABLE      65537
X$KGLCURSOR_CHILD_SQLID          4294952684 TABLE      65537
X$KGLCURSOR_CHILD_SQLIDPH        4294952680 TABLE      65537
X$KGLCURSOR_CHILD                4294952683 TABLE      65537
X$JOXFS                          4294951597 TABLE      65537

X$JOXFC                          4294951598 TABLE      65537
X$JOXFR                          4294951599 TABLE      65537
X$JOXFD                          4294951621 TABLE      65537
X$JOXOBJ                         4294952364 TABLE      65537
X$JOXSCD                         4294952365 TABLE      65537
X$JOXRSV                         4294952366 TABLE      65537
X$JOXREF                         4294952367 TABLE      65537
X$JOXDRC                         4294952368 TABLE      65537
X$JOXDRR                         4294952369 TABLE      65537
X$JOXMOB                         4294952370 TABLE      65537

X$JOXMIF                         4294952371 TABLE      65537
X$JOXMIC                         4294952372 TABLE      65537
```

```
X$JOXMFD                         4294952373 TABLE        65537
X$JOXMMD                         4294952374 TABLE        65537
X$JOXMAG                         4294952375 TABLE        65537
X$JOXMEX                         4294952376 TABLE        65537

798 rows selected.

SQL> spool off
```

Now that there is a complete listing of the *x$* tables within Oracle 11g release, run some example scripts to obtain useful database internal reports. One useful script that can be used by the busy Oracle DBA to monitor complex Oracle 11g database environments from within SQL*Plus is to access the Oracle 11g *alert.log* file from a script against the *x$*. This is used to reference the Oracle 11g alert log without using the 11g ADR.

In Oracle 11g, the settings for the ADR and *alert.log* are stored in an XML file called *log.xml* located under the operating system directory structure governed by the Oracle 11g database initialization parameter, *diagnostic_dest*. Searching for the *alert.log* file can be a tricky task, but fortunately for power Oracle DBAs, the undocumented *x$* tables provide a quick solution. If one queries the *x$dbgalertext* table, it will give the information quickly and painlessly from the current database *alert.log* files.

```
SQL> DESCRIBE X$DBGALERTEXT

Name                                      Null?    Type
----------------------------------------- -------- ----------------
ADDR                                               RAW(4)
INDX                                               NUMBER
INST_ID                                            NUMBER
ORIGINATING_TIMESTAMP                              TIMESTAMP(3) WITH TIME ZONE
NORMALIZED_TIMESTAMP                               TIMESTAMP(3) WITH TIME ZONE
ORGANIZATION_ID                                    VARCHAR2(64)
COMPONENT_ID                                       VARCHAR2(64)
HOST_ID                                            VARCHAR2(64)
HOST_ADDRESS                                       VARCHAR2(16)
MESSAGE_TYPE                                       NUMBER
MESSAGE_LEVEL                                      NUMBER
MESSAGE_ID                                         VARCHAR2(64)
MESSAGE_GROUP                                      VARCHAR2(64)
CLIENT_ID                                          VARCHAR2(64)
MODULE_ID                                          VARCHAR2(64)
PROCESS_ID                                         VARCHAR2(32)
THREAD_ID                                          VARCHAR2(64)
USER_ID                                            VARCHAR2(64)
INSTANCE_ID                                        VARCHAR2(64)
DETAILED_LOCATION                                  VARCHAR2(160)
PROBLEM_KEY                                        VARCHAR2(64)
UPSTREAM_COMP_ID                                   VARCHAR2(100)
DOWNSTREAM_COMP_ID                                 VARCHAR2(100)
EXECUTION_CONTEXT_ID                               VARCHAR2(100)
```

```
EXECUTION_CONTEXT_SEQUENCE                      NUMBER
ERROR_INSTANCE_ID                               NUMBER
ERROR_INSTANCE_SEQUENCE                         NUMBER
VERSION                                         NUMBER
MESSAGE_TEXT                                    VARCHAR2(2048)
MESSAGE_ARGUMENTS                               VARCHAR2(128)
SUPPLEMENTAL_ATTRIBUTES                         VARCHAR2(128)
SUPPLEMENTAL_DETAILS                            VARCHAR2(128)
PARTITION                                       NUMBER
RECORD_ID                                       NUMBER

SQL>


SQL> SELECT MESSAGE_TEXT FROM X$DBGALERTEXT WHERE ROWNUM<=30;

MESSAGE_TEXT
--------------------------------------------------------------------
Starting ORACLE instance (normal)
LICENSE_MAX_SESSION = 0
LICENSE_SESSIONS_WARNING = 0
Shared memory segment for instance monitoring created
Picked latch-free SCN scheme 2
Using LOG_ARCHIVE_DEST_1 parameter default value as C:\win11g1\RDBMS
Using LOG_ARCHIVE_DEST_10 parameter default value as
USE_DB_RECOVERY_FILE_DEST
Autotune of undo retention is turned on.
IMODE=BR
ILAT =18
LICENSE_MAX_USERS = 0

MESSAGE_TEXT
--------------------------------------------------------------------
SYS auditing is disabled
Starting up ORACLE RDBMS Version: 11.1.0.6.0.
Using parameter settings in client-side pfile
C:\WIN11G1\ADMIN\WIN11G\PFILE\INIT
.ORA on machine KARMA

System parameters with non-default values:
  processes            = 150
  memory_target        = 816M
  control_files        = "C:\WIN11G1\ORADATA\WIN11G\CONTROL01.CTL"
  control_files        = "C:\WIN11G1\ORADATA\WIN11G\CONTROL02.CTL"
  control_files        = "C:\WIN11G1\ORADATA\WIN11G\CONTROL03.CTL"

MESSAGE_TEXT
--------------------------------------------------------------------
  db_block_size            = 8192
  compatible               = "11.1.0.0.0"
  db_recovery_file_dest     = "C:\win11g1\flash_recovery_area"
  db_recovery_file_dest_size= 2G
  undo_tablespace          = "UNDOTBS1"
  remote_login_passwordfile= "EXCLUSIVE"
  db_domain                = ""
  dispatchers              = "(PROTOCOL=TCP) (SERVICE=win11gXDB)"
  audit_file_dest          = "C:\WIN11G1\ADMIN\WIN11G\ADUMP"
  audit_trail              = "DB"

30 rows selected.

SQL>
```

The above query returns details from the *alert.log* based on the first 30 occurrences in the 11g *alert.log*. If one wants more historical data mined from the *alert.log*, simply change the predicate for ROWNUM to a larger value based on how much detail is desired from the 11g *alert.log*. One also can query the *x$dbgdirext* table to obtain the file and directory names for the Oracle 11g diagnostic and trace files with the following query:

```
SQL> desc x$dbgdirext

Name                                      Null?    Type
----------------------------------------- -------- -----------------
ADDR                                               RAW(4)
INDX                                               NUMBER
INST_ID                                            NUMBER
PHYSICAL_PATH                                      VARCHAR2(444)
LOGICAL_PATH                                       VARCHAR2(444)
PHYSICAL_FILE                                      VARCHAR2(68)
LOGICAL_FILE                                       VARCHAR2(68)
CREATION_TIME                                      TIMESTAMP(3) WITH TIME ZONE
MODIFY_TIME                                        TIMESTAMP(3) WITH TIME ZONE
LVL                                                NUMBER
TYPE                                               NUMBER

SQL> select lpad (' ',lvl,' ')||logical_file file_name
  2   from x$dbgdirext
  3   where rownum<=30;

FILE_NAME
--------------------------------------------------------------------
asm
clients
user_mixxalot
host_1792144485_11
alert
log.xml
cdump
incident
incpkg
lck

am_1096102193_3488045378.lck
am_1096102262_3454819329.lck
am_3216668543_3129272988.lck
metadata
adr_control.ams
inc_meter_impt_def.ams
inc_meter_pk_impts.ams
stage
sweep
trace

sqlnet.log
user_unknown
host_411310321_11
alert
cdump
incident
incpkg
```

```
FILE_NAME
--------------------------------------------------------------------
lck
am_1762783_4031814035.lck
am_3216668543_3129272988.lck

30 rows selected.
```

One excellent usage of the *x$* tables in the previous two queries would be to set up a custom monitoring system for problem tracking with Oracle 11g issues. The result sets of the previous *x$* queries can then be spooled into a database table for monitoring on a regular basis by the support DBA team.

Summary

This chapter has provided insight into the following topics regarding *x$* tables for Oracle 11g database:

- Exploring Oracle 11g new features and internals with the *x$* tables

- Using the *x$* tables for Oracle 11g database analysis

- Scripts using *x$* $ tables with Oracle 11g

In the appendices, some useful tips are given that will be essential to the expert Oracle DBA as part of troubleshooting toolkit to complement the journey to *v$* and *x$* tables for Oracle 11g.

Book Conclusion

It is my hope that you, the reader, have enjoyed this voyage to the world of Oracle 11g database internals. In summary, you have been provided with a solid introduction to the database internal structures, tools and methods for troubleshooting complex database issues with your Oracle 11g database system environments. Furthermore, this book has also provided a methodology that will allow you to perform root cause analysis to quickly isolate and pinpoint the cause of your performance and database failures to ensure stability and successful implementations and ongoing database maintenance.

Cheers,

Ben Prusinski

Appendix A: Internal Tools for Oracle 11g

DBX

Using DBX for core analysis with Oracle 11g:

- http://docs.sun.com/app/docs

Syntax:

- *$ dbx - process_id*

Worked Example:

```
[oracle@suntest bin]$ pwd
/opt/sun/sunstudio12/bin
[oracle@suntest bin]$ ./dbx
For information about new features see `help changes'
```

Command Summary:

Use commands to see a command summary consisting of one-line descriptions of each DBX command.

```
Execution and Tracing
  cancel      catch       clear        cont       delete
  fix         fixed       handler      ignore     intercept
  next        pop         replay       rerun      restore
  run         runargs     save         status     step
  stop        trace       unintercept  when       whocatches
```

Using DBX for Debugging Oracle

First, log on to SQL*Plus and create a table:

```
SQL> create table foo(a number);


Table created.
```

Next, find the Oracle processes to trace:

```
[oracle@raclinux1 bin]$ ps -ef|grep oracle

oracle   19994 19993  0 00:31 ?        00:00:00 oracleORA11G
(DESCRIPTION=(LOCAL=YES)(ADDRESS=(PROTOCOL=beq)))
oracle   19993  3834  0 00:31 pts/2    00:00:00 sqlplus
```

Then get a trace with DBX:

```
[oracle@raclinux1 bin]$ ./dbx $ORACLE_HOME/bin/oracle 19994

Reading ld-linux.so.2
Reading libskgxp11.so
Reading librt.so.1
Reading libnnz11.so
Attached to process 19994
t@3086931648 (l@19994) stopped in _dl_sysinfo_int80 at 0x90a7a2
0x0090a7a2: _dl_sysinfo_int80+0x0002:   ret
(dbx)

(dbx) collector enable
```

Now return back to the DBX trace session:

```
(dbx) cont
```

Using DBX for Tracing Oracle 11g Memory Process:

Use the DBX thread command as shown below.

```
(dbx) thread t@3086931648
t@3086931648 (l@24976) stopped in _dl_sysinfo_int80 at 0x90a7a2
0x0090a7a2: _dl_sysinfo_int80+0x0002:   ret
(dbx) where
current thread: t@3086931648
=>[1] _dl_sysinfo_int80(0xf493504, 0xe5b652e, 0x9, 0xf5a684e, 0x2010,
0xf493504) , at 0x90a7a2
[2] __read_nocancel(0xf59d318, 0xf59d980, 0xf59ab08, 0xf5a684e, 0xbfffb8b4,
0x 0), at 0xb5c4c3
[3] ntpfprd(0xf59a9a0, 0xf5a684e, 0x2010, 0xbfffbb48, 0x8), at 0xe5b64cf
[4] nsbasic_brc(0xf591fd8, 0xf5920f4, 0xbfffc5d8, 0x0), at 0xe59b3c7
[5] nsbrecv(0xf591fd8, 0xf5920f4, 0xbfffc5d8, 0x0), at 0xe59e20e
[6] nioqrc(0xf5523e4, 0x0, 0xbfffe658, 0x1, 0x0), at 0xe5a2d20
[7] __PGOSF20_opikndf2(0xf5523e4, 0x2, 0xbfffe658, 0x1, 0x0, 0x0), at
0xe39da6 5
[8] opitsk(0x0, 0x0), at 0x8988d90
[9] opiino(0x3c, 0x4, 0xbffff518), at 0x898b294
[10] opiodr(0x3c, 0x4, 0xbffff518, 0x0), at 0xe39eeb3
[11] opidrv(0x3c, 0x4, 0xbffff518), at 0x898570a
```

```
[12] sou2o(0xbffff4fc, 0x3c, 0x4, 0xbffff518), at 0x8bf6b03
[13] opimai_real(0x2, 0xbffff610), at 0x851a37f
[14] ssthrdmain(0x2, 0xbffff610), at 0x8bfa2d6
[15] main(0x2, 0xbffff6d4, 0xbffff6e0, 0x915b46, 0x2eaff4, 0x0), at
0x851a2fc
[16] 0x1dae33(0x851a288, 0x2, 0xbffff6d4, 0xa54ff04, 0xa54ff58, 0x9163d0),
at 0x1dae33

(dbx) thread -info
        Thread t@3086931648 (0x0) at priority 0
        state: active on l@3107
        base function: 0x0: 0x00000000() stack: 0x0[0]
        flags: (none)
        masked signals: (none)
        Currently active in _dl_sysinfo_int80

(dbx) trace -file tracedbx
All trace output redirected to "tracedbx"

(dbx) debug -f
Debugging: oracle (process id 24976)
```

Truss

Truss is the Sun Solaris operating system level tool that can be used to trace Oracle 11g process activities for all system calls performed by the Oracle background processes. Truss provides the ability to walk through trace at step-by-step level for Oracle 11g internal processes.

Syntax:

```
truss [-fcaeil] [-[tvx] [!]syscall...] [-s [!]signal...] [-m [!]fault...] [-
[rw] [!]fd...] [-o outfile] command | -p pid
```

Typical options for truss:

- -o output to file

- -f trace child processes

- -c count system calls

- -p trace calls based on Unix PID

Example:

```
solaris02$ truss -cp 3316
^C
```

```
Syscall          seconds calls errors
read             .000       2
Write            .000              2
times            .000      33
yield            .000     226
```

Appendix B: Oracle 11g Trace Events

Oracle 11g has hundreds of undocumented trace events. The following is a comprehensive listing of these trace events which can be used for performance tuning and debugging issues for the experienced Oracle database professional. Since many of these trace events place load on production systems and may cause unforeseen consequences, this author advocates that Oracle support analysts be consulted before running most traces with these events.

Oracle 11g Database Trace Level Events

Event	Description
10000	controlfile debug event, name *'control_file'*
10001	controlfile crash event1
10002	controlfile crash event2
10003	controlfile crash event3
10004	controlfile crash event4
10005	trace latch operations for debugging
10006	testing - block recovery forced
10007	log switch debug crash after new log select, thread
10008	log switch debug crash after new log header write, thread
10009	log switch debug crash after old log header write, thread
10010	Begin Transaction
10011	End Transaction
10012	Abort Transaction

10013	Instance Recovery
10014	Roll Back to Save Point
10015	Undo Segment Recovery
10016	Undo Segment Extend
10017	Undo Segment Wrap
10018	Data Segment Create
10019	Data Segment Recovery
10020	partial link restored to linked list (KSG)
10021	latch cleanup for state objects (KSS)
10022	trace ktsgsp
10023	Create Save Undo Segment
10024	Write to Save Undo
10025	Extend Save Undo Segment
10026	Apply Save Undo
10027	Specify Deadlock Trace Information to be Dumped
10028	Dump trace information during lock / resource latch cleanup
10029	session logon (KSU)
10030	session logoff (KSU)
10031	sort debug event (S*)
10032	sort statistics (SOR*)
10033	sort run information (SRD*/SRS*)
10035	parse SQL statement (OPIPRS)
10036	create remote row source (QKANET)
10037	allocate remote row source (QKARWS)
10038	dump row source tree (QBADRV)
10039	type checking (OPITCA)

10040	dirty cache list
10041	dump undo records skipped
10042	trap error during undo application
10043	check consistency of owner/waiter/converter lists in KSQ
10044	free list undo operations
10045	free list update operations - ktsrsp, ktsunl
10046	enable SQL statement timing
10047	trace switching of sessions
10048	Undo segment shrink
10049	protect library cache memory heaps
10050	sniper trace
10051	trace OPI calls
10052	do not clean up obj$
10053	CBO Enable optimizer trace
10054	trace UNDO handling in MLS
10055	trace UNDO handing
10056	dump analyze stats (kdg)
10057	suppress file names in error messages
10058	use table scan cost in *tab$.spare1*
10059	simulate error in logfile create/clear
10060	CBO Enable predicate dump
10061	disable SMON from cleaning temp segment
10062	disable usage of OS Roles in osds
10063	disable usage of DBA and OPER privileges in osds
10064	thread enable debug crash level, thread
10065	limit library cache dump information for state object dump

10066	simulate failure to verify file
10067	force redo log checksum errors - block number
10068	force redo log checksum errors - file number
10069	Trusted Oracle test event
10070	force datafile checksum errors - block number
10071	force datafile checksum errors - file number
10072	protect latch recovery memory
10073	have PMON dump info before latch cleanup
10074	default trace function mask for kst
10075	CBO Disable outer-join to regular join conversion
10076	CBO Enable cartesian product join costing
10077	CBO Disable view-merging optimization for outer-joins
10078	CBO Disable constant predicate elimination optimization
10079	trace data sent/received via SQL*Net
10080	dump a block on a segment list which cannot be exchanged
10081	segment High Water Mark has been advanced
10082	free list head block is the same as the last block
10083	a brand new block has been requested from space management
10084	freelist becomes empty
10085	freelists have been merged
10086	CBO Enable error if kko and qka disagree on oby sort
10087	disable repair of media corrupt data blocks
10088	CBO Disable new NOT IN optimization
10089	CBO Disable index sorting
10090	invoke other events before crash recovery

10091	CBO Disable constant predicate merging
10092	CBO Disable hash join
10093	CBO Enable force hash joins
10094	before resizing a data file
10095	dump debugger commands to trace file
10096	after the cross instance call when resizing a data file
10097	after generating redo when resizing a data file
10098	after the OS has increased the size of a data file
10099	after updating the file header with the new file size
10100	after the OS has decreased the size of a data file
10101	atomic redo write recovery
10102	switch off anti-joins
10103	CBO Disable hash join swapping
10104	dump hash join statistics to trace file
10105	CBO Enable constant pred trans and MPs w *where*-clause
10106	CBO Disable evaluating correlation pred last for NOT IN
10107	CBO Always use bitmap index
10108	CBO Do not use bitmap index
10109	CBO Disable move of negated predicates
10110	CBO Try index rowid range scans
10111	Bitmap index creation switch
10112	Bitmap index creation switch
10113	Bitmap index creation switch
10114	Bitmap index creation switch
10115	CBO Bitmap optimization use maximal expression
10116	CBO Bitmap optimization switch

10117	CBO Disable new parallel cost model
10118	CBO Enable hash join costing
10119	QKA Disable GBY sort elimination
10120	generate relative file # different from absolute
10121	CBO Do not sort bitmap chains
10122	Disable transformation of count(col) to count(*)
10123	QKA Disable Bitmap And-EQuals
10124	Force creation of segmented arrays by kscsAllocate
10125	Disable remote sort elimination
10126	Debug oracle java xa
10127	Disable remote query block operation
10128	Dump Partition Pruning Information
10129	Alter histogram lookup for remote queries
10130	sort disable readaheads
10131	use *v$sql_plan* code path for explain plan
10132	dump plan after compilation
10133	testing for SQL Memory Management
10134	tracing for SQL Memory Management for session
10135	CBO do not count 0 rows partitions
10136	CBO turn off fix for bug 1089848
10137	CBO turn off fix for bug 1344111
10138	CBO turn off fix for bug 1577003
10139	CBO turn off fix for bug 1386119
10140	CBO turn off fix for bug 1332980
10141	CBO disable additional keys for inlist in bitmap optimization
10142	CBO turn off advanced OR-expansion checks

10143	CBO turn off hints
10144	CBO turn off cost based selection of bji over bsj subquery
10145	test auditing network errors
10146	enable Oracle TRACE collection
10147	enable join push through UNION view
10148	Use pre-7.3.3 random generator
10149	allow the creation of constraints with illegal date constants
10150	import exceptions
10151	Force duplicate dependency removal
10152	CBO do not consider function costs in plans
10153	Switch to use public synonym if private one does not translate
10154	Switch to disallow synonyms in DDL statements
10155	CBO disable generation of transitive OR-chains
10156	CBO disable index fast full scan
10157	CBO disable index access path for in-list
10158	CBO preserve predicate order in post-filters
10159	CBO disable order-by sort pushdown into domain indexes
10160	CBO disable use of join index
10161	CBO recursive semi-join on/off-switch
10162	CBO join-back elimination on/off-switch
10163	CBO join-back elimination on/off-switch
10164	CBO disable subquery-adjusted cardinality fix
10165	mark session to be aborted during shutdown normal
10166	trace long operation statistics updates
10167	CBO use old index MIN/MAX optimization

10168	CBO disable single-table predicate predicate generation
10169	CBO disable histograms for multi partitions
10170	CBO use old bitmap costing
10171	CBO disable transitive join predicates
10172	CBO force hash join back
10173	CBO no constraint-based join-back elimination
10174	view join-back elimination switch
10175	CBO star transformation switch
10176	CBO colocated join switch
10177	CBO colocated join switch
10178	CBO turn off hash cluster filtering through memcmp
10179	CBO turn off transitive predicate replacement
10180	temp table transformation print error messages
10181	CBO disable multi-column in-list processing
10182	CBO disable generation of implied predicates
10183	CBO disable cost rounding
10184	CBO disable OR-exp if long inlist on bitmap column
10185	CBO force index joins
10186	CBO disable index join
10187	CBO additional index join switch
10188	CBO additional index join switch
10189	CBO turn off FFS null fix
10190	Analyze use old frequency histogram collection and density
10191	Avoid conversion of in-lists back to OR-expanded form
10192	nopushdown when number of groups exceed number of rows

10193	Force repeatable sampling with specified seed
10194	CBO disable new LIKE selectivity heuristic
10195	CBO do not use check constraints for transitive predicates
10196	CBO disable index skip scan
10197	CBO force index skip scan
10198	check undo record
10199	set parameter in session
10200	consistent read buffer status
10201	consistent read undo application
10202	consistent read block header
10203	block cleanout
10204	signal recursive extend
10205	row cache debugging
10206	transaction table consistent read
10207	consistent read transactions' status report
10208	consistent read loop check
10209	enable simulated error on controlfile
10210	check data block integrity
10211	check index block integrity
10212	check cluster integrity
10213	crash after controlfile write
10214	simulate write errors on controlfile
10215	simulate read errors on controlfile
10216	dump controlfile header
10217	debug sequence numbers
10218	dump uba of applied undo

10219	monitor multi-pass row locking
10220	show updates to the transaction table
10221	show changes done with undo
10222	row cache
10223	transaction layer - turn on verification codes
10224	index block split/delete trace
10225	free/used extent row cache
10226	trace CR applications of undo for data operations
10227	verify (multi-piece) row structure
10228	trace application of redo by kcocbk
10229	simulate I/O error against datafiles
10230	check redo generation by copying before applying
10231	skip corrupted blocks *on _table_scans_*
10232	dump corrupted blocks symbolically when kcbgotten
10233	skip corrupted blocks on index operations
10234	trigger event after calling kcrapc to do redo N times
10235	check memory manager internal structures
10236	library cache manager
10237	simulate ^C (for testing purposes)
10238	instantiation manager
10239	multi-instance library cache manager
10240	dump dbas of blocks that we wait for
10241	remote SQL execution tracing/validation
10242	suppress OER 2063 (for testing distrib w/o different error log)
10243	simulated error for test of K2GTAB latch cleanup

10244	make tranids in error msgs print as 0.0.0 (for testing)
10245	simulate lock conflict error for testing PMON
10246	print trace of PMON actions to trace file
10247	Turn on scgcmn tracing (VMS ONLY)
10248	turn on tracing for dispatchers
10249	turn on tracing for multi-stated servers
10250	Trace all allocate and free calls to the topmost SGA heap
10251	check consistency of transaction table and undo block
10252	simulate write error to data file header
10253	simulate write error to redo log
10254	trace cross-instance calls
10255	PL/SQL parse checking
10256	turn off shared server load balancing
10257	trace shared server load balancing
10258	force shared servers to be chosen round-robin
10259	get error message text from remote using explicit call
10260	Trace calls to SMPRSET (VMS ONLY)
10261	Limit the size of the PGA heap
10262	Do not check for memory leaks
10263	Do not free empty PGA heap extents
10264	Collect statistics on context area usage (*x$ksmcx*)
10265	Keep random system generated output out of error messages
10266	Trace OSD stack usage
10267	Inhibit KSEDMP for testing
10268	Do not do forward coalesce when deleting extents
10269	Do not do coalesces of free space in SMON

10270	Debug shared cursors
10271	distributed transaction after COLLECT
10272	distributed transaction before PREPARE
10273	distributed transaction after PREPARE
10274	distributed transaction before COMMIT
10275	distributed transaction after COMMIT
10276	distributed transaction before FORGET
10277	Cursor sharing (or not) related event (used for testing
10278	Internal testing
10279	Simulate block corruption in kdb4chk
10280	Internal testing - segmentation fault during crash recovery
10281	maximum time to wait for process creation
10282	Inhibit signaling of other backgrounds when one dies
10283	simulate asynch I/O never completing
10284	simulate zero/infinite asynch I/O buffering
10285	Simulate controlfile header corruption
10286	Simulate controlfile open error
10287	Simulate archiver error
10288	Do not check block type in ktrget
10289	Do block dumps to trace file in hex rather than formatted
10290	kdnchk - checkvalid event - not for general purpose use
10291	die in tbsdrv to test controlfile undo
10292	dump uet entries on a 1561 from dtsdrv
10293	dump debugging information when doing block recovery
10294	enable PERSISTENT DLM operations on non-compliant systems

10295	die after file header update durning cf xact
10296	disable ORA-379
10297	customize dictionary object number cache
10298	ksfd I/O tracing
10299	Trace prefetch tracking decisions made by CKPT
10300	disable undo compatibility check at database open
10301	Enable LCK timeout table consistency check
10302	trace create or drop internal trigger
10303	trace loading of library cache for internal triggers
10304	trace replication trigger
10305	trace updatable materialized view trigger
10306	trace materialized view log trigger
10307	trace RepCat execution
10308	replication testing event
10309	Trigger Debug event
10310	trace synchronous change table trigger
10311	Disable Flashback Table Timestamp checking
10312	Allow disable to log rows into the mapping table
10313	Allow Row CR operations for single instance
10314	Enable extra stats gathering for CR
10316	Events for extensible txn header, non zero ext header size
10317	Events for extensible txn header, zero ext header size
10318	Trace extensible txn header movements
10319	Trace PGA statistics maintenance
10320	Enable data layer (kdtgrs) tracing of space management calls
10321	Datafile header verification debug failure

10322	CBO do not simplify inlist predicates
10323	before committing an add datafile command
10324	Enable better checking of redo logs errors
10325	Trace control file record section expand and shrink operations
10326	clear logfile debug crash at, log
10327	simulate ORA-00235 error for testing
10328	disable first-to-mount split-brain error, for testing
10329	simulate lost write, test detection by two-pass recovery
10330	clear MTTR statistics in checkpoint progress record
10331	simulate resilvering during recovery
10332	force *alter_system* QUIESCE RESTRICTED command to fail
10333	dump MTTR statistics each time it is updated
10334	force FG to wait to be killed during MTTR advisory simulation
10336	Do remote object transfer using remote SQL
10337	enable padding owner name in slave sql
10338	CBO do not use inlist iterator with function-based indexes
10339	CBO disable DECODE simplification
10340	Buffer queues sanity check for corrupted buffers
10341	Simulate out of PGA memory in DBWR during object reuse
10342	Raise unknown exception in ACQ_ADD when checkpointing
10343	Raise an out of memory exception-OER 4031 in ACQ_ADD
10344	Simulate kghxal returning 0 in ACQ_ADD but no exception
10345	validate queue when linking or unlinking a buffer

10346	check that all buffers for checkpoint have been written
10347	dump active checkpoint entries and checkpoint buffers
10348	test abnormal termination of process initiating file checkpoint
10349	do not allow ckpt to complete
10350	Simulate more than one object & tsn id in object reuse
10351	size of slots
10352	report direct path statistics
10353	number of slots
10354	turn on direct read path for parallel query
10355	turn on direct read path for scans
10356	turn on hint usage for direct read
10357	turn on debug information for direct path
10358	Simulate out of PGA memory in cache advisory reset
10359	turn off updates to control file for direct writes
10360	enable dbwr consistency checking
10365	turn on debug information for adaptive direct reads
10370	parallel query server kill event
10371	disable TQ hint
10372	parallel query server kill event proc
10373	parallel query server kill event
10374	parallel query server interrupt (validate lock value)
10375	turn on checks for statistics rollups
10376	turn on table queue statistics
10377	turn off load balancing
10378	force hard process/range affinity

10379	direct read for rowid range scans (unimplemented)
10380	kxfp latch cleanup testing event
10381	kxfp latch cleanup testing event
10382	parallel query server interrupt (reset)
10383	auto parallelization testing event
10384	parallel dataflow scheduler tracing
10385	parallel table scan range sampling method
10386	parallel SQL hash and range statistics
10387	parallel query server interrupt (normal)
10388	parallel query server interrupt (failure)
10389	parallel query server interrupt (cleanup)
10390	Trace parallel query slave execution
10391	trace PX granule allocation/assignment
10392	parallel query debugging bits
10393	print parallel query statistics
10394	generate a fake load to test adaptive and load balancing
10395	adjust sample size for range table queues
10396	circumvent range table queues for queries
10397	suppress verbose parallel coordinator error reporting
10398	enable timeouts in parallel query threads
10399	trace buffer allocation
10400	turn on system state dumps for shutdown debugging
10401	turn on IPC (ksxp) debugging
10402	turn on IPC (skgxp) debugging
10403	fake CPU number for default degree of parallelism
10404	crash dbwr after write

10405	emulate broken mirrors
10406	enable datetime TIMESTAMP, INTERVAL datatype creation
10407	enable datetime TIME datatype creation
10408	disable OLAP builtin window function usage
10409	enable granule memset and block invalidation at startup
10410	trigger simulated communications errors in KSXP
10411	simulate errors in IMR
10412	trigger simulated errors in CGS/CM interface
10413	force simulated error for testing purposes
10414	simulated error from event level
10425	enable global enqueue service open event trace
10426	enable global enqueue service convert event trace
10427	enable global enqueue service traffic controller event trace
10428	enable tracing of global enqueue service distributed resource
10429	enable tracing of global enqueue service IPC calls
10430	enable tracing of global enqueue service AST calls
10431	enable verification messages on pi consistency
10432	enable tracing of global cache service fusion calls
10433	global enqueue service testing event
10434	enable tracing of global enqueue service multiple LMS
10435	enable tracing of global enqueue service deadlock detection
10436	enable global cache service duplicate ping checking
10437	enable trace of global enqueue service S optimized resources
10442	enable trace of kst for ORA-01555 diagnostics
10450	signal ctrl-c in kdddca (drop column) after n rows

10498	disable fix for 2645455
10499	revert to old scale behavior
10500	turn on traces for SMON
10501	periodically check selected heap
10502	CBO disable the fix for bug 2098120
10503	enable user-specified graduated bind lengths
10504	CBO disable the fix for bug 2607029
10510	turn off SMON check to offline pending offline rollback segment
10511	turn off SMON check to cleanup undo dictionary
10512	turn off SMON check to shrink rollback segments
10513	turn off wrap source compression
10515	turn on event to use physical cleanout
10520	recreate package/procedure/view only if definition has changed
10550	signal error during create as select/create index after n rows
10560	block type"
10561	block type ", data object#
10562	Error occurred while applying redo to data block (file#, block#)
10563	Test recovery had to corrupt data block (file#, block#) in order to proceed
10564	tablespace
10565	Another test recovery session is active
10566	Test recovery has used all the memory it can use
10567	Redo is inconsistent with data block (file#, block#)
10568	Failed to allocate recovery state object: out of SGA memory

10570	Test recovery complete
10571	Test recovery canceled
10572	Test recovery canceled due to errors
10573	Test recovery tested redo from change to
10574	Test recovery did not corrupt any data block
10575	Give up restoring recovered datafiles to consistent state: out of memory
10576	Give up restoring recovered datafiles to consistent state: some error occurred
10577	Cannot invoke test recovery for managed standby database recovery
10578	Cannot allow corruption for managed standby database recovery
10579	Cannot modify control file during test recovery
10580	Cannot modify datafile header during test recovery
10581	Cannot modify redo log header during test recovery
10582	The control file is not a backup control file
10583	Cannot recovery file renamed as missing during test recovery
10584	Cannot invoke parallel recovery for test recovery
10585	Test recovery cannot apply redo that may modify control file
10586	Test recovery had to corrupt 1 data block in order to proceed
10587	Invalid count for ALLOW n CORRUPTION option
10588	Can only allow 1 corruption for normal media/standby recovery
10589	Test recovery had to corrupt data blocks in order to proceed
10590	kga (argus debugger) test flags
10591	kga (argus debugger) test flags

10592	kga (argus debugger) test flags
10593	kga (argus debugger) test flags
10594	kga (argus debugger) test flags
10595	kga (argus debugger) test flags
10596	kga (argus debugger) test flags
10597	kga (argus debugger) test flags
10598	kga (argus debugger) test flags
10599	kga (argus debugger) test flags
10600	check cursor frame allocation
10601	turn on debugging for *cursor_sharing* (literal replacement)
10602	cause an access violation (for testing purposes)
10603	cause an error to occur during truncate (for testing purposes)
10604	trace parallel create index
10605	enable parallel create index by default
10606	trace parallel create index
10607	trace index rowid partition scan
10608	trace create bitmap index
10609	trace for array index insertion
10610	trace create index pseudo optimizer
10611	causes migration to fail - testing only
10612	prints debug information for auto-space managed segments
10613	prints debug information for auto-space managed segments
10614	Operation not allowed on this segment
10615	Invalid tablespace type for temporary tablespace
10616	Operation not allowed on this tablespace

10617	Cannot create rollback segment in dictionary managed tablespace
10618	Operation not allowed on this segment
10619	Avoid assertions when possible
10620	Operation not allowed on this segment
10621	data block does not belong to the segment
10622	test/trace online index (re)build
10623	Enable Index range scan Prefetch - testing only
10624	Disable UJV invalidation on drop index
10625	Turn off redo log dump for the index when OERI 12700
10627	Dump the content of the index leaf block
10628	Turn on sanity check for kdiss index skip scan state
10640	Operation not permitted during SYSTEM tablespace migration
10641	Cannot find a rollback segment to bind to
10642	Found rollback segments in dictionary managed tablespaces
10643	Database should be mounted in restricted mode and Exclusive mode
10644	SYSTEM tablespace cannot be default temporary tablespace
10645	Recursive Extension in SYSTEM tablespace during migration
10646	Too many recursive extensions during SYSTEM tablespace migration
10647	Tablespace other than SYSTEM,, not found in read only mode
10650	disable cache-callback optimization
10651	incorrect file number block number specified
10666	Do not get database enqueue name

10667	Cause sppst to check for valid process ids
10690	Set shadow process core file dump type (Unix only)
10691	Set background process core file type (Unix only)
10700	Alter access violation exception handler
10701	Dump direct loader index keys
10702	Enable histogram data generation
10703	Simulate process death during enqueue get
10704	Print out information about what enqueues are being obtained
10705	Print Out Tracing information for every I/O done by ODSs
10706	Print out information about global enqueue manipulation
10707	Simulate process death for instance registration
10708	print out trace information from the RAC buffer cache
10709	enable parallel instances in create index by default
10710	trace bitmap index access
10711	trace bitmap index merge
10712	trace bitmap index or
10713	trace bitmap index and
10714	trace bitmap index minus
10715	trace bitmap index conversion to rowids
10716	trace bitmap index compress/decompress
10717	trace bitmap index compaction trace for index creation
10718	event to disable automatic compaction after index creation
10719	trace bitmap index dml
10720	trace db scheduling
10721	Internal testing - temp table transformation

10722	set parameters for CPU frequency calculation (debug)
10723	Internal testing - release buffer for buffer cache shrink
10724	trace cross-instance broadcast
10730	trace row level security policy predicates
10731	dump SQL for CURSOR expressions
10740	disables fix for bug 598861
10750	test rollback segment blksize guessing for index array insert
10800	disable Smart Disk scan
10801	enable Smart Disk trace
10802	reserved for Smart Disk
10803	write timing statistics on cluster database recovery scan
10804	reserved for ksxb
10806	Switch to 7.3 mode when detaching sessions
10807	Disable user id check when switching to a global transaction
10810	Trace snapshot too old
10811	Trace block cleanouts
10812	Trace Consistent Reads
10826	enable upgrade/downgrade error message trace
10827	database must be opened with MIGRATE option
10830	Trace group by sort row source
10831	Trace group by rollup row source
10841	Default un-initialized character set form to SQLCS_IMPLICIT
10842	Event for OCI Tracing and Statistics Info
10850	Enable time manager tracing
10851	Allow Drop command to drop queue tables

10852	Enable tracing for Enqueue Dequeue Operations
10853	event for AQ statistics latch cleanup testing
10856	Disable AQ propagator from using streaming
10857	Force AQ propagator to use two-phase commit
10858	Crash the AQ propagator at different stages of commit
10859	Disable updates of message retry count
10860	event for AQ admin disable new name parser
10861	disable storing extended message properties
10862	resolve default queue owner to current user in enqueue/dequeue
10871	dump file open/close timestamp during media recovery
10900	extent manager fault insertion event #
10902	disable seghdr conversion for ro operation
10903	Force tablespaces to become locally managed
10904	Allow locally managed tablespaces to have user allocation
10905	Do cache verification (kcbcxx) on extent allocation
10906	Unable to extend segment after insert direct load
10907	Trace extent management events
10908	Trace temp tablespace events
10909	Trace free list events
10910	inject corner case events into the RAC buffer cache
10911	Locally managed SYSTEM tablespace bitmaps
10912	Used to perform admin operations on locally managed SYSTEM tablespace
10913	Create locally managed database if compatible > 920 by default
10924	import storage parse error ignore event

10925	Trace name context forever
10926	Trace name context forever
10927	Trace name context forever
10928	Trace name context forever
10929	Trace name context forever
10930	Trace name context forever
10931	Trace name context forever
10932	Trace name context forever
10933	Trace name context forever
10934	Reserved. Used only in version 7.x.
10935	Reserved. Used only in version 7.x.
10936	Trace name context forever
10937	Trace name context forever
10938	Trace name context forever
10939	Trace name context forever
10940	Trace name context forever
10941	Trace name context forever
10943	Trace name context forever
10944	Trace name context forever
10945	Trace name context forever
10970	backout event for bug 2133357
10975	trace execution of parallel propagation
10976	internal package related tracing
10977	trace event for RepAPI
10979	trace flags for join index implementation

10980	prevent sharing of parsed query during Materialized View query generation
10981	dscn computation-related event in replication
10982	event to turn off CDC-format MV Logs
10983	event to enable *create_change_table* debugging
10984	subquery materialized view-related event
10985	event for NULL refresh of materialized views
10986	do not use *hash_aj* in refresh
10987	event for the support of caching table with object feature
10988	event to get exclusive lock during materialized view refresh in IAS
10989	event to internally create statistics MV
10996	event to make a process hold a latch in ksu
10999	do not get database enqueue name

Appendix C: ORA-0600 Troubleshooting

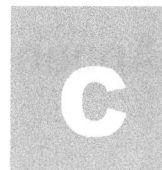

Oracle Metalink provides an excellent support tool to lookup the root cause of ORA-0600 Internal errors. The lookup tool is available from Oracle Support on Metalink Note 153788.1: Troubleshoot an ORA-600 Error using the ORA-600 Argument Lookup Tool. Below is a sample of the tool for diagnosing ORA-0600 internal errors for Oracle 11g.

ORA-600/ORA-7445 Troubleshooter

Lookup By Code

Error Code: ORA-600

ORA-600 First Argument: ORA-00600: internal error code, ar

Database Version (optional): 11.1.x

[Lookup Error] [Reset Form]

Search Call Stack

☐ Show Search Criteria

[Search Call Stack] [Reset Form]

Figure C.1: *Sample of the ORA-0600 Argument Lookup Tool*

Appendix D: References

Chapter 1: Introduction

Oracle Metalink Note #466931.1: 11g Top New Features Summary

Oracle Metalink Note #454927.1: Using and Disabling the Automatic Diagnostic Repository (ADR) with Oracle Net for 11g

Oracle Metalink Note #443529.1: 11g How To Package And Send ORA-00600/ORA-07445 Diagnostic Information To Support

Oracle Metalink Note #438148.1: Finding *alert.log* file in 11g

Oracle Metalink Note #422893.1: 11g Understanding Automatic Diagnostic Repository

Oracle Metalink Note #453125.1: 11g Diagnosability: Frequently Asked Questions

Oracle Metalink Note #454442.1: 11g Install - Understanding about Oracle Base, Oracle Home and Oracle Inventory Locations

Oracle® Database Utilities
11g Release 1 (11.1)
Part Number B28319-02
http://tahiti.oracle.com/

Chapter 2: Oracle 11g Memory

Oracle Metalink Note #44376.1: Automatic Memory Management (AMM) on 11g

Oracle Metalink Note #6820317.8: Bug 6820317- DBVERIFY fails with DBV-0600 [22] if no write permissions on file

Oracle Metalink Note #255409.1: Size Shared Pool using *v$shared_pool_advice*

Oracle Metalink Note #558671.1: Getting ORA-01461 while INSERT INTO WWV_THINGS

Oracle Metalink Note #148511.1: Oracle Dynamic Buffer Cache Advisory

Oracle Metalink Note #453567.1: 11g New Feature: SQL Query Result Cache

Oracle Metalink Note #311302.1: How to Generate A Stack Trace of A Hanging Discoverer Session or Core Dump File Using GDB

Oracle Metalink Note #225349.1: Implementing Address Windowing Extensions (AWE) or VLM on Windows Platforms

Oracle Metalink Note #46001.1: Oracle Database and the Windows NT memory architecture, Technical Bulletin

Oracle® Database Reference
11g Release 1 (11.1)
Part Number B28320-02

Oracle® Database Concepts
11g Release 1 (11.1)
Part Number B28318-05

Chapter 3: Database Locks

Oracle® Database Concepts
11g Release 1 (11.1)
Part Number B28318-05

Oracle® Database Reference
11g Release 1 (11.1)
Part Number B28320-02

Oracle 8i Internal Services, Steve Adams
1999, O'Reilly Press

Oracle Wait Interface: A Practical Guide to Performance Diagnostics
and Tuning
Shee, et al, Oracle Press, 2004

Chapter 4: Database Latches

Oracle Metalink Notes:

ML #22908.1: What are Latches and What Causes Latch Contention

ML #104426.1: Short Wait and Long Wait Latches

Oracle® Database Concepts
11g Release 1 (11.1)
Part Number B28318-05

Oracle® Database Reference
11g Release 1 (11.1)
Part Number B28320-02

Oracle 8i Internal Services, Steve Adams
1999, O'Reilly Press

Oracle Wait Interface: A Practical Guide to Performance Diagnostics and Tuning, Shee, et all, Oracle Press, 2004

Chapter 5: Hidden Oracle 11g Parameters

Burleson, D., Oracle 11g Hidden Undocumented Parameters, April 2009
http://www.dba-oracle.com/t_11g_hidden_parameters.htm

Chapter 6: V$ Views

Oracle Metalink Note #220021.1: V$ View Definitions Library
Oracle Database 10g Performance Tuning - Tips and Techniques
Niemec, Richard, Oracle Press, 2007

Chapter 7: X$ Tables for 11g

Burleson, Donald K., Oracle Tips: Querying the X$ Structures
http://www.oracle-training.cc/oracle_tips_x$.htm

Poder, Tanel, Reading Alert Log Via SQL
http://blog.tanelpoder.com

Oracle Metalink: various notes
Oracle Metalink Note #34405.1: Buffer Busy Waits

Oracle Metalink Note #22241.1: Subject: List of X$ Tables and how the names are derived

Oracle Database 10g Performance Tuning: Tips and Techniques
Niemec, Richard, Oracle Press, 2007

Appendix A: Oracle 11g Database Internal Toolkit

Oracle Metalink Note #396940.1: Troubleshooting and Diagnosing ORA-4031 Error

Oracle Metalink Note #118252.1: How to Process an Express Core File Using dbx, dbg, dde, gdb

Oracle Metalink Note #46001: Oracle Database and the Windows NT memory architecture

Oracle Metalink Note #17613.1: ORA-03113 on UNIX

Oracle Metalink Note #224176.1: How to use OS commands to diagnose Database Performance Issues

Oracle Metalink Note #233869.1: Diagnosing and Resolving ORA-4030 Errors

Oracle Metalink Note #29786.1: Suptool Oradebug

Oracle Metalink Note #1812.1: TECH - Getting a Stack Trace from a CORE file

Oracle Metalink Note #69882.1: Windows NT - Killing an Oracle Thread

Appendix B: Oracle 11g Trace Events

Oracle Trace Events
https://netfiles.uiuc.edu/jstrode/www/oraparm/events.html

Oracle Metalink Support Notes

Appendix C: ORA-0600

Oracle Metalink Note #260459.1: How to Analyze Problems Related to Internal Errors (ORA-600) and Core Dumps (ORA-7445)

Oracle Metalink Note #153788.1: Troubleshoot an ORA-600 or ORA-7445 Error Using the Error Lookup Tool

Appendix E: Strace

Oracle Metalink Note #1078106.6: How to Get a Trace File From a Proc Core Dump on Linux

Appendix F: Using GDB for Oracle 11g

Oracle Metalink Note #362791.1: STACKX User Guide

Oracle Metalink Note #278173.1: How to generate and analyze the core files on Linux

Oracle Metalink Note #311302.1: How to Generate A Stack Trace of A Hanging Discoverer Session or Core Dump File Using GDB

Appendix G: Orakill for Windows and Oracle 11g

Oracle Metalink Note #69882.1: Windows NT - Killing an Oracle Thread

Oracle Metalink Note #110751.1: How to Kill Oracle Threads within the Microsoft Management Console (MMC)

Appendix E: Using Strace

E

Strace for Oracle 11g and Linux

One of the best system tools for internal troubleshooting of Oracle 11g problems on Linux platform is the Strace tool. Some examples and syntax will be provided on how to get started with this powerful tracing tool for Oracle 11g on the Linux platform. With the push from Oracle to develop on the Linux platform as their prime choice for operating systems, Strace will be the system tool of choice with Oracle 11g environments running on Red Hat Linux (RHEL) and Oracle Enterprise Linux (OEL) among many other popular flavors of the Linux operating system.

Command Options for Strace with Linux for Oracle 11g

```
[oracle@raclinux1 ~]$ strace

usage: strace [-dffhiqrtttTvVxx] [-a column] [-e expr] ... [-o file]
              [-p pid] ... [-s strsize] [-u username] [-E var=val]
              [command [arg ...]]
   or: strace -c [-e expr] ... [-O overhead] [-S sortby] [-E var=val] ...
              [command [arg ...]]
-c -- count time, calls, and errors for each syscall and report summary
-f -- follow forks, -ff -- with output into separate files
-F -- attempt to follow vforks, -h -- print help message
-i -- print instruction pointer at time of syscall
-q -- suppress messages about attaching, detaching, etc.
-r -- print relative timestamp, -t -- absolute timestamp, -tt -- with usecs
-T -- print time spent in each syscall, -V -- print version
-v -- verbose mode: print unabbreviated argv, stat, termio[s], etc. args
-x -- print non-ascii strings in hex, -xx -- print all strings in hex
-a column -- alignment COLUMN for printing syscall results (default 40)
-e expr -- a qualifying expression: option=[!]all or
option=[!]val1[,val2]...
   options: trace, abbrev, verbose, raw, signal, read, or write
-o file -- send trace output to FILE instead of stderr
-O overhead -- set overhead for tracing syscalls to OVERHEAD usecs
-p pid -- trace process with process id PID, may be repeated
-s strsize -- limit length of print strings to STRSIZE chars (default 32)
-S sortby -- sort syscall counts by: time, calls, name, nothing (default
time)
-u username -- run command as username handling setuid and/or setgid
```

```
-E var=val -- put var=val in the environment for command
-E var -- remove var from the environment for command
```

Perform a full trace for Oracle Process with Strace for Oracle 11g:

```
[oracle@raclinux1 ~]$ strace oracle

execve("/u01/app/oracle/product/11.1.0/11g/bin/oracle", ["oracle"], [/* 41
vars */]) = 0
uname({sys="Linux", node="raclinux1.us.oracle.com", ...}) = 0
brk(0)                                  = 0xf56b000
access("/etc/ld.so.preload", R_OK)      = -1 ENOENT (No such file or
directory)
open("/u01/app/oracle/product/11.1.0/11g/lib/tls/i686/sse2/libskgxp11.so",
O_RDONLY) = -1 ENOENT (No such file or directory)
stat64("/u01/app/oracle/product/11.1.0/11g/lib/tls/i686/sse2", 0xbfffecd8) =
-1 ENOENT (No such file or directory)
open("/u01/app/oracle/product/11.1.0/11g/lib/tls/i686/libskgxp11.so",
O_RDONLY) = -1 ENOENT (No such file or directory)
stat64("/u01/app/oracle/product/11.1.0/11g/lib/tls/i686", 0xbfffecd8) = -1
ENOENT (No such file or directory)
open("/u01/app/oracle/product/11.1.0/11g/lib/tls/sse2/libskgxp11.so",
O_RDONLY) = -1 ENOENT (No such file or directory)
stat64("/u01/app/oracle/product/11.1.0/11g/lib/tls/sse2", 0xbfffecd8) = -1
ENOENT (No such file or directory)
open("/u01/app/oracle/product/11.1.0/11g/lib/tls/libskgxp11.so", O_RDONLY) =
-1 ENOENT (No such file or directory)
stat64("/u01/app/oracle/product/11.1.0/11g/lib/tls", 0xbfffecd8) = -1 ENOENT
(No such file or directory)
open("/u01/app/oracle/product/11.1.0/11g/lib/i686/sse2/libskgxp11.so",
O_RDONLY) = -1 ENOENT (No such file or directory)
stat64("/u01/app/oracle/product/11.1.0/11g/lib/i686/sse2", 0xbfffecd8) = -1
ENOENT (No such file or directory)
open("/u01/app/oracle/product/11.1.0/11g/lib/i686/libskgxp11.so", O_RDONLY)
= -1 ENOENT (No such file or directory)
stat64("/u01/app/oracle/product/11.1.0/11g/lib/i686", 0xbfffecd8) = -1
ENOENT (No such file or directory)
open("/u01/app/oracle/product/11.1.0/11g/lib/sse2/libskgxp11.so", O_RDONLY)
= -1 ENOENT (No such file or directory)
stat64("/u01/app/oracle/product/11.1.0/11g/lib/sse2", 0xbfffecd8) = -1
ENOENT (No such file or directory)
open("/u01/app/oracle/product/11.1.0/11g/lib/libskgxp11.so", O_RDONLY) = 3
read(3, "\177ELF\1\1\1\0\0\0\0\0\0\0\0\0\3\0\3\0\1\0\0\0\3204\0"..., 512) =
512
fstat64(3, {st_mode=S_IFREG|0644, st_size=274114, ...}) = 0
old_mmap(NULL, 206592, PROT_READ|PROT_EXEC, MAP_PRIVATE|MAP_DENYWRITE, 3, 0)
= 0x9f4000
old_mmap(0xa25000, 8192, PROT_READ|PROT_WRITE,
MAP_PRIVATE|MAP_FIXED|MAP_DENYWRITE, 3, 0x31000) = 0xa25000
close(3)                                = 0
open("/u01/app/oracle/product/11.1.0/11g/lib/librt.so.1", O_RDONLY) = -1
ENOENT (No such file or directory)
open("/u01/app/oracle/product/11.1.0/11g/lib/librt.so.1", O_RDONLY) = -1
ENOENT (No such file or directory)
open("/lib/tls/i686/sse2/librt.so.1", O_RDONLY) = -1 ENOENT (No such file or
directory)
```

```
stat64("/lib/tls/i686/sse2", 0xbfffecbc) = -1 ENOENT (No such file or
directory)open("/lib/tls/i686/librt.so.1", O_RDONLY) = -1 ENOENT (No such
file or directory)
stat64("/lib/tls/i686", {st_mode=S_IFDIR|0755, st_size=4096, ...}) = 0
open("/lib/tls/sse2/librt.so.1", O_RDONLY) = -1 ENOENT (No such file or
directory)
stat64("/lib/tls/sse2", 0xbfffecbc)     = -1 ENOENT (No such file or
directory)
open("/lib/tls/librt.so.1", O_RDONLY)    = 3
read(3, "\177ELF\1\1\1\0\0\0\0\0\0\0\0\0\3\0\3\0\1\0\0\0\320\220"..., 512) =
512fstat64(3, {st_mode=S_IFREG|0755, st_size=47851, ...}) = 0
old_mmap(NULL, 4096, PROT_READ|PROT_WRITE, MAP_PRIVATE|MAP_ANONYMOUS, -1, 0)
= 0xb7fff000
old_mmap(0xdd7000, 81656, PROT_READ|PROT_EXEC, MAP_PRIVATE|MAP_DENYWRITE, 3,
0) = 0xdd7000
old_mmap(0xddf000, 8192, PROT_READ|PROT_WRITE,
MAP_PRIVATE|MAP_FIXED|MAP_DENYWRITE, 3, 0x7000) = 0xddf000
old_mmap(0xde1000, 40696, PROT_READ|PROT_WRITE,
MAP_PRIVATE|MAP_FIXED|MAP_ANONYMOUS, -1, 0) = 0xde1000
close(3)                                 = 0


[oracle@raclinux1 ~]$ clear

[oracle@raclinux1 ~]$ strace oracle

execve("/u01/app/oracle/product/11.1.0/11g/bin/oracle", ["oracle"], [/* 41
vars */]) = 0
uname({sys="Linux", node="raclinux1.us.oracle.com", ...}) = 0
brk(0)                                   = 0xf56b000
access("/etc/ld.so.preload", R_OK)       = -1 ENOENT (No such file or
directory)
open("/u01/app/oracle/product/11.1.0/11g/lib/tls/i686/sse2/libskgxp11.so",
O_RDONLY) = -1 ENOENT (No such file or directory)
stat64("/u01/app/oracle/product/11.1.0/11g/lib/tls/i686/sse2", 0xbfffecd8) =
-1 ENOENT (No such file or directory)
open("/u01/app/oracle/product/11.1.0/11g/lib/tls/i686/libskgxp11.so",
O_RDONLY) = -1 ENOENT (No such file or directory)
stat64("/u01/app/oracle/product/11.1.0/11g/lib/tls/i686", 0xbfffecd8) = -1
ENOENT (No such file or directory)
open("/u01/app/oracle/product/11.1.0/11g/lib/tls/sse2/libskgxp11.so",
O_RDONLY) = -1 ENOENT (No such file or directory)
stat64("/u01/app/oracle/product/11.1.0/11g/lib/tls/sse2", 0xbfffecd8) = -1
ENOENT (No such file or directory)
open("/u01/app/oracle/product/11.1.0/11g/lib/tls/libskgxp11.so", O_RDONLY) =
-1 ENOENT (No such file or directory)
stat64("/u01/app/oracle/product/11.1.0/11g/lib/tls", 0xbfffecd8) = -1 ENOENT
(No such file or directory)
open("/u01/app/oracle/product/11.1.0/11g/lib/i686/sse2/libskgxp11.so",
O_RDONLY) = -1 ENOENT (No such file or directory)
stat64("/u01/app/oracle/product/11.1.0/11g/lib/i686/sse2", 0xbfffecd8) = -1
ENOENT (No such file or directory)
open("/u01/app/oracle/product/11.1.0/11g/lib/i686/libskgxp11.so", O_RDONLY)
= -1 ENOENT (No such file or directory)
stat64("/u01/app/oracle/product/11.1.0/11g/lib/i686", 0xbfffecd8) = -1
ENOENT (No such file or directory)
open("/u01/app/oracle/product/11.1.0/11g/lib/sse2/libskgxp11.so", O_RDONLY)
= -1 ENOENT (No such file or directory)
```

```
stat64("/u01/app/oracle/product/11.1.0/11g/lib/sse2", 0xbfffecd8) = -1
ENOENT (No such file or directory)
open("/u01/app/oracle/product/11.1.0/11g/lib/libskgxp11.so", O_RDONLY) = 3
read(3, "\177ELF\1\1\1\0\0\0\0\0\0\0\0\0\3\0\3\0\1\0\0\0\3204\0"..., 512) =
512
fstat64(3, {st_mode=S_IFREG|0644, st_size=274114, ...}) = 0
old_mmap(NULL, 206592, PROT_READ|PROT_EXEC, MAP_PRIVATE|MAP_DENYWRITE, 3, 0)
= 0x2c9000
old_mmap(0x2fa000, 8192, PROT_READ|PROT_WRITE,
MAP_PRIVATE|MAP_FIXED|MAP_DENYWRITE, 3, 0x31000) = 0x2fa000
close(3)                                = 0
open("/u01/app/oracle/product/11.1.0/11g/lib/librt.so.1", O_RDONLY) = -1
ENOENT (No such file or directory)
open("/u01/app/oracle/product/11.1.0/11g/lib/librt.so.1", O_RDONLY) = -1
ENOENT (No such file or directory)
open("/lib/tls/i686/sse2/librt.so.1", O_RDONLY) = -1 ENOENT (No such file or
directory)
[oracle@raclinux1 ~]$
```

Check for system call errors for Oracle 11g with Strace:

```
[oracle@raclinux1 bin]$ strace -c oracle

% time     seconds  usecs/call     calls    errors syscall
------ ----------- ----------- --------- --------- ----------------
  4.19    0.865232       41202        21           write
  4.02    0.831352      207838         4           lstat64
  4.02    0.831329      207832         4           _llseek
  4.02    0.831327      207832         4           times
  3.42    0.707903      707903         1           io_setup
  3.42    0.707867      707867         1           _sysctl
  3.42    0.707864      707864         1           socket
  3.42    0.707843      707843         1           bind
  3.42    0.707839      707839         1           set_thread_area
  3.42    0.707837      707837         1           futex
  3.42    0.707836      707836         1           dup
  3.42    0.707836      707836         1           set_tid_address
  3.42    0.707835      707835         1           gettid
  3.42    0.707833      707833         1           fcntl64
  3.42    0.707831      707831         1           getuid32
  3.42    0.707831      707831         1           geteuid32
  3.21    0.662962       82870         8           mprotect
  3.21    0.662671       82834         8           gettimeofday
  2.77    0.572299       26014        22           fstat64
  2.71    0.560835       12192        46           old_mmap
  2.66    0.549201      109840         5           shmdt
  2.61    0.539206      107841         5           shmat
  2.61    0.539194      107839         5         5 access
  2.61    0.539158      107832         5           rt_sigprocmask
  2.46    0.509131        2204       231           close
  2.39    0.494136       41178        12         9 shmget
  2.01    0.415677      207839         2           uname
  1.57    0.325381       20336        16        16 mkdir
  1.30    0.268287        5708        47        17 stat64
  1.27    0.263489         909       290        61 open
  1.19    0.246993       41166         6           getrlimit
```

```
 1.19    0.246990       41165        6          rt_sigaction
 0.87    0.179247        2938       61          read
 0.60    0.123500       41167        3          brk
 0.60    0.123500       41167        3          setrlimit
 0.60    0.123494       41165        3          lseek
 2.70   -1.1557161       2786      200           mmap2
 1.52   -1.1313491       2986      105           munmap
------  -----------  -----------  ---------  ---------  ----------------
100.00   20.669398                1134       108 total
```

Tracing Single Oracle 11g Process for Database Writer (DBWR):

```
[oracle@raclinux1 ~]$ ps -ef|grep dbw

oracle    3873    1  0 Aug23 ?        00:00:02 ora_dbw0_ORA11G
oracle    1650 32699  0 02:13 pts/6   00:00:00 grep dbw

[oracle@raclinux1 ~]$ strace -p 3873

Process 3873 attached - interrupt to quit
gettimeofday({1219558406, 240152}, NULL) = 0
gettimeofday({1219558406, 240431}, NULL) = 0
gettimeofday({1219558406, 240647}, NULL) = 0
gettimeofday({1219558406, 240847}, NULL) = 0
gettimeofday({1219558406, 241046}, NULL) = 0
gettimeofday({1219558406, 254813}, NULL) = 0
gettimeofday({1219558406, 255022}, NULL) = 0
times(NULL)                              = 1193596
gettimeofday({1219558406, 255477}, NULL) = 0
gettimeofday({1219558406, 255678}, NULL) = 0
semtimedop(98304, 0xbfffe084, 1, {2, 920000000}) = -1 EAGAIN (Resource
temporarily unavailable)
```

Find System calls for Oracle 11g DBWR process:

```
[oracle@raclinux1 ~]$ strace -c -p 3873

Process 3873 attached - interrupt to quit
Process 3873 detached

% time     seconds  usecs/call     calls    errors syscall
------  ----------- -----------  ---------  --------- ----------------
 82.95    0.003289          12       282           gettimeofday
  7.92    0.000314           8        40           times
  5.42    0.000215           8        26           getrusage
  1.99    0.000079           6        13        13 semtimedop
  0.76    0.000030          30         1           open
  0.68    0.000027          27         1           read
  0.28    0.000011          11         1           close
------  ----------- -----------  ---------  --------- ----------------
100.00    0.003965                   364        13 total
```

Appendix F: Using GDB with Oracle 11g

F

Linux provides a potent debugger called GDB that can be used to discover root level problems with Oracle system processes. While a full discussion is beyond the scope of this book, some examples will be provided to show how to use this useful tool. Please consult the Oracle Metalink Support notes for additional details. The main page for GDB shows the syntax help menu. In addition, http://linux.die.net/man/1/gdb provides basics on using GDB.

Introduction to GDB with Oracle 11g

First one needs to find the Oracle 11g process that will be traced with GDB for Oracle 11g and Linux. In this case study, trace SQL*Plus activity.

> 💣 Warning: Please be careful to use these low-level system level tools ONLY under the guidance of Oracle Support for production systems as they affect memory and the Oracle 11g kernel and, without caution, may cause serious unintended consequences!

```
[oracle@raclinux1 ~]$ ps -ef|grep sqlplus

oracle    3106  2809  0 02:23 pts/4    00:00:00 sqlplus
oracle    3171  3110  0 02:23 pts/5    00:00:00 grep sqlplus


[oracle@raclinux1 ~]$ ps -ef|grep 3106

oracle    3106  2809  0 02:23 pts/4    00:00:00 sqlplus
oracle    3107  3106  0 02:23 ?        00:00:00 oracleORA11G
(DESCRIPTION=(LOCAL=YES)(ADDRESS=(PROTOCOL=beq)))
oracle    3173  3110  0 02:23 pts/5    00:00:00 grep 3106
```

Now that the process ID (3106) for SQL*Plus is obtained, it is time to begin the debug session with GDB for Oracle 11g and Linux.

```
[oracle@raclinux1 ~]$ gdb $ORACLE_HOME/bin/oracle 3107

GNU gdb Red Hat Linux (6.1post-1.20040607.62rh)
Copyright 2004 Free Software Foundation, Inc.
GDB is free software, covered by the GNU General Public License, and you are
welcome to change it and/or distribute copies of it under certain
conditions.
Type "show copying" to see the conditions.
There is absolutely no warranty for GDB.  Type "show warranty" for details.
This GDB was configured as "i386-redhat-linux-gnu"...(no debugging symbols
found)...Using host libthread_db library "/lib/tls/libthread_db.so.1".

Attaching to program: /u01/app/oracle/product/11.1.0/11g/bin/oracle, process
3107
Reading symbols from
/u01/app/oracle/product/11.1.0/11g/lib/libskgxp11.so...(no debugging symbols
found)...done.
Loaded symbols for /u01/app/oracle/product/11.1.0/11g/lib/libskgxp11.so
Reading symbols from /lib/tls/librt.so.1...(no debugging symbols
found)...done.
Loaded symbols for /lib/tls/librt.so.1
Reading symbols from
/u01/app/oracle/product/11.1.0/11g/lib/libnnz11.so...(no debugging symbols
found)...done.
Loaded symbols for /u01/app/oracle/product/11.1.0/11g/lib/libnnz11.so
Reading symbols from
/u01/app/oracle/product/11.1.0/11g/lib/libclsra11.so...done.
Loaded symbols for /u01/app/oracle/product/11.1.0/11g/lib/libclsra11.so
Reading symbols from
/u01/app/oracle/product/11.1.0/11g/lib/libdbcfg11.so...done.
Loaded symbols for /u01/app/oracle/product/11.1.0/11g/lib/libdbcfg11.so
Reading symbols from
/u01/app/oracle/product/11.1.0/11g/lib/libhasgen11.so...done.
Loaded symbols for /u01/app/oracle/product/11.1.0/11g/lib/libhasgen11.so
Reading symbols from
/u01/app/oracle/product/11.1.0/11g/lib/libskgxn2.so...done.Loaded symbols
for /u01/app/oracle/product/11.1.0/11g/lib/libskgxn2.so
Reading symbols from
/u01/app/oracle/product/11.1.0/11g/lib/libocr11.so...done.
Loaded symbols for /u01/app/oracle/product/11.1.0/11g/lib/libocr11.so
Reading symbols from
/u01/app/oracle/product/11.1.0/11g/lib/libocrb11.so...done.Loaded symbols
for /u01/app/oracle/product/11.1.0/11g/lib/libocrb11.so
Reading symbols from
/u01/app/oracle/product/11.1.0/11g/lib/libocrutl11.so...done.
Loaded symbols for /u01/app/oracle/product/11.1.0/11g/lib/libocrutl11.so
Reading symbols from /usr/lib/libaio.so.1...done.
Loaded symbols for /usr/lib/libaio.so.1
Reading symbols from /lib/libdl.so.2...done.
Loaded symbols for /lib/libdl.so.2
Reading symbols from /lib/tls/libm.so.6...done.
Loaded symbols for /lib/tls/libm.so.6
Reading symbols from /lib/tls/libpthread.so.0...done.
```

```
[Thread debugging using libthread_db enabled]
[New Thread -1208035648 (LWP 3107)]
Loaded symbols for /lib/tls/libpthread.so.0
Reading symbols from /lib/libnsl.so.1...done.
Loaded symbols for /lib/libnsl.so.1
Reading symbols from /lib/tls/libc.so.6...done.
Loaded symbols for /lib/tls/libc.so.6
Reading symbols from /lib/ld-linux.so.2...done.
Loaded symbols for /lib/ld-linux.so.2
Reading symbols from /usr/lib/libnuma.so...done.
Loaded symbols for /usr/lib/libnuma.so
Reading symbols from /lib/libnss_files.so.2...done.
Loaded symbols for /lib/libnss_files.so.2
Reading symbols from
/u01/app/oracle/product/11.1.0/11g/lib/libnque11.so...done.Loaded symbols
for /u01/app/oracle/product/11.1.0/11g/lib/libnque11.so
0x0090a7a2 in _dl_sysinfo_int80 () from /lib/ld-linux.so.2

(gdb) stepi

[Switching to Thread -1208035648 (LWP 3107)]
0x0090a7a2 in _dl_sysinfo_int80 () from /lib/ld-linux.so.2

(gdb) call ksudss(10)

$1 = 0

(gdb) detach

Detaching from program: /u01/app/oracle/product/11.1.0/11g/bin/oracle,
process 3107
(gdb)
```

Oracle 11g Trace Stack with GDB

Now one needs to attach the Oracle process to GDB debugger to trace
further details for Oracle 11g by using the *attach* command with GDB as
shown below.

```
(gdb) attach 3107

Attaching to program: /u01/app/oracle/product/11.1.0/11g/bin/oracle, process
3107
[New Thread -1208035648 (LWP 3107)]
Symbols already loaded for
/u01/app/oracle/product/11.1.0/11g/lib/libskgxp11.so
Symbols already loaded for /lib/tls/librt.so.1
Symbols already loaded for
/u01/app/oracle/product/11.1.0/11g/lib/libnnz11.so
```

```
Symbols already loaded for
/u01/app/oracle/product/11.1.0/11g/lib/libclsra11.so
Symbols already loaded for
/u01/app/oracle/product/11.1.0/11g/lib/libdbcfg11.so
Symbols already loaded for
/u01/app/oracle/product/11.1.0/11g/lib/libhasgen11.soSymbols already loaded
for /u01/app/oracle/product/11.1.0/11g/lib/libskgxn2.so
Symbols already loaded for
/u01/app/oracle/product/11.1.0/11g/lib/libocr11.so
Symbols already loaded for
/u01/app/oracle/product/11.1.0/11g/lib/libocrb11.so
Symbols already loaded for
/u01/app/oracle/product/11.1.0/11g/lib/libocrutl11.soSymbols already loaded
for /usr/lib/libaio.so.1
Symbols already loaded for /lib/libdl.so.2
Symbols already loaded for /lib/tls/libm.so.6
Symbols already loaded for /lib/tls/libpthread.so.0
Symbols already loaded for /lib/libnsl.so.1
Symbols already loaded for /lib/tls/libc.so.6
Symbols already loaded for /lib/ld-linux.so.2
Symbols already loaded for /usr/lib/libnuma.so
Symbols already loaded for /lib/libnss_files.so.2
Symbols already loaded for
/u01/app/oracle/product/11.1.0/11g/lib/libnque11.so
[Switching to Thread -1208035648 (LWP 3107)]
0x0090a7a2 in _dl_sysinfo_int80 () from /lib/ld-linux.so.2
```

To get the stack dump, issue the *bt* command for the GDB session.

```
(gdb) bt

#0   0x0090a7a2 in _dl_sysinfo_int80 () from /lib/ld-linux.so.2
#1   0x003d14c3 in __read_nocancel () from /lib/tls/libpthread.so.0
#2   0x0e5b652e in sntpread ()
#3   0x0e5b64cf in ntpfprd ()
#4   0x0e59b3c7 in nsbasic_brc ()
#5   0x0e59e20e in nsbrecv ()
#6   0x0e5a2d20 in nioqrc ()
#7   0x0e39da65 in __PGOSF20_opikndf2 ()
#8   0x08988d90 in opitsk ()
#9   0x0898b294 in opiino ()
#10  0x0e39eeb3 in opiodr ()
#11  0x0898570a in opidrv ()
#12  0x08bf6b03 in sou2o ()
#13  0x0851a37f in opimai_real ()
#14  0x08bfa2d6 in ssthrdmain ()
#15  0x0851a2fc in main ()
(gdb)
```

Basic knowledge of using debuggers for Linux such as GDB will help one to identify the root cause for bugs and other issues with the Oracle 11g environments on Linux. By providing stack trace dumps to Oracle support analysts, they can better help the DBA with these problems to a speedy solution.

Appendix G: Orakill for Windows

Orakill for Windows

The Microsoft Windows platform provides a useful tool called Orakill for terminating runaway and zombie Oracle 11g sessions.

Syntax:

orakill <sid> <thread>

One can also use the graphical user interface (GUI) called Quickslice or *qslice.exe* to find threads since one needs to be sure that one only kills the process that needs to be shutdown. QSlice is available on Windows NT Resource Kit from Microsoft.

> 💣 Warning: please be careful that the wrong session is not killed! The below example shows QSLICE in action.

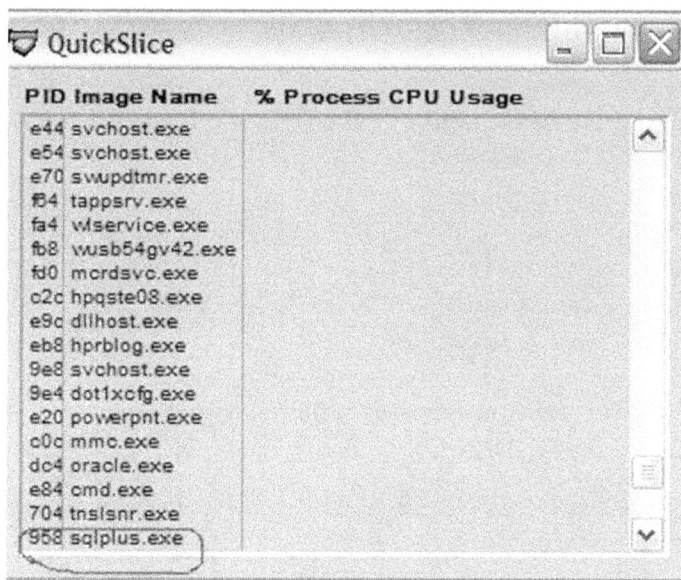

Figure G.1: *Snapshot of QuickSlice*

Query if not using *qslice.exe* for details:

```
C:\>orakill

Usage:  orakill sid thread

  where sid    = the Oracle instance to target
        thread = the thread id of the thread to kill
```

The thread ID should be retrieved from the spid column of a query such as:

```
        select spid, osuser, s.program from
        v$process p, v$session s where p.addr=s.paddr

C:\ >sqlplus "/as sysdba"

SQL*Plus: Release 11.1.0.6.0 - Production on Sun May 24 18:16:43 2009

Copyright (c) 1982, 2007, Oracle.  All rights reserved.


Connected to:
Oracle Database 11g Enterprise Edition Release 11.1.0.6.0 - Production
With the Partitioning, OLAP, Data Mining and Real Application Testing
options
```

```
SQL> select spid, osuser, s.program from
  2  v$process p, v$session s where p.addr=s.paddr;

SPID                    OSUSER     PROGRAM
----------------------- ---------- ----------------------
888                     SYSTEM     ORACLE.EXE (PMON)

3276                    SYSTEM     ORACLE.EXE (VKTM)

3480                    SYSTEM     ORACLE.EXE (DIAG)

SPID                    OSUSER     PROGRAM
----------------------- ---------- ----------------------
2536                    SYSTEM     ORACLE.EXE (DBRM)

1048                    SYSTEM     ORACLE.EXE (PSP0)

2552                    KARMA\     mixxalot sqlplus.exe
```

Now one needs to kill the zombie session which, in this case, is a user
who forgot to logoff from SQL*Plus!

```
C:\>orakill WIN11G 2552
```

```
Kill of thread id 2552 in instance WIN11G successfully signaled.
```

Index

$

$database_block_corruption.......................... 40

/

/dev/shm 69

—

_diag_hm_tc_enabled................................... 144
_hang_detection 143
_hang_resolution.. 143
_hm_analysis_oradebug_node_dump_level 143
_hm_analysis_output_disk 143

1

11g ASM 151
11g Concurrency and SQL Tuning.............. 152
11g Data Guard.. 150
11g Health Monitor 178
11g Memory Tuning..................................... 152
11g Streams 151
11gRAC... 151

A

ACID model 77
ADR Memory Monitor................................. 142
adrci.. 21
adrci> show home... 22
alert.log 22, 103, 198
alert.log file.. 196
alter index...invisible 10
alter index...visible 8
archive control latches................................. 108
attach.. 245
Automatic Diagnostic Database Monitor 121
Automatic Diagnostic Repository 20, 165
automatic segment space management.......... 38
Automatic Workload Repository................. 121

B

background_dump_dest.................................. 21
Backup and Recovery 150
block media recovery................................... 143
bt 246

C

cache buffers chain latch 110
cache buffers LRU chain latch 110
catalog.sql 147
catldr.sql.. 147
core_dump_dest 21
Cost Based Optimizer.................................... 7
cpu_count... 111
cursor:mutex 63
cursor:pin 64

D

data dictionary 147, 164
data dictionary cache 49
Data Guard.. 20
Data Recovery Advisor................................ 143
database buffer cache.................................... 52
database locks 79
db_block_buffers 126
db_block_hash_buckets 127
db_block_lru_latches 127
db_block_size 52, 126
db_cache_size 41
dba_extents 37
dba_hist_latch 117
dba_objects.object_id 94
dba_segments... 36
dbms_repair 40
dbms_xplan... 17
DBVERIFY 38
DBWR 61
DBX.. 201
ddl_lock_timeout... 98
deadlock... 103
diag_adr_auto_purge 142
diag_adr_enabled... 142

diag_adr_test_param 142
diag_hm_rc_enabled 142, 144
diagnostic_dest 21, 196
dirty reads 78
DML locks 81
dra_bmr_number_threshold 143
dra_bmr_percent_threshold 143
dra_enable_offline_dictionary 143
dumpsga 74

E

EM Support Workbench 29
Enterprise Manager 101
exclusive 119
explicit locking 80

F

fk_empno 19
flashback memory buffer 57
fuzzy reads 78

G

GDB 243
global cache services 116
global enqueue services 116
global lock conflicts 93
gv$dlm_latch 114
gv$latch 114
gv$lock 92
gv$resource 92

H

health monitor 143, 149
help 24
help extended 23
hm_analysis_oradebug_sys_dump_level 144

I

index-organized tables 16
initrans 101
interested transaction list 169
interprocess communication model 67
interval partitioning 13
invisible index 6
ipc 73

ipcs 67
ips create package 26
ips show 27

J

Java pool buffer 56

K

Kernal Database Layers 168
Kernel Access 169
Kernel Cache 169
Kernel Compilation 168
Kernel Data 169
Kernel Distributed Transaction 168
Kernel Execution 168
Kernel Generic 169
Kernel Locking 169
Kernel Query 169
Kernel Security 169
Kernel Services 168
Kernel Transactions 169
kgl_latch_count 111
kgllkreq 176
kglnaobj 176

L

large pool buffer 55
large_pool_size 55
latch contention issues 121
latch hit ratio 126
latch request mode 107
latch_wait_posting 109
latches 108, 119
Latches 106
level 107
library cache 48, 107
library cache latch 111
local lock conflicts 93
Locally Managed Tablespaces 49
lock escalation 91
lock table 99
locks 76, 119
log.xml 21, 22, 196
log_buffer 41, 55
log_small_entry_max_size 112
long wait latches 109
LRU 52
LRU chain latches 126

M

Maximum Availability Architecture 150
maxtrans 101
memory management 29
Memory Management Units......................... 66
memory_max_target.................................... 43
memory_target.................................... 43, 60
mutex 64
mutex_type 62
mutexes.. 62

N

Network Attached Storage 121
NFS configuration 149
nowait 107
no-wait mode... 107
null... 119

O

optimizer_use_invisible_indexes 7
ORA-0600 231
Oracle Call Interface.................................. 30
Oracle SGA 108
Orakill... 248

P

pct_free.. 38
pct_used.. 38
pga_aggregate_target................................. 58
pga_target 29
phantom reads.. 78
physical address area 66
pk_emp invisible 10
pmap 68
PMON process... 108
Program Global Area.................................. 34
prop_old_enabled..................................... 142
pstack... 71

Q

qslice.exe 248
Quickslice 248

R

Recovery Manager....................................... 39
redo allocation latches 108, 112
Redo copy latch 108
redo copy latches 112
redo log buffer 55
reference partitioning.................................. 18
reference_emp.. 19
result cache 51
row cache objects latch.............................. 112
row exclusive 119
row share.. 119
row-level locks.. 81

S

serialization mechanisms........................... 106
sga_max 29
sga_max_size..................................... 41, 43
sga_target.. 29, 41
share... 119
share locks 80
share row exclusive.................................. 119
shared pool 107
shared pool latches................................... 111
Short wait latches..................................... 109
show alert.. 25
spin count.. 107
spin_count.. 124, 127
SQL*Plus.. 164
SQL*Plus interface................................... 146
statistics_level.. 50
Storage Area Network 121
Strace tool 238
Streams Pool 54
streams_pool_size..................................... 54
SYS level privileges 170
sysresv.. 67
System Global Area................................... 34
system partitioning.................................... 11

T

table locks 83
Trace Level Events 205
transaction locks 83
Truss 203

U

undocumented parameters 129
User Program Interface 30
user_dump_dest 21
user_part_tables 19
user_tab_partitions 12

V

v$ dynamic performance views 146, 153
v$ views 165
v$db_cache_advice 53
v$diag_info 22, 179
v$fixed_table 153, 180
v$fixed_view_definition 147
v$ir_repair 165
v$java_pool_advice 56
v$javapool 56
v$latch 124
v$latchholder 116
v$latchname 116, 117
v$library_cache_memory 48
v$librarycache 48
v$lock 93, 176
v$memory_dynamic_components 57, 164
v$memory_target_advice 60
v$mutex_sleep 62
v$mutex_sleep_history 63
v$pgastat 58, 59
v$rowcache 51
v$segment_statistics 103
v$sga_target_advice 42

v$shared_pool_advice 49
v$streams_pool_advice 54
virtual 16
virtual column based partitioning 14

W

wait events 152
willing-to-wait request mode 107
Windows Virtual Memory Manager 66

X

x$ tables 167, 170, 180
x$dbgalertext 196
x$dbgdirext 198
x$diag_info 179
x$ir_repair_option 178
x$kcbfwait 172
x$kgllk 174
x$kglpn 65
x$kq 173
x$kqfvi 173, 174
X$KS 170
x$ksmsp 171
x$ksppi 130
x$kzspr 176
x$kzsrt 176, 177

Y

yearly_sal 15

About the Author

Ben Prusinski

Ben Prusinski is an Oracle Certified Professional with 10 years of full-time experience as a database administrator and has written numerous articles and white papers on database management. Ben is also an active member of the San Diego and Orange County Oracle and IBM DB2 User Group community, and he has published various articles for customers and user groups on data management.

Ben has been working with databases including Oracle, Microsoft SQL Server, IBM DB2 UDB, Informix, MySQL, and PostgreSQL since 1996 and has accumulated over a decade of practical knowledge and experience with complex database migrations and support on how to best achieve results with large database migrations to the Oracle platform.

Ben enjoys training in martial arts and tai chi as well as travel to exotic locations in his free time outside of working on Oracle databases. He has traveled to over 15 countries in Latin America and Asia and has a passion for learning new foreign languages as well as cultural traditions.